Carrie Welton

For Jarn—

hope you enjoy this

story—

Charles Monagan

# Carrie Welton

by

Charles Monagan

www.penmorepress.com

Carrie Welton by Charles Monagan
Copyright © 2016 March : Charles Monagan

ISBN-13: 978-1-942756-64-4(Paperback)
ISBN :-978-1-942756-65-1 (e-book)

BISAC Subject Headings:
BIO022000BIOGRAPHY/Women
BIO006000BIOGRAPHY /Historical
BIO000000BIOGRAPHY/ General

Editing: Chris Wozney
Cover Illustration by Christine Horner

Address all correspondence to:

Penmore Press LLC
920 N Javelina Pl
Tucson AZ 85748

For Marcia

## Disclaimer

This novel is based in part upon the lives of real people. Certain characters and actions, events and timelines have been created or changed for dramatic effect.

## Credit for author photo

Liss Couch-Edwards

## Permission for Carrie Welton portrait

Abraham Archibald Anderson (1847-1940)
*Miss Caroline Welton*, c. late 1880s
Oil on canvas
Collection of the Mattatuck Museum, Gift of the Society for
Prevention of Cruelty to Animals, 1940

*Prologue*

In May 1877, Caroline Josephine Welton sat, or rather stood, for a portrait in the Manhattan studio of a promising young painter named Abraham Archibald Anderson. At the time, Carrie was 34 years old and in the full flower of mature womanhood, a condition clearly evident in Anderson's finished work. Her form is pleasing and athletic, her bearing open. The tasseled fan held lightly in her left hand, the pearls and gold cross arrayed around her neck and upon her breast, the kid gloves, the luxuriant, snug-waisted, ivory dress with its sweeping train all serve to mark what had been for her a life of the greatest material comfort and privilege. Even the delicate pink rose painted just above Anderson's signature, a sly reference to Carrie's palace and prison, Rose Hill, speaks to her genteel upbringing.

But what of the face we see? Isn't that where Carrie's essential spark resides, and where one's real story is so often found? What do we find when we look there?

Some years ago, I had the pleasure of viewing the portrait once again as it was about to be carried out of Rose Hill for shipping to the American Society for the Prevention of Cruelty to Animals in New York. I happened to be out walking our dogs in the warm evening (I live across the street) when I noticed the delivery carriage on the estate's great front drive. As I knew Jane Porter Welton, Carrie's mother, to be away at her Watch Hill cottage, I hailed one of the deliverymen and asked their purpose. When he told me, I hastily tied the dogs to the iron hitching post and went inside for one last look—for one last goodbye to my dear young friend.

I had of course seen the painting before. In fact, I had spoken with Carrie the morning she was to leave for New York to have it done. She told me that the work had been commissioned by the ASPCA and its founder Henry Bergh in recognition of her great and continuing generosity to them, with the expectation that it would one day hang in the society's headquarters. Then Carrie very animatedly described to me the details of what she was going to wear for the sitting—the gown, the gloves, the pearls, the gold cross. She even mentioned the fan.

"They think of me as their queen, so I must look regal," she'd concluded, and I couldn't tell if she meant it seriously or for a laugh. When she wanted, which was often the case at that late, unstable stage of her life, she could be just that hard to read.

How hard? Consider the expression she wears in her portrait, as I did on that summer evening in the empty, high-ceilinged drawing room of Rose Hill. The frame had been taken down and was leaning up against the wall, ready to be wrapped for shipping. With her feet on the floor, or nearly so, the image of Carrie took on a hauntingly lifelike appearance in the day's fading light. She was almost as I'd seen her in this very room, or elsewhere in the house, at one of her mother's many social gatherings, lurking in a back hallway as guests arrived and departed. And I must say that on more than a few of those occasions—when she was bravely fighting her family demons, or feeling especially determined to persist in her own vexing course through life, or harboring the most unimaginable secrets—she wore the very same look on her face.

How to describe it when there is such a range of possibilities? One could start off by calling her visage "imperious," although "impudent" might do as well—and one could not dismiss her own wish to appear "regal." Her largish ears, the delicate cleft in her chin and pile of brown ringlets atop her head are all endearing, but the arched eyebrows and chilly forecast in the lines of her mouth, in my judgment, are not.

So where do we look for the truth?

Her eyes, blue and luminous, are perfectly captured by Anderson, and they carry us right in to the core. Here the hauteur that one sees in Carrie at first glance disappears, replaced by something that approaches the most pitiable longing and sadness. Do I draw these conclusions because I know her full, heartbreaking story? That is a possibility, of course. One could hardly be coldly objective under the circumstances. But I ask you, I ask you in all seriousness, have you ever seen such beauty and unhappiness combined? And have you ever sensed a story, however tragic it might turn out to be, so begging to be told?

—F.J.K.

# Part 1

## Chapter One

$\mathcal{I}$ was first introduced to Carrie Welton on a snowy winter afternoon in Waterbury in 1858. So great was her first impression upon me that it's a day I recall with total clarity even now, after forty-five years. I was seated in my study on Prospect Street, snug and self-satisfied in my armchair before a good oak fire. I had the comfortable feeling of the day at last dimming and drawing to a close beyond the room's thick draperies, and of my needing to take no part in that quickening hour that occurs just before nightfall. I had moments earlier put the finishing touches on a long note regarding the evolution of our town common area known as "the Green" and was reaching for the decanter of Madeira when Abel entered the room.

"Mr. Lamson Scovill is in the vestibule, sir, shaking, or might I say stomping, the snow off his boots," he announced with a lightning glance of disapproval. "He has his three-seat bobsled standing under the porte-cochere and he seems to be in something of a hurry."

At that, Lamson himself flew into the room, his face flushed with exertion, his hands cutting the air with excitement, and his wet boots throwing globules of slush onto the Tabriz carpet.

"Come, Frederick, get your overcoat on," he nearly shouted. "I want to show you something"—his eyes were bulging—"an epic wrong, a case of nearly criminal tardiness and neglect!"

Lamson always had something he wanted to show to someone, and usually with just this sense of urgency. And as he was a neighbor of ours and the older brother of my late father-in-law, William Scovill, I was often at the very top of his invitation list. At his behest, I had not long ago witnessed his excited installation of the first coal furnace in Waterbury, and several months later memorably tasted the first ice cream ever hand-cranked in the town. And since I was in line to one day become president of the cash-belching industrial concern—Scovill Manufacturing Company—that he and William had founded and grown to many times its original size, and further, because we were standing in a very handsome house William had built as a wedding gift for my wife and me, I was almost never in a position to refuse.

By the time I had thrown on a coat and gotten into a pair of boots and out the door, Lamson was already seated in the sleigh, impatiently slapping the reins onto his palm. I climbed up into the front seat next to him, and with the pleasurable hiss of fresh snow against the metal runners we set off at once down the hill.

"It's been coming down since eleven this morning!" Lamson shouted into the wind. "And by early afternoon, we were done! You could feel the town grinding to a halt! An absolute halt!"

So there it was—of course. As was so often the case with Lamson's grievances, both in his factories and at home, the bugaboo was an inefficiency that needed immediate correction. We soon arrived at the Green, a central rectangle planted with elms and lined on all four sides with homes, including Lamson's, as well as municipal and commercial buildings. I thought of my warm study, the monograph I had just completed and the wine I'd nearly put to my lips as Lamson drew the horses to a halt and turned to face me. Snow was beginning to accumulate on the brim of his stovepipe.

"What do you notice, Frederick?" he asked, theatrically sweeping his arm around in a circle, taking in all of the town center.

I looked out over the quiet, snowy scene, the lone dark figure of Donnelly the lamplighter beginning to make his rounds down by the stone church, the clattering black tree branches high above. But I couldn't guess what Lamson was getting at, and in any case he wasn't patient enough to wait for me.

"I'll tell you what it is," he said. "There's no one about. It's a Tuesday afternoon in January in the very center of our town and there is no one at all about!"

"No one can *get* about, sir," I responded mildly. "Not enough own sleighs, and no one wants to trudge."

"They're not trudging in New Haven," he shot back. "They're certainly not trudging in New York. It's business as usual in those two places. And do you know why?"

In this instance, I did.

"They have tracks and horse trolleys, and we don't."

"Exactly so!" he bellowed. "We are laggards, Frederick, perpetual laggards, and I've brought you out because this is

6

something you should be addressing. You are a director of the company now, freshly minted, and you must attend to its best interests. Put down tracks and the entire city will thrive!"

I was not about to disagree, and in fact I didn't. I was going to say so when we were interrupted quite incongruously by the approaching shouts of children. Just released from the center school, they were now crossing the Green to begin the long walk up the hill back home. To say they were slowing down to dawdle in the snow would be a great understatement.

"Now there's some life!" Lamson exclaimed with sudden joy. Characteristically, he had, in an instant, progressed from one enthusiasm to the next. He raised up the reins and smiled. "Let's show 'em the way home," he said.

He swung the bobsled out and rounded the corner toward where the children were now running in ragged circles, throwing snowballs and snuffling in the drifts like piglets. We drew abreast of them and stopped.

"Climb aboard, my little ones!" Lamson cried. "Your snow clipper has arrived and is setting sail for home!"

The children hurriedly clambered up into the sleigh, and why wouldn't they? This was a hearty, bearlike man whom they greatly adored, who often gave them rides home from school in any weather, and who only a month ago had passed out nearly 200 dolls and toys as Christmas gifts to what seemed like the entire town. They quickly filled the bobsled's two back benches, with some standing and even spilling over the sides. We made ready to leave.

And then that extraordinary thing happened.

From behind us came a sudden high-pitched shriek and the hard pounding of hoofs on the snow. Before we could turn fully around, a black stallion was even with us and shot very quickly past, almost with a roar in its wake. There was no time to discern the rider. I saw only a blur of a white face, the smudge of a mouth opened wide in reckless laughter as it passed. As the stallion disappeared into the snow down the street and its thundering faded, the children, whose raucous excitement had been stopped cold, remained uncomfortably silent.

"That boy will kill himself riding like that," I said.

"It was no boy, sir," answered a little voice from the sleigh. "It was Carrie."

I knew at once it was true. Of course it was. Welton's girl. Even as late as 1858, I knew nearly everyone in Waterbury, where I'd been born thirty-five years earlier, and I certainly had heard of Carrie. A handful, they said. The talk of the town. No discipline. Her mother can't control her, her father won't be bothered. Refused to go to school with other children. A free spirit who loved wild sport and risk. She'd be, what, fifteen or sixteen now? A young woman with an unshackled air—a most dangerous situation. A powder keg.

Lamson was uncharacteristically subdued as he piloted the bobsled up the hill, but eventually regained some of his cheer as he dropped off each child. As for me, I was happy to return to my predictable household and cozy lair. As I resumed my place before the fire and at last sipped my wine, I realized just how thoroughly I'd been unsettled by the sight of Carrie Welton racing so heedlessly through the snow. Try as I might, I couldn't truly account for the power of the vision, or why it had taken such a hold. And even as I lay in bed that night, the clouds having moved off and hard moonlight pouring through the window and across my blankets, I kept seeing it over and over, like a specter before me—that white face and the smudge of a mouth—and hearing the wild cry.

In the days following that memorable excursion to the Green, three things happened in fairly rapid succession.

First, with the greatest alacrity, plans were made for the placement of trolley tracks on the major streets of downtown Waterbury. With Lamson's words ringing in my ears, and the understanding that he was more than justified in his dismay, I marshaled the support of the leaders of the town's business interests, procured financial backing and presented the scheme pretty much as a *fait accompli* to Waterbury's political hierarchy. Having already been embarrassingly late —or "laggard," as Lamson would have it—to the building of a railroad into town (at one time, someone had stood up at a meeting and declared "The only way to get to Waterbury is to be born here"), the politicos were quick to approve the whole thing. Work would commence in the spring and be finished by summer. It was my first foray into local head-knocking, and I found it, in the end, exhilarating. When it was over, Alathea and I shared a private Champagne toast while standing before the big portrait of her father that graced (or dominated, as I sometimes complained) our front parlor. Although neither of us spoke of it directly, the clinking of crystal that night rang with a sense of my expanding role in the local juggernaut.

The second thing that happened was that Lamson Scovill, who had taken to his bed with fever the day after our sleigh ride, after two weeks of ferocious sweats and suffering, died of pneumonia at the age of sixty-seven. It was a great shock to see a man of such energy, of such a mighty physical presence, extinguished so quickly and irrevocably—and it was an enormous loss not only to those of us who knew him well, but for the community at large, each member of which felt some real kinship with the man and his work, or at least sensed the warmth of his benevolence.

The tributes to Lamson came in like a tide. His fine physique, indomitable energy, perseverance, retentive memory and hearty manner were all recalled and lauded. One commenter praised him as "quick to the rescue" because he had once horsewhipped a farmer he'd witnessed mistreating a young hired hand. The local newspaper declared in a glowing editorial that "he carried others on his shoulders." It was noted that he was only 22 years old when he bought a failing gilt-button business and began transforming it into the present-day success story. Perhaps most telling, on the day of his funeral all of Waterbury's factories, schools, stores and public buildings were closed in his honor. To this day, I have never heard of such a tribute being paid to anyone less than a king, queen, president or potentate.

Which leads me directly to the third thing that occurred in the wake of that auguring blizzard: I once again saw Carrie Welton, and spoke with her, and was exposed to her remarkable presence.

On the afternoon of Lamson's service, many in the town who had known him, who were counted among his friends or important associates, had gathered at his house at the invitation of his widow, Sarah Morton Scovill. We were a large group, mostly men, easily filling the front rooms that looked out upon West Main Street and the snowy Green. I found myself standing by the Chickering piano with a smaller group of contemporaries, drinking flip and smoking, and listening with some amusement, I must admit, as Judge Stephen Kellogg retold one more time, for the benefit of a relative newcomer in our ranks, the remarkable story of Lamson's romantic life.

"When he was in his twenties and running the button company, Lamson considered himself full of promise and good looks and charm, and in all respects a catch on the scale of a leviathan," Kellogg began. "Unfortunately, those females with their poles set out did not see him quite the same way."

He then recounted the story of how Lamson had asked Miss Ann Buckingham for her hand, only to be turned down. She went on to marry Charles Merriman, and together they soon produced a daughter, Sarah. Although in many respects an impatient and even impetuous man, Lamson bided his time and grew his fortune, and when the year, month, day and hour seemed propitious he stepped up gamely and asked to marry Sarah, the daughter of his first intended. But, alas, she followed her mother's lead and also said no, and shortly thereafter went on to marry Mr. Morton. It wasn't until Morton died that she gave in to yet another passionate bid by Lamson, who, at age sixty, clearly did not fear looking foolish in old age, or at least knew exactly what he wanted and was not afraid to ask for it more than once.

Kellogg's delivery of all this was quite amusing, even if familiar, and of course it was dead inappropriate under the circumstances, but we young men—although we loved Lamson and owed much to him and were standing in his very parlor—would have our laugh, even if it had to be up our sleeves. Indeed, as Kellogg at last finished his tale, I turned away in just that snickering manner only to be struck nearly still by the sight of a female form, young yet somehow stately and composed, standing not ten feet away and staring directly at me.

I at first turned back to my group and attempted to rejoin the fray, but it was of no use. The figure's presence tugged at me like a magnet. I looked again and saw that she was staring still. Here I ask you to return once again to the

Anderson portrait described at the outset of this account and you will see pretty much what I saw in Scovill's parlor, except half the age and wearing the plainer fashion of a pre-War girl, and somber colors, as befitted the occasion. But the confident bearing (for she had already grown to her full height), the face, the uncanny expression were all the same. And, unlike that earlier snowy afternoon on the Green, this time I knew who she was—although I did not want her to know it. I excused myself from the group and stepped over to where she stood. I addressed myself to her with a lightly scolding tone, as a full-grown man might speak to a misbehaving young niece.

"You know, it is not considered polite for a girl of your age to stare as you are doing," I said.

Remarkably, she held her ground and did not look away, nor did she make any effort to answer. I hoped that I did not show how taken aback I was. After the briefest of moments, I tried a slightly more "grown-up" tack.

"Is it the nature of our conversation that sets your lines so?" I asked.

"I couldn't hear your words, only your laughter," she replied. "My mother had warned me this would not be an occasion for laughter, only of great sadness, and yet here you are."

Her words and the manner in which she delivered them threw me back yet again. The admonition was so assured and clearly spoken, it was if she felt herself to be in every respect my equal, if not superior to me. I felt astonishment and even a disadvantage. I dug awkwardly for a rejoinder.

"But you are staring at me in particular," I said. "What is the reason for that? Do I offend in some peculiar way?"

"You are Mr. Frederick Kingsbury, and you do not offend in the least," she said evenly but with a knowing, impish light in her blue eyes. "You will soon be my across-the-street neighbor and I was merely trying to get a good look at you."

Again I tried to hide my surprise, but this time it was mostly at the news she conveyed. I considered myself then, when the town was still small, as one who knew of all its movements and transactions, especially property transfers, almost before they occurred. Now this girl with scuffed shoes and chewed fingernails (I was looking more closely) was informing me that the Weltons were about to purchase the magnificent Rose Hill.

She took a step toward me and put out her hand, an unheard-of gesture under the circumstances.

"I am Caroline Welton," she said. Her grip seemed effortlessly straightforward and natural. "I hope we can be friends."

I would have liked the conversation to continue, uncomfortable as it may have been at my end, but just then Jane Welton entered the room in a typical squawking confusion of silk and feathers.

"Carrie, I've been looking for you all up and down this house," she said with far more drama than the moment called for. "I must say that the men's smoking room is the last place I expected to find you." And looking at me with her famously beautiful smile, "I'm sure that Mr. Kingsbury won't object if I pull you away now and take you home."

I might have objected, if only to ascertain details of the family's impending move, but of course I didn't. The facts would present themselves soon enough, or perhaps I would have to go ferret them out. In any event, I'd met the girl on the stallion, and instead of resolving the mystery she'd only deepened it. How confounding it was for me to square the howling nightrider with the extraordinarily grounded young woman I'd met in the parlor! And how in the world had she escaped my notice up to this point? I knew many young people her age in the town. I knew both her flighty mother and sullen father. I'd even been to their house once or twice, although I couldn't remember when or why. But Carrie had remained, for me, elusive in plain sight, like a minor actress in a stage play whom one never notices until she accidentally drops her basket of posies while making her exit. Now, in the little play *à deux* just enacted in the smoky Scovill parlor, Carrie had dropped her posies, and not at all by accident. She had set out to be noticed, and she had been. But what would further be expected of me, and just how thoroughly her topsy-turvy life would eventually intertwine with mine, and my wife's, I could not possibly have guessed.

The Weltons and their noisy trailing caravan of servants, livestock (four horses, two lambs and a goat, three geese) and household essentials did in fact arrive at Rose Hill in several weeks' time. For what seemed like days and days, our little street was busy with comings and goings, including those of Carrie herself, who could be seen dashing about on her handsome young stallion, Knight. Early on, while the Welton household was still in a somewhat confused transitional state, Alathea and I made a perfunctory Saturday afternoon call of welcome and good wishes. Jane Welton kindly received us with tea and much talk of the house and grounds, with the two women trading a great deal of domestic intelligence. Neither Carrie nor her father seemed to be at home. When I at last asked after Carrie, her mother said she didn't know her whereabouts at present, but that she would soon be going off to a school in New Haven run by a Miss Averill. I said I'd never heard of it.

"It's set up for difficult girls," Jane said with a sigh. "And Carrie, as you no doubt are aware, is difficult. She won't say 'yes' when she can say 'no,' and won't be found when she needs to be at hand. She's either alone, brooding in some dark corner of this house, or out riding the streets at any time or in any weather. There's no normal in-between life for Carrie. That's where most of us live—the in-between—but she's always at the top or bottom. If we're lucky, they'll give her some taste of discipline at this place, and of how a girl is to act. That's what her father says she wants more than anything."

Jane Welton was known for speaking injudiciously; you could even call it one of her greatest talents, but this was an especially discomfiting outburst and certainly no way for a mother to, in effect, introduce us to her daughter. We didn't pursue it, of course. We finished our tea and said our goodbyes.

When we were out on the front walk and safely out of earshot, Alathea turned to me and asked, "Does this still sound like the girl you described to me?"

I had spoken to her with some wonderment of my first two encounters with Carrie.

"It tallies with what I saw," I said. "I could easily imagine each Carrie I witnessed—the one on horseback and the one in the drawing room—being what her mother calls "difficult." But Mrs. Welton views her simply as a disobedient child, while I am beginning to think of her as something a little more grown-up and far more complicated."

"You have the luxury of not being her parent," said Alathea.

"True enough. No doubt we can afford her more leeway than a mother or father can," I said. "Still, the way Mrs. Welton described her—it's not the way a mother should be speaking of her child before virtual strangers."

"I hope she doesn't make a habit of it," agreed Alathea, "or I won't be crossing the street very regularly in the future."

We had just reached the end of the Welton's walk when Carrie herself stepped out from behind the great chestnut tree by the front gate. She looked windswept and miserable, and her eyes were red and swollen. It was a bitingly chilly March afternoon and she had clearly been outdoors for some time, perhaps ever since we'd arrived, without adequate protection. She walked directly toward us.

"What did she say about me?" she asked.

"Carrie, this is Mrs. Kingsbury," I said. "I don't believe you've met."

Carrie acknowledged Alathea's presence with a distracted nod. We could see plainly that her tears had not been caused by the wind.

"Please, what did my mother say?" she asked again.

"She told us she was delighted to be in her new house in her new neighborhood," Alathea said brightly, and fished out a handkerchief for Carrie's watery eyes.

"Did she tell you she hates me?"

She wanted to say this matter-of-factly, and came close, but it was easy to see that she had just that moment regained her composure enough to speak at all. I reflexively reached for her as one would to someone about to fall, but she held her ground.

"They both do. Did she tell you that?"

"No, she didn't," I said evenly. "She told us you were going to school in New Haven."

"Prison, you mean. They are sending me from one prison to another."

"I'm sure it's a very fine school," I said without much conviction.

Carrie looked back and forth between the two of us.

"I won't go. I can't go. I've met the warden and she is a villainess. I can see how she will forever be called a Miss because I don't reckon any man would ever have her."

"But if you don't go—" Alathea began.

"I know, I'm doomed," Carrie said. There was a flicker of wit in her eyes, and then she offered a wan smile. "Story of my young life," she said, and wiped her tears with Alathea's handkerchief.

As we stood in a momentary silence, watching Carrie dry her cheeks, I noticed again that her fingernails had been bitten down to the nubs—a sign, to me, always, of a nervous, wandering, careless disposition. And I could not help but note that, as she had done in the Scovill parlor a month earlier, Carrie was speaking to Alathea and me with the most disarming directness, even as the confiding "friend" that she had hoped on that afternoon she might become. Why us? Maybe we seemed that much younger and approachable than her parents were, and with no siblings or even school friends with whom she could share her intimacies and frustrations, she had nowhere else to turn.

At last, Alathea spoke.

"You must get indoors, Carrie, or you'll doom yourself to pneumonia. If you wish, we can speak of this at another time."

Carrie's eyebrows shot up and a sudden warmth came into her face, as if she had not dared to hope for so much.

"Do you promise?" she asked. "Can I really come see you? I'd like nothing more."

"I promise. Come visit."

"Be careful, I might come at any time."

"Please feel welcome."

With that, Carrie's features softened further. She gave us each a last look, a *beseeching* look, I'd call it, then turned and walked rapidly back to her house.

When we got home, Alathea paused in the entrance hall to remove her bonnet.

"There is great disharmony in that house, Frederick," she said. "The girl seems genuinely distressed. She's accustomed to using her wits and wants to be brave, but she's not fooling anyone. What on earth could be making her so miserable?"

I thought of her poor, puffy eyes and the dreaded exile to New Haven.

"Well, her mother can be a fool, as we saw, Alla; and her father is never seen, except in his pin shop, or his brass shop, or going from one to the other. Add a bright, sensitive child to that mix and you will soon enough have drama. On the other hand, she could also just be a sixteen-year-old girl *acting* like a sixteen-year-old girl. It's really none of our concern."

I took the evening paper from the entry hall table and walked to my study. Despite what I'd just said, I knew I wouldn't be able to keep thoughts of Carrie from intruding on whatever I planned to do next. By force of her personality and her overwhelming neediness, she had already burrowed in, like a stray cat finding a saucer of milk and a comfortable spot by the fire. In the briefest possible time, Carrie had made us care about her. I already felt sure that neither my wife nor I would be successful in keeping her from becoming at least in part "our concern."

But it was Alathea who put a cap on it for the day when she stuck her head through the study doorway.

"Perhaps it's just Rose Hill," she said. "Perhaps it's just meant to be a great weepy place."

And if anyone were entitled to say such a thing about that big house, and claim kinship with the ghosts that resided there, it was she.

My own familiarity with Rose Hill could not have been more complete unless I had lived there myself. During our engagement, Alathea and I had liked to stroll up Prospect Hill together. Nearly all the land that stretched up and back from the Scovill and Merriman houses on the Green was open country then, an almost unimaginable vision today. About halfway up, there was a red gate that led into a meadow and small orchard, and we'd sometimes go through to catch a lovely view of the sunset and talk about the future. We'd known each other all our lives. In fact, I remembered her as a six-month-old baby when I would have been just turning six. She in turn recalled my taking her home from school in a fine little sleigh when I was sixteen and she was ten, and all the other girls wishing they were the one sitting next to me. We had much in common, but not everything. I was more worldly after my travels and my years at Yale, and my words or behavior sometimes shocked her. But at all times, you must believe, I was very ready to yield, and invariably did yield, to what I knew were her superior standards.

In any event, in the course of one of our walks together, Alathea expressed the hope of one day building a house right there, right in "our" meadow. By the way she said it, I knew she had been doting on the idea for some time. What I did not anticipate was how soon the meadow would indeed become ours. Several days later, when Alathea happened to mention our now shared dream to her father, he not only thought it a splendid idea, but he immediately insisted on buying the property and building the house for us as a wedding gift, which will give you some idea of the magnitude of the Scovill fortune in those days.

His one request was that we allow him to hire the architect, and we of course agreed. His choice was Henry Austin, of New Haven, who had just designed the new St. John's Church on the Green, a project for which William Scovill had served prominently on the building committee. (The Scovills were such ardent, influential Episcopalians that the church was sometimes referred to behind their backs as St. Scovill's.) Austin was then Connecticut's fashionable architect of choice, his highly detailed, even florid designs being very much à la mode in the region. He did not let us down. In due course he gave us an appropriately fashionable and handsome Italianate marvel, layered like a *torta claudia* and perfect for our hillside, with light in every corner and space enough for our needs, including all the various requirements of what would turn out to be our five children and several generations of servants. I can assert without hesitation that we have lived here happily ever since.

But my by-now father-in-law had something further in mind. Once our house had been finished off to his satisfaction, he and Austin embarked on another project right across the street from us. It was the design and construction of a highly dramatic Gothic residence that, with its gardens, sloping lawns, winding paths, wooded perimeters and multiple outbuildings, would become known collectively as Rose Hill.

It is my understanding that William Scovill paid something on the order of $70,000 for his new estate. As a comparison, our substantial property, house, barn and all furniture had come to about $11,000. Rose Hill was widely considered by Waterburians to be a marvel along the lines of the Great Pyramid or the Lighthouse of Alexandria. People flocked up the hill for a look during its construction, and when it was completed, with its sidewalk running all the way down to the town center, they returned to loiter and try for a peek inside. The house was finally made ready for occupancy in December of 1853, and with a great sense of ceremony we crossed what was now known as Prospect Street and took part in Rose Hill's first Christmas. We arrived at that blazing palace of light on Christmas Eve with eight-month-old Willie in our arms and dazzled him with all its finery and frippery, and an ebbing and flowing tide of relatives, until he finally began crying and wouldn't stop. In the morning, we gathered again and all went to church together and then came back for gifts, family gossip, a roast goose and cheery visitations from select Bronsons, Buckinghams and Benedicts.

But along with this official "opening" of Rose Hill, there was a very strong secondary theme felt by all, and it was that Alathea's father was terribly ill and for most of the time was not seen. He suffered a fever and complained of sharp abdominal pain, but doctors could find no cause and thus could prescribe no cure. In early January, he was taken to South Carolina, where it was thought he might convalesce in a more favorable clime. But things only got worse. Alathea planned a visit to Charleston, but never got to make the trip; William Scovill, the brilliantly organized inside planner and calculator of the brass company's great successes, died in mid-March at age fifty-eight. To make matters worse, William's second wife, Rebecca (Alathea's mother had died when she was eleven), who had been sickly for some time, died in August. Rose Hill, for all its grandeur and high hopes, was thus abandoned and put into a forlorn state almost before it was born.

It sat brooding over the town for well over two years. As a duty to his dead brother, Lamson saw to Rose Hill's care and paid a small staff to keep up the house and grounds. But even before Lamson himself died, under circumstances I have already described, the estate had become a burden to all in the family. Alathea and her sister were William's only surviving heirs, four siblings having died in childhood. They decided to get rid of the house as quickly as possible.

"Every time I look out a window, I see that empty place," Alathea said to me suddenly one day, "and my dead father, and stepmother, and also my own mother and Thomas, Sarah, James and Nathan. It feels like a punishment I did not earn." At least with the property sold, she reasoned, there would be new life across the street, and her memories might grow less painful over time. Having been greatly enriched by the passing of her father, she seemed determined to sell at almost any price just to have it done with, and that's essentially what she did. Joseph Welton, sensing a once-in-a-lifetime opportunity, and perhaps at the urging of his wife, who saw a properly grand setting for her grand social imaginings, paid $16,000 for the estate. Thus we had our new neighbors—and an entirely new chapter of thoughts and feelings as we looked out our windows and across to Rose Hill.

# Chapter 2

Carrie took to heart Alathea's offer to speak with her again "at another time." We saw her quite often, my wife far more frequently than I, in the weeks that followed and before she was trundled off to school in New Haven. Her moods seemed to shift as often as the weather did during that flighty spring. And like clothes flapping on a drying line, they sometimes swung every which way during the course of a single visit. She could be friendly and bright and really very funny at one moment, and then dark and nearly inconsolably sad the next. In appearance she could vary from woefully unkempt, in the manner almost of a mucking stable boy, to quite agreeably handsome and fashionable. To make things even more complicated, her mood did not necessarily match her appearance.

Her first visit came a couple of days after our memorable meeting on Rose Hill's front walk. I was downtown in my office at the savings bank, the town's first, which I had recently incorporated and which was naturally requiring a great deal of my time, but Alathea was home when she heard footsteps on our gravel drive and then the sounds of the bell and of Abel taking a visitor in to the small sitting room by the front entrance. When Alathea got down the stairs, she was surprised to find Carrie, conventionally attired in a long cotton print dress and carrying a rather large canvas under one arm.

"Carrie, good morning," she said. "What have you got there?"

Carrie held out the unframed painting.

"It's for you, ma'am," she said. "I'd like to pretend that this is our first meeting rather than the other day. I made it yesterday and this morning."

It was a likeness of our house and grounds. It was rather sketchily rendered, but in the line and proportions, in the branches of the trees and the shadowing cross the house's façade, there was evidence of at least a little talent. Alathea took it and stood it against an armchair.

"It's lovely, Carrie, thank you. But there was really no need. If you'd like me to forget our meeting the other day, I'll promptly do so."

"Well, maybe not forget entirely. But it was not a way to make an acquaintance, and certainly did not represent what Mrs. Draper taught me about making a good first impression. But thinking ahead, thinking of consequences, they are things that don't seem to come naturally to me, or even unnaturally."

Carrie laughed openly at her own unplanned wordplay. She was ready on this morning to be cheerful and chatty and in every respect endearing. Indeed, she seemed an entirely different being from the one we'd encountered in tears beneath the chestnut tree. My wife had spoken to me of Carrie several times during the interim, and no doubt had thought of her situation frequently. In recent years, I'd noticed that Alathea had become increasingly drawn to the lives of girls we knew and had frankly expressed an interest in helping them through the difficult steps they had to take as they maneuvered their way into womanhood—not always an easy journey, then or now. She readily sought the girls' confidence, and they hers. I'm not sure from what noble impulse this behavior sprang, but here, with Carrie, she thought she saw a special case, and a door opening, perhaps one that had been closed for a long time. With a smile and a wholly sympathetic tilt of the head, she planted her foot firmly into the threshold.

"Who is Mrs. Draper?" she asked.

"Ever since I was too disruptive for the schoolroom and they wouldn't let me stay, she comes into the house and works on me with poems and Greek sayings and such, and also manners and how to appear genteel."

"Well, let's have a morning tea together. We can see how you do."

Alathea steered her across the house and onto a sunny window seat in the dining room, where our second child, Mary, was napping peacefully in a day crib. She gave orders to Abel to see to a simple tea service with biscuits.

"Does Mrs. Draper teach painting as well?" Alathea asked as they settled into positions opposite each other with a small Bombay tea table between them. Carrie laughed again. It was a delightful laugh, natural and unrehearsed.

"I don't think she could paint a barn door, although I'd like to see her try," she said. "There's another woman, Miss Beechum, who paints with me and shows me technique. I have a studio on the third floor, but I had to paint yours by looking out my bedroom window."

"Well, I hope you didn't get any paint on your bedclothes."

"Only a few drops of blue on the floor. But I hid them with my old toy box. No one will see, I don't think."

"Will you paint when you go to the school in New Haven —was it Miss Averill's?"

Carrie darkened noticeably and turned slightly inward on her chair. She hadn't shown it up to this moment, but she'd crossed a very unsteady bridge to come here today, my wife realized.

"I haven't asked what they'll be doing with me. I suppose they have great plans to turn me into my mother, or at least someone my mother could be seen with."

"I think your mother is quite proud of you."

"Hah!" Carrie exclaimed. "That's why she's going off to the Rhode Island shore this summer and sending me miles away to a boarding school in New Haven. I don't see how that shows pride in me."

"We heard her speak of you the other day, as you know. She's concerned about your well-being. She wants you to be happy."

"Well if that's true, and I doubt it's much of a concern of hers, she's keeping it a secret from me. Of course we are a family of very many secrets."

Just then, Abel brought in a tray of tea and small ginger biscuits and placed it between them on the small table. Alathea turned the teapot handle toward Carrie. She decided to let the Welton "secrets" await another occasion.

"Show me some of Mrs. Draper's training, Carrie," she said.

Carrie expertly handled the pot and cups, the pouring of tea and measuring out of sugar and cream. She even proffered the plate of biscuits.

"I think you are ready for whatever comes next," Alathea teased when Carrie was done. "Although I do not see how you will turn into your mother."

This seemed to be exactly the sort of conversation Carrie was looking for when she dared to befriend the Kingsburys, Alathea later told me. The girl exuded a perfect sense of ease as they drank their tea, feeling the season's first warm sun on their backs, and continued chattering on, mostly about the children of other Waterbury families—who was smart, or shy, or always late, or bound for great things. It was a conversation she could never have at home, where she said her mother saw the children of others merely as pieces on her social chessboard. As they droned on pleasantly, Alathea saw nothing further of Carrie's troubled side—only that she was an astute observer and an enjoyable companion, especially for one so young.

At length, the baby began to stir and fret in her crib, and anyway the sun had gradually shifted to another spot in the house. As she rose to leave, Carrie extended her hand to Alathea just as she had to me at Lamson's memorial. It was the rarest of gestures between two women.

"I hope we can have more talks like this," she said.

Alathea took her hand.

"I'm sure we will, Carrie. Living in such close proximity, we can hardly avoid each other."

But Carrie wanted to strike a more serious note.

"I know I am not always in such fine control of my feelings as I have been this morning," she said with some effort. "My circumstances..."

But her voice trailed off. Even after so much pleasant talk, she could not get to that inner chamber—not quite, not yet.

"Maybe we can finish that sentence the next time you are here," Alathea said.

Carrie smiled and turned to where Abel was waiting to show her to the door.

"I'd like that," she said as she left. "But I'm not so sure that you would. Or poor Mrs. Draper, who would be appalled!"

That evening, as Alathea spun out for me the events of the morning tea, I began to feel quite satisfied about the order of things. It sounded to me as if Carrie might have found a safe harbor in our house, a place she could resort to whenever she felt the need, as long as it wasn't too often, of course. We could not at that early stage profess to know about, much less understand, the demons that resided within her, nor the melancholia that possessed her from time to time, but we felt that we might be doing some good. It made us feel useful, especially Alathea who, even with two youngsters, had, and always would have, an admirable appetite for further complications in her life.

Did our attraction to Carrie go deeper than that? Retrospection tells me that it did. In the years ahead, Alathea was to mention to me on numerous occasions how much Carrie reminded her of her younger sister, Sarah, who had been born at around the same time and had lived long enough to prove herself beautiful, bright, headstrong and somewhat spoiled before being struck down fatally by scarlet fever at the age of eight. Alathea had been old enough to carry and burp Sarah when she was a baby and eventually feed her and watch over her, and, as she put it, "boss her" whenever her mother and the nursemaid allowed. She did not go into great detail, but I believe Alathea thought she could have treated her little sister with more kindness and care during her brief life. This, I believe, lurked beneath her eagerness to take Carrie under her wing.

As to my own attraction, I might pin it to the fact that both Carrie and I were what are called "only children."

Although our parents were vastly different in their natures and their methods of child-rearing, I felt there were situations and feelings that children without siblings shared, and that I could be of some service to Carrie in that way. But of course there was more to it than that. It was plain to see that Carrie was a remarkably attractive, cultivated young woman with a wild streak—not a combination one encounters often in a life, certainly not in my own life. My actions were always above board and properly motivated, but perhaps I might be forgiven for gazing wonderingly upon the girl from time to time and eagerly anticipating her appearances at our door.

"You realize that a conventional response would have us hurrying across the street to tell the Weltons all about their daughter's visit with you for tea," I offered at one point as we sat in the parlor after dinner, gazing into the fire. "Isn't that our duty in a situation like this?"

"I cannot imagine doing that, Frederick," Alathea said with some feeling. She had very little use for duty in its societal sense, and anyway, Carrie had become a confidante.

"But it would be the expected thing, wouldn't it?" I insisted. "We are neighbors, we are of the same class—isn't there an unspoken code?"

She saw that I was making an argument for its own sake, an irritating practice of mine that she blamed on my Yale education.

"If you had sat across from her as I did and witnessed her wit and intelligence and felt her wonderful youthful spirit, I don't think you would suggest such a thing, not even in jest."

I tossed the stub of my cheroot into the fire and watched it flare up briefly.

"I am not serious about it, and don't intend to do it, as you have guessed," I said. "But still there is something to it. I feel it nagging at me."

"Well, it's not nagging at me," said my wife, as if that was all that mattered. And of course, in this case, it was—or near enough.

As we retired that night, and in the nights ahead, we continued to feel good and even complacent about the course we had taken. Carrie came to visit from time to time, or we saw her as we took a turn through the neighborhood. As I have mentioned, her moods and appearance were not always on an even keel. We continued to wonder at her gloomy spells, or the times she enigmatically rode by without a word. When she was with us and in a talkative frame of mind, she spoke little about her problems at home, although there was what we took to be an occasional meaningful glance or veiled reference. She hadn't yet completed the forbidden thought that she had begun during her tea with Alathea. Still, we believed that we had done our job, as it were, and perhaps had made a lasting young friend into the bargain.

As it turned out, however, in our contented self-congratulations Alathea and I were so far from understanding the depth of Carrie's feelings and the true nature of her unhappiness that we may just as well have never spoken with her at all.

That realization came like a clap of thunder on a Friday in late June, the day before she was to go off to New Haven to Miss Averill's School. I was walking up the steep hill from the bank, headed home at last, enjoying the warmth and the long dusky light of that season. As I drew near our front gate, I became aware of a rising commotion across the street in Rose Hill. From behind the house, in the vicinity of the stable, I heard loud angry voices, one being that of a female, certainly Carrie, and the other a male's. The exchange quickly escalated to near screaming on both sides. I don't think I'd ever experienced the sounds of such murderous anger. Thinking Carrie might be in danger, I started to cross the street, but checked myself. Then I saw Jane Welton fly down the side porch steps in her long skirts and run toward the scene of the dispute, and next heard her voice raised as well. I couldn't make out any of the words or the nature of the disagreement. After a moment the arguing ceased, and I heard only the sound of Carrie crying—great, loud sobbing echoing along the ground and up into the trees between the stable and the house. I lingered to hear if there would be more. I saw Jane hurry back to the house alone, head downcast, without a look in my direction. And then I heard the sound of hoofs as Carrie emerged from the shadows on Knight. As she reached the head of the drive, she turned back toward the house and shouted something, but she was still crying and her miserable voice caught and slurred and I could not get the words. She galloped her horse out and up the hill and into the highest reaches of the wilderness beyond. A profound silence fell across the neighborhood, as at the end of an extended volley of cannon fire.

I all but ran into the house and called out for Alathea.

"Did you hear that?" I asked excitedly once she came down the stairs. "A battle across the street! Shouting and crying, and now Carrie is off in a terrible state! I've never witnessed such a thing!"

But Alathea hadn't heard. She'd been in the back of the house, overseeing a rearrangement of linens in a large walk-in closet. I poured out a glass of whiskey and tried to settle my thoughts. I resumed in a calmer voice, but not without a feeling of incredulity.

"He had no control. He was screaming at her with a monstrous voice. I tell you, Alla, when I was in the South I once witnessed a station master put a horsewhip to an African slave for no reason, just to entertain those standing nearby—and I don't think that what I heard just now was any more civil."

"Could you tell what they were fighting over?"

"No, I couldn't make it out. They were at the stable. Their voices were so strained and agitated that there seemed no sense to what they were saying."

"Could Carrie have been at fault?"

I took a good drink of whiskey.

"Of course she could have been," I said. "But I can't imagine a fault so grave that it would lead to this—this display!"

"Carrie is going away tomorrow to a place she doesn't want to be."

"It could not be any worse than where she is right now."

"That may be, but she's going away, to a strange school, just as summer is beginning—the last thing a high spirited girl wants to do. She has told me it's because her mother doesn't want her at Watch Hill with her and doesn't want her alone all summer with her father."

"Now I see why," I said.

"It's a situation that could grow into real anger, and clearly did so this evening."

There was nothing I could add, except to mutter the word "disgraceful" under my breath. As I looked into my glass, I wondered how long we could countenance such barbarity just beyond our own front door.

When Carrie returned after dark, it was to our house and not her own. She must have dismounted and walked Knight up our drive, for we did not hear her approach. She came to the side door and begged entrance from Abel, who, well attuned to the events of the day, as always, wisely showed her into the kitchen, where she could not be spotted from across the street. Although her appearance was wild, her long night ride had given her a chance to calm down. We sat at the servants' table, again with hot tea as a balm. It was clear that Carrie had something she wanted to tell us, and when she at last spoke her mood was nearly solemn.

"I hope you will not forget me after I leave tomorrow," she said. "I need to know that there's someone who cares for me. "

It was the saddest thing we had ever heard.

"I don't know what I shall do if there's no one."

We glanced at each other and then leaned forward with disorganized words of support.

She was not just being dramatic. It seemed to us both that she was very nearly at the end of her rope and was merely stating her thoughts as clearly as she knew how.

"I witnessed from a distance much of what transpired this evening," I said. "Your disagreement—and that is a hopelessly mild word for what I heard—was with your father, I take it?"

"Yes."

We gave her a chance to further compose herself. With swift, nervous strokes she pushed her unruly hair back from her brow several times and then brought the teacup to her lips, her hand trembling as she did so.

"And what was the nature of it—of this disagreement?" I asked.

"It will always be the same," said Carrie. She paused as if on a precipice and then forged ahead. "He wished for his first born—his only born—to be a boy and did not get one, and he has always blamed me."

At last, after our months in each other's company, the dreadful secret had been revealed and a singular burden lifted. A first whisper of understanding, an exhalation, circled the kitchen table. After a long moment, we began to navigate our way slowly through this new territory. Alathea spoke first, calmly and carefully.

"Whether that is true or not, it certainly could not have been the subject of today's dispute," she said to Carrie.

"Oh, it is true, ma'am. He has said it to me directly and he has punished me steadily for it. It's at the root of almost all our disagreements, even if on the surface they are about something else. It's just the way he sees me. Now you are the only other ones who know it. I'm sorry to put it upon you like this."

Alathea shook her head as if not quite believing. "What did you argue about today?" she asked.

"It doesn't matter. It will be buried deep with all the others, all the other arguments and angry words. It will not be spoken of when I return home."

"And what of your mother, Carrie dear?" I asked. "What is her role in this infamy?"

"She will do as he tells her. She is the one who had me and could not have another, and so they were stuck." Carrie paused. "And his money comes between any understanding my mother and I might have had. If there is one thing true about her, it is that she will travel and hold galas and have fine things."

"You have given this much thought, haven't you?" I said. "I don't think someone your age should have to bear such a weight. Nothing could be more unfair."

We sipped our tea and listened to the steady hiss of the gas lamps.

"You will not abandon me," Carrie said at last, looking up from her cup. "I must go now, but you will keep me in your thoughts while I am gone?"

We offered the gravest assurances that we would always do so, that we wished her well and promised she would one day find happiness. Then we said goodbye in the doorway and sent her back across the street and away.

# Chapter 3

*Is* it possible to fall in love with a smile? By that I mean, is it possible to be so taken by the smile of another, in this instance a woman, that you would toss all else aside in order to make it a part of your life forever? The mere parting of the lips, the bowing up in their corners, the concomitant broadening and lightening of the face, the softening of the eyes, the demure showing of teeth and perhaps just the darting pink tip of the tongue, the delicate flaring of the nostrils, the dimpled cheeks, animated brow, supple curves of the jaw and neck—I mean all of it—is it—and I mean just it and only it—enough to drive an otherwise sensible man to the altar?

Such were the questions—the one question, really—I contemplated as I began my study of Joseph Welton and Jane Porter Welton, our neighbors, inhabitants of Rose Hill, and now known to us as obstacles to Carrie Welton's happiness. As Alathea and I said our goodbyes to Carrie from our doorstep on that terrible night in early summer, I had already determined that I had to learn more about these two. Without overstepping my bounds too obviously—and I assure you, in our little social circle there were bounds aplenty to consider—I felt a real obligation to find out how such misery and anger had come into their lives as a family, and how we might best advise and possibly even protect Carrie as she entered young womanhood. And if, as I thought over such things, I was only at the very beginning of a long, difficult course of study—as I felt I might be—Jane Welton's famous smile seemed like the easiest place to start.

It was a smile that was radiant and expressive, although her mouth did not open, or only slightly. It was what she offered one in greeting at her front door or upon a chance meeting in town, or as she moved you toward a cup of punch or looked you over and sized up the cut of your waistcoat. It's how she smoothed over an awkward social situation, as when she had rescued Carrie from the company of men at Lamson Scovill's memorial, or, more often, it was how she hid her ignorance on a political, philosophical or literary point. I'd heard it said that her smile was the first thing to enter a room and the last to leave it, and, more practically, that it's how she got things and then kept them. In short, her smile was both a natural wonder and a useful tool, and years ago it had trapped her future husband just as surely as a baited hook will bring in a fine, flapping fish for dinner.

How could that be, you ask? How could something so superficial have such an impact upon whole lives and fates? Well, I'll tell you. Have you never read of the Trojan "face that launched a thousand ships" or wondered about the legendary Egyptian queen's "infinite variety"? I think it likely that the fearsome power that both Helen of Troy and Cleopatra exercised over their respective realms began with, and was sustained by, a seducing smile. Not that our own fluttering and flighty Jane Welton could in any way be compared to these rare, magnificent figures from history and poetry. Of course not. Never. It would be a travesty to think so. And yet...

"You are getting too involved in your study of our neighbors," Alathea interrupted my thoughts one night late that summer as we took a turn through the meadow, or what was left of it after our house had been built. "You speak of it all the time now, and I can tell when you are thinking about it, which is often. I don't see how it will be of much help to Carrie."

"You did not hear them argue," I said.

"No, I didn't, but I don't see what difference that would make."

A firefly that had separated itself from the pulsing swarm by the apple trees now landed on Alathea's sleeve.

"If you'd heard her father's voice, you would have a better sense of the potential danger of Carrie's situation. You would see that her bravery would take her only so far."

"She is brave," my wife allowed. She induced the firefly onto the tip of her index finger and drew it up to her face for a closer look. The creature blinked twice amiably and then flew away. "But say you learn that her father is a bad man and her mother negligent?" she continued. "What would you propose to do about it? And how would it benefit the girl?"

I didn't have an answer to that. Wishing for a boy or regretting a girl were not criminal offenses —unless you were then to behead the mother, as has been the case among caliphs and certain English kings.

"It's a study of human behavior," I said, as if that would be sufficient.

"And what have you learned in your studies so far?"

"Not enough to satisfy you, I am certain."

We resumed our stroll and I organized a summary as I went.

Both Joseph and Jane were descended from the founding families of our town. The Weltons and the Porters were in that group of hardy souls who had trekked down from Farmington in 1673 to build a small settlement along the banks of the Naugatuck River, first called Mattatuck and then Waterbury. Some of the families died out or left, but the Weltons and Porters persisted. They farmed, they operated stores, they learned manufacturing skills, and they produced offspring enough to keep the line alive through flood and pestilence and contribute in ways large and small to the town's present prosperous state.

Jane's own father was an exemplar of the breed. Deacon Timothy Porter was born in 1792, taught school and worked on his father's farm as a young man. Although he always considered himself primarily to be a farmer, he built a small factory dedicated to the carding of wool, made horn and bone buttons, manufactured bricks from a clay deposit on his property, and sold ice from his pond. And if that weren't enough, he also financed the building of a successful brass mill, became a Baptist preacher, and was widely known as a vocal anti-slavery man. He opened his house as a stop on the Underground Railroad, was elected as a state legislator, selectman and town agent, purchased property for the local poor farm, and was able to quote Pope's "Essay on Man" at length. Such was the fiber of Carrie's maternal grandfather, still vital and involved in local affairs even as she set out that day for Miss Averill's School. It is not hard to see where Carrie had gotten her strength of character.

But because of his abolitionist views, Deacon Porter was not welcome at Rose Hill, where his son-in-law vehemently held the opposing view. Joseph C. Welton, whose father had been a simple farmer and shopkeeper, was a self-made striver as well. As a young man, he had traveled through the

South, selling Yankee clocks with enough success to eventually come back to Waterbury, purchase an interest in the Oakville Pin Company, and soon become its president. A few years after that, he was selected as president of the Waterbury Brass Company as well. Both have proven to be extraordinarily profitable ventures. But as I asked about Welton among my friends and associates in town, I soon discovered that he was a very hard case, indeed.

"He has no interests beyond the executive office and the shop floor," offered one of my manufacturing colleagues. "Because of this, he is the subject of much wonder and agitation among his own workers, for he will labor in terrible heat and cold, and without food or sleep, in order to take care of whatever work is at hand. And he expects the same from those who earn far less."

I was seated at a table at the Nosahogan Lodge of the Odd Fellows, one of Waterbury's rising wave of new fraternal organizations, in their hall on the top floor of my own bank building. Four of us, all prominent in the community, had been drinking brandies and engaging in congenial conversation when I stealthily brought up the subject of our neighbors, saying it strange that I had never seen Welton, except fleetingly, upon his own premises.

"He has been known on several occasions to brag that he has never taken a vacation or even a day off from work," said another. "I always thought that a point of honor among those with few other distinctions."

"And yet, they have a cottage at Watch Hill," I interjected.

"But he doesn't go. He's never gone once. He considers it *her* place."

"And so does she, I'm sure." The speaker paused to consider. "He's a dark cloud anyway, the way he hovers so awkwardly at social occasions."

"Or retreats completely."

"I would like to have been there the day the two of them were first introduced. She must have taken one good look at his circumstances and lit up like—what's the phrase?—a thousand suns for him."

"He was surely no match for her in that department."

"And their paths have rarely crossed since. He's the office, she's the house, and that's the way they must like it."

Over another round of drinks our conversation strayed. We agreed loudly upon the importance of vacations to family happiness and personal health, the superiority of Watch Hill to Newport, and the long-term prospects of any politician named Fish, one of whom was then running locally for mayor. And then one in our party, not I, came back to the subject of Rose Hill and, in particular, Carrie Welton.

"She's such an unusual creature, very game and attractive," he offered a bit unsteadily. "Do you ever see her, Kingsbury?"

"From time to time," I answered, not showing my hand. "She is away at school now in New Haven."

"Our Mary Elizabeth and she were particular friends as little girls," said another. "A little later, Carrie had episodes at school when she could not be controlled, and others when she could not stop crying. Finally, her parents took her out and wouldn't even allow our daughter to visit, or have Carrie visit us. Irene and I wondered whether it had been something she had seen or heard, something that had happened in her family life, or was it a malformation, an abnormality, of her brain."

A silence fell among us.

"Yet she is a smart girl, a very talented one," I said despite myself. "You cannot keep a spirit like that locked up."

"Tell that to Joe Welton," said the man. "He's got two in his gilded cage."

Alathea and I had retreated to our garden bench from which we regarded the deepening summer night in silence. Behind us, gas flame spluttered in several of our windows and in the servants' quarters, but not in the darkened nursery, where Mary slept, or from Willie's room. In front of us and below, the town spread out to the south, east and west. Light came up the hill from the modest rows of lamps in the center, and from three or four factories working late with urgent orders to fill. The feeling that a war was coming was growing stronger every day. One read about it in the newspapers or heard it in gossip among salesmen arriving back in town from the South. For Waterbury, it would one day mean great grieving and sacrifice, but for now and always a war also meant money—cash from both sides of the accelerating dispute was coming in for tools, conveyances, uniform buttons and munitions. Out to the east, our own Scovill's was lit up from foundation to turret that night after taking on an urgent order from Washington for brass infantry buttons featuring arrow-brandishing warbirds on the obverse.

But however worthy, these were not my primary thoughts at that moment.

"I don't know what to make of Jane Welton," I finally said.

I felt Alathea's hand tighten in mine just to the slightest degree, a mild rebuke for my continuing on the subject.

"I do," she said.

"Her father is so substantial in every way," I went on. "He is admired for his unwavering character and his courage in speaking out, even among those who disagree with him. Yet

Jane will not speak or act in support of her own daughter! She puts more energy into her azaleas!"

"She is weak. A strong parent may have a weak child, and vice versa," my wife replied. "In her youth she'd gotten used to fine things, but as a female with six brothers she would get none of the Porter fortune, such as it is. She was left to use whatever weapons she had at her disposal, and then somewhere along the line she chanced upon poor, unwary Welton. She dazzled him for his money, it is true, and found her safe harbor, but now she must live with him and his ways."

"'Poor, unwary Welton,' you say, Alla. You cannot expect me to have sympathy for him."

"I only mean it in the way he was so easily bowled over by her advances."

"Her smile, yes. Or what some people we know see more as a calculating mask."

"It was enough for him. He was not one to prolong the exercise of acquiring a wife. Her smile would be enough, and he would not try to see behind it."

I mentioned that someone at the lodge had referred to Rose Hill as a gilded cage.

"Yes, I agree that there is something in the way he keeps them," she said. "They are not chained, but they have the aspect of being not entirely free in their words and movements. I do not doubt that there are more secrets over there, Frederick, than just the one Carrie has revealed to us."

As we rose at last to walk inside, I took my wife's commentary as a tacit approval of my inquiries, which I would continue as time and circumstances allowed. But as Carrie was away now, and her mother too, I felt less urgency regarding the matter. And then several days later, we received this in the mail:

My Dear Mr. and Mrs. Kingsbury,

Here I am at my little desk in my little room writing this little note to you. I miss Knight terribly and our rides together out into the town. Could one of you ever find the time to go over to Rose Hill and make sure from Michael Walsh, our groom, that Knight is fit and not pining for me too much? As for the school, it appears I am the only one here along with Miss Averill. She says there will be more after the summer, and then we will have proper classes. Now it is the two of us reading at opposite ends of her parlor, and sometimes I will make a painting or walk in the town. It is very hot. I do want to thank you for taking an interest in me. No one else knows my "boy" secret and I hope we can keep it strictly between us. And, please, my father can never know I told you! Remember, the groom's name is Michael.

Respectfully,
Carrie

Could we be forgiven for seeing this as nothing more than a typical letter from a young woman of Carrie's age? It was calm and direct, set off no real alarms, and was, in its own way, charming. After all, we weren't planning on sharing her revelations with anyone, least of all her father. Taken as a whole, it made us think hopefully of Carrie's situation, and we agreed that she might even be able to find some form of happiness while away from home.

# Chapter 4

*In* 1842, Lamson Scovill, in one of his characteristic flashes of civic altruism, financed from his own pocket the planting of dozens of elm trees on the Waterbury green, which to that point had been rocky, virtually treeless, and altogether haphazard in appearance and utility. Over time, the trees matured and gave the town center, and by extension the town as a whole, an organized look. The turning of their color every October came to mark, for me, the arrival of autumn to Waterbury. As those graceful, flutelike, high arching limbs dropped their golden coins all around us, we put away our summer longueurs and turned once again fully to the business at hand.

As I have indicated, there was much business to attend to in the autumn of 1858. The factories were full of urgent manufacturing orders—so many that a profusion of new concerns had sprung up to compete for them, and soon there were dozens of shops located in our valley. The subsequent call for workers brought men and their families to town from the countryside and from further afield in Connecticut, New England and, increasingly, from overseas (one of our main thoroughfares had already been informally christened Dublin Street for the sudden, spectacular influx of Irish).

And because many of these wage earners, and their bosses, wanted a safe place to put their money, our Waterbury Savings Bank, whose charter I had secured as a state legislator in 1850 and whose treasurer I would be for more than 50 years, was thriving as well.

All this manufacturing wealth meant new people earning substantial money, their families clamoring to live on our hill, and, eventually, a churning in the town's social order. The old families like mine and Alathea's had not disappeared so much as our positions were being assailed by newcomers. Successful and altogether worthy factory owners, inventors, salesmen, bankers, doctors and attorneys were being created every week, and they were not especially mindful of, or interested in, the way things had been done in the past. One could see them casting their eyes upon New York, Boston, Philadelphia, and perhaps even London and Paris, for the houses, furnishings, clothing, equipages and social conventions they could bring to Waterbury. They were determined to drag the town into the main stream, and in retrospect it is hard to blame them for wanting to do so.

But for the time being, before the war, the old order still held sway, and our social calendar remained predictable and, to our minds, perfectly adequate. Each new season would have its proscribed dance, banquet or outing (with fireworks or barrels of oysters or ice skating) during which the young would pose, flirt and frolic, while their elders shook their heads gravely on the sidelines and recalled better days. In between these ritualized events there would be regular visiting between houses, or afternoon teas, or sometimes even a dinner. And when I say "houses," there were not more than twenty of them that mattered, and we could easily walk among them all during a Sunday afternoon stroll. There was Charles Benedict's "Grove Hill" and H.W. Hayden's

"Maplewild," and then the unnamed but equivalent estates of Leavenworth, Holmes, Brown, Merriman, Buckingham, Kellogg and Scovill—and ours, and Rose Hill. And even as Waterbury was officially incorporated as a city, even as its population more than doubled in eight years, even as trains began running night and day carrying both freight and passengers, we continued to think rather securely of ourselves, our little group, rightly or wrongly, in our old, simple, homespun way. As I look back from later years, it is not hard for me to imagine a young vagabond soul like Carrie's feeling trapped and finding these complacent goings-on unbearable. But at the time, we knew no better. We thought our existing social calendar and our unambitious approach to life would hold sway for a long time to come.

Which is why Jane Porter Welton's invitation that autumn took us all by such complete surprise. It wasn't that she didn't belong in our social group—she did. It wasn't that she couldn't be the life of a party—she could. But with this invitation—hand-delivered by a servant dressed as a Prussian officer, no less!—she was announcing the birth of a new social order in Waterbury with herself right at the top, like a sultana riding high on the lead elephant in the procession.

"Grand Thanksgiving Ball!" the invitation read in large lettering at its head, and beneath it was an engraving of Rose Hill followed by, in somewhat smaller type, the words, "You are cordially invited to attend a Thanksgiving Ball to be given at the home of J.C. and J.P. Welton, Rose Hill, on Thursday Evening, November 25th, 1858, in the Grand Manner of the Duchess of Richmond's Ball!" There was more printed below about music and food, but it's not likely that many got that far. Certainly Alathea did not.

"The Duchess of Richmond's Ball?" she exclaimed loudly, and then said again, "The Duchess of Richmond's Ball?"

I had to laugh at the extent of her disbelief.

"Say it three times and it will still be true," I said.

"Surely she reaches too far," Alathea managed to say. "And on Thanksgiving!"

It was unusual to see my wife so flummoxed. She held the invitation before her with both hands and read it again, then gazed up at the ceiling, then walked over to the window and looked out across our leaf-strewn lawn to Rose Hill. At last, with the shock partially chewed and digested, she spoke:

"What on earth will one be expected to wear to such an affair? I must go speak with Lucia Kellogg about this immediately. I just hope I can beat the Prussian soldier up the hill to her door!"

Was this an overreaction on my wife's part? I'll leave that for you to decide. The Duchess of Richmond's Ball was perhaps the most famous in history, and the subject of poetry and painting alike in the years since. It had been held June 15, 1815, in Brussels, on the eve of what turned out to be the Battle of Quatre Bras, in which nearly 10,000 French troops under Napoleon and British/Prussian forces led by the Duke of Wellington died, two days before the decisive Battle of Waterloo. Brussels at that time was the swarming center of British interests on the continent, thus a lively gathering place for titled officers and their many aides, ambitious men of affairs, society schemers (the cost of living a luxurious life in Brussels was far less than it was in London), those with recent fortunes, those seeking fortunes by any means, and far-roaming royals from all across Europe.

The Duchess's extensive guest list was made up of princes, dukes (including Wellington himself), lords, counts and countesses, barons, viscounts, generals, majors and many sirs and ladies. Virtually every one of them attended, gathering in what Lord Byron would later call "that high hall." There, many performed gaily that night. The Gordon Highlanders danced reels. There was a lavish ball supper. But the smell of impending battle was strong in the air. Officers had to say their goodbyes during the course of the evening in order to pack up and make their way out to the front. Wellington rose from the table to take the breathless news from the field that Napoleon had crossed the frontier and was already engaging the forward lines—moving him to say famously to his host: "Napoleon has humbugged me, by God; he has gained twenty-four hours march on me!" Even he was forced to leave.

What poet could resist the imagery of gallant soldiers in uniform dancing as if without care, then dying in battle the next day, as many did? Or of young men "full of military ardour" in such a rush to get to battle that they fought in their evening clothes? Or of noble doom and death and lost love in general?

Such was the task that Jane Welton had set before herself to re-create in some sense on our hillside in Waterbury within a month's time. But as word of her enormously ambitious plan raced through our little community, as tongues wagged and eyebrows flew high, she got to work. And like Wellington and Napoleon, Jane Welton had an army. Her troops arrived the day after the invitations were delivered and immediately set to the task of building a ballroom.

It was to be a freestanding, temporary hall, put up just to the rear of the main house, 160 feet long and 90 feet broad, with arching windows, gas lighting, a 30-foot-high ceiling, architectural embellishments and even a faux grand stairway that led to the top stair and nowhere beyond. Needless to say, Waterbury had never seen anything like it, and soon seemed determined to see it as often as possible. Our street, including my own front sidewalk, became a part of the attraction, and I must admit it was something to witness as the workmen flew to their task. Sometimes they flew too fast. I was at the bank one day when a man fell from the scaffolding. When I got home, Abel told me my wife "was there with a bottle of camphor about the time the man struck the ground." So despite her doubts about the whole enterprise, Alathea was clearly watching the events across the street with close interest, probably even closer than my own.

As Thanksgiving approached, our thoughts turned not to our own table, but to the one across the street—the long, long one in the new ballroom. By the beginning of Thanksgiving Week, exterior work had been essentially completed on the new building, with only a little painting left to do. Inside, the paper had been hung—a trellis pattern with roses—the flooring laid down, and now furniture and lighting were being brought in. Only odds and ends were left: a few large Indian rugs, cloak and hat racks, statuary, fainting couches, hanging draperies, music stands, ash receptacles, and finally, at the last, fresh flowers and food.

On the day before Thanksgiving, I took it upon myself to pay a visit. I did not wish to get in the way, of course, but now almost everything appeared to be in readiness. I took Willie and our Maltese terrier Cherry as a sort of social protection. We walked up Rose Hill's drive to the new ballroom building, and I was looking in one of the windows when Joeseph Welton happened to step right in front of me on the other side of the glass. We startled each other, and I saw his instinctive look of disapproval. He probably wanted to flee, as did I, but then he motioned me to come join him inside.

"Now you can see for yourself what one determined woman can accomplish," he said as we all came through the massive entrance and into the hall. He meant it as a light comment, but he wore a disagreeable expression on his face, which was set in an eternal, hawkish frown to begin with. I couldn't tell if his look was meant for me or for the massive expense of time and money on behalf of this most fleeting of vanities.

"Maybe you can use it as a coach house afterward, or a racquets court," I said, intending to be humorous. But Welton ignored the remark.

"He is your oldest?" he asked, indicating Willie, who was running and shouting with Cherry through the pavilion's vast, echoing expanse, his blond hair flashing in and out of the late morning sunshine.

"Yes, and a good, growing boy," I replied with a smile. "I am not afraid to say that he is my greatest source of pride. I sometimes wonder that I deserve him at all."

He watched my son intently. He was suddenly miles away.

"Never—" he began, but did not finish the thought. In the years that followed, I wondered about the thousands of paths he could have taken from that opening declarative. As I've considered Joseph Welton's murky depths and tragic fate, I've provided dozens myself, even scores, headed in all sorts of directions, but not with anything that felt truly conclusive. In the event, he turned to face me with a quick change back to the subject at hand.

"All this will be taken down before Christmas," he said, gesturing toward the ceiling. "I am sorry for any inconvenience its construction may have caused you and your household."

I shook my head and murmured something reassuring. He spoke again.

"I must confess, I have no head for society in any event," he said. "The niceties, the small conversation—I don't see how it gets you anywhere." He looked at me with piercing blue eyes. "Tell me, Kingsbury, where does it get you?"

"I'm not a great one for it, either," I said without much conviction, "although as a banker and a one-time elected official I like to see people and hear different views on things. And I will admit that I like to dance on occasion."

He regarded me now as one would a lunatic raving in the street.

"Well, you will have your opportunity tomorrow, I can assure you. We have a twelve-piece orchestra that has made a great study of the music played in Belgium in 1815. I hope you have made a similar study of the steps."

"I did not think to do that," I replied with a smile. "I fear I will be at a loss."

I could sense Welton agitating to remove himself from our harmless little conversation, and I had seen what I'd come over to see.

"I mustn't get in your way any further," I said. "Until tomorrow, then."

But Welton, rather than retreating, took a step closer to me.

"You and your wife have spent a great deal of time with Caroline," he said with what I took to be real, sudden menace. "I want you to know that I do not approve and do not want you to continue doing so."

I was startled but decided to stand my ground.

"Carrie is a wonderful, very talented girl—a joy to know, really—and we cannot make apologies for our behavior," I said.

But Welton was in no mood for a discussion.

"She is not your daughter, she is mine. She has many difficulties in her life and your meddling will not help solve them. We are neighbors, but you must take this as a warning. There will be consequences if you continue."

He now stepped back and with an outstretched arm indicated the way back out beneath the Duchess of Richmond's gilded archway.

"I wish you a good day, sir," he said. "I will greet you tomorrow evening as if we have not spoken of this, but I assure you I am not one to forget."

"And if you threaten me, sir, I know how to return a threat," I said, feeling a strange dark force boiling inside me and crowding into my head. Such was my nature and the even keel of my life that I didn't know what real rage was until that moment.

I hurried Willie and Cherry back across the street. Alathea was upstairs, giving her gown a final trial before the ball. When I came bursting into the room so apparently full of news, she asked Georgiana—our woman of all work who had been helping with the many buttons—to leave the room. She then turned her attention fully to me as I described the events that had just transpired. I went into every detail, fresh as it was in my mind, including even the scar beneath Welton's right eye that turned bright purple as he angered. When I finished, Alathea ran her hands along the folds of her red silk evening gown. She hadn't wanted me to see it until the evening of the ball, but events have a way of intruding.

"I don't see how we can abandon Carrie now," she said with a force and clarity that greatly became her.

I thought first how lucky Carrie was to have someone like Alathea in her corner. Then I thought how awful the Welton house must be with such a wretched, antagonizing creature at its head. I thought a lot of things, one after the other and then all at once. I was still in some sense across the street, standing toe to toe with Joseph Welton.

"It is agreed then," I said at last. "Whether we are called her friends or her guardians, or both, Carrie's interests to some degree need our protection."

"As does her heart."

"And we will be here if she needs us, regardless of the consequences."

"Yes, certainly, insofar as we can judge it now."

"Even if we have a busy household and two children of our own to watch over."

"And another on the way."

Shock was now following upon shock like thunder rolling across a plain.

"It was to be a Thanksgiving surprise, my love, like my gown," Alathea said, coming to me, suddenly radiant, her arms outstretched. "But today we seem to be opening all our presents at once."

Her gown enveloped me like a billowing red cloud. We held each other close, our cheeks touching intimately.

"'Another on the way'—such happy words," I said softly into her ear.

We lingered a moment, then Alathea pulled away to face me.

"What can be going on at Rose Hill?" she asked.

"Well, for one thing, a very large ball," I answered, and left her to her many preparations.

The Thanksgiving Ball at Rose Hill exceeded even our elevated expectations. There were more than 200 guests, some traveling from as far as Hartford, Litchfield and New Haven. Welton put carriages at the rail depot to ferry train travelers up the hill. We arrived on foot, needless to say, and were swept under the glowing archway and into the hall with the Colt party, ten strong, from Hartford. I took a good long look at Samuel Colt and his wife, Elizabeth, whose wedding two years earlier had taken place aboard a steamship in the Connecticut River and featured fireworks and rifle salutes. They could give Jane Welton a run for her money and then some I thought as we followed them in, although perhaps not tonight.

Jane was just inside the entrance, buzzing from guest to guest like a bright blue bumblebee on a rhododendron bush. Alathea immediately noted to me that Mrs. Welton had chosen a high-waisted gown in the style of 1815, after the original ball. It had been a question of some gravity and much discussion among Alathea and her friends, and by extension their husbands, as to whether to follow the fashion dictates of 1815 or 1858. Guidance had not been provided in the invitation. Striking a note of practicality, to say nothing of frugality, we ultimately decided on the latter, and at first glance so had most of the other early arrivals: We saw only a few bare bosoms, including Jane's, among the ladies, and but a handful of men in silk stockings and cravats wrapped up to their chins.

As for the great hall itself, it was now magnificently festooned with flowers and illuminated by candlelit chandeliers and strings of gaslights within frosted globes. The orchestra was easing pleasantly through the beginnings of what would become an intoxicating lineup of waltzes, reels and quadrilles. To one side of the hall, the supper was laid out, with roasts of lamb, beef and fowl, raised pies, lobsters and prawns, galantines, custards, and fruit ices, with claret, ale, cider and other drinks nearby. Some of the older guests were already milling about the feast and loading up their plates.

But what dazzled most audaciously were the extraordinary touches Jane Welton had employed to bring us closer to that fateful night in Brussels. There were men in uniform scattered throughout the hall—actors she had hired from somewhere, now done up as British or Prussian officers toasting and carousing as if on the eve of battle. I believe a fictive Mayor of Brussels was in attendance as well. Moreover, she had placed a cannon way up at the top of our hill, and at intervals it would fire just loud enough for all to hear, much as French guns were heard in the distance on the night of the Duchess of Richmond's gala. After the big gun made its noise, several of the "officers" would come over to a group of guests and announce regretfully they had to leave and report to duty on the front lines.

"There has surely been nothing like this, at least not on our side of the Atlantic!" I shouted to my friend and fellow banker Willard Spencer over the growing din of the assembly.

"And I hope we never shall see it again!" he shouted back. "I've never witnessed such vulgarity and waste!"

Spencer was twenty years older than I, and seemed an old Yankee, nearly a Colonial, by comparison. But with his wide-ranging interests, cool judgment and good head for facts, he was highly respected as one of the local sachems. He had advised me wisely in business matters and was a regular visitor to my study, where we usually spoke of large events. Now he leaned in toward me again.

"Do they not see that we are on the threshold of a great war ourselves, and that these scenes they take such pains to re-create for our amusement will soon come to pass—except with real anguish and our own sons and husbands as fodder?"

As he glared at me, I noticed over his shoulder, across the room, an unmistakable figure. She was standing in the shadow of the great false staircase that dominated the hall's southwest corner, speaking with one of the young hired officers. With a bow and a hasty acknowledgement of his wise words, I excused myself from Spencer's presence. I wanted to rush over to Carrie with the warmest of greetings, but now I felt I could no longer do such a thing, at least not spontaneously, and not in this setting. I looked around for her father, but could not spot him—in fact, I had not seen him all evening and wasn't even sure he was present. It would be like him to avoid the big party and then personally be present for and even supervise the hall's destruction. I kept an eye on Carrie, for I did not want to lose her in the crowd. I was also on the lookout for Alathea so I could give her the news. I felt like an octopod, so stretched I was in all directions. At just that moment, Welton's brother George happened by, his severe visage, so much like Joseph's, easily identifiable amid all the general gaiety.

"I say, Welton!" I shouted, putting an arresting hand on his arm. "Do you know where your brother is? I want to congratulate him on this miraculous achievement!"

"He is gone!" George Welton shouted back. "Called away at the last moment to New York on business!"

"Called away on Thanksgiving?"

"So it would seem!"

He moved off into the crowd as the orchestra started up a reel and the dance floor quickly filled with swirling petticoats. I remained uncertain about what to do. I did not doubt that Joseph Welton was not present, but I could not be sure he was truly away. He could be lurking somewhere, standing just outside the building in a spot where he could see but not be seen. Alathea caught me deep in my considerations.

"You are not dancing, Freddie," she scolded me. I could tell by the way she'd addressed me that she'd had a second glass of wine. "Surely we have not grown so old that we cannot dance!"

I held up a hand.

"Look over there to the left of the staircase, a little in its shadow, and tell me what you see," I said, indicating the way.

She followed my gaze and watched for a moment.

"She has just spotted us, and me looking at her, and yet turned away," said Alathea. "We must go see her."

"Mightn't that put her in danger?" I asked. "Welton was very blunt."

"Guests may speak freely with each other at a ball—in fact that is one of its primary purposes—and I have not spoken with Carrie in more than five months. I cannot believe we wouldn't be allowed to go say hello to her."

Alathea rushed off in Carrie's direction, but I didn't follow. I held back, looking out for Welton or even his wife, although Jane was surely not thinking of her daughter on this evening.

Carrie didn't flee at Alathea's approach, but she regarded it uneasily. She held out a hand, which my wife took warmly. Carrie gestured toward her companion.

"Mrs. Kingsbury, are you acquainted with Gilbert Stocking? He is the son of Deacon Stocking and is now at Yale."

Alathea and Stocking exchanged pleasantries.

"Carrie and I were schoolmates as children, and it was she who recruited me and many of my classmates from the streets of New Haven into her mother's regiment," the young man said brightly.

Alathea smiled as she took his elbow and turned him gently, as if he were a toy sailboat on a pond.

"Do you see that man standing across the room watching us? He is an Eli, too. I'm sure you and he will discover much in common to talk about."

She gave Stocking a little shove in the right direction and he went where he was told. She then turned her attention upon Carrie.

"Step out into the light and let me see you," she said.

Carrie took a cautious step and then lurched forward and threw herself into Alathea's arms, sobbing.

"What ever is the matter, child?" Alathea asked, drawing Carrie away and looking into her eyes.

"All has ended in failure," Carrie cried. "And I am back at Rose Hill, where every minute is endless, to say nothing of the hours and days."

"What about school?"

"Miss Averill was not what she claimed. Despite her promises, only two other students ever arrived, and she was not inclined to teach us anything of any use. I wrote to Mrs. Draper and she told me that this is a common scandal for educating girls. They charge enough to seem legitimate, but they aren't. All they do is provide meals and a bed and a place to read. Eventually, of course, they are discovered and put out of business. Why is it that they don't treat boys so poorly?"

"How long have you been back in Waterbury?"

"A week."

"How have we not noticed you?"

"I've stayed in my room, I am ashamed to say. I painted a canvas of your house again, and as I did so I thought of our conversation in your kitchen and envied the warmth within your walls. And I rode out very late at night so you wouldn't know."

"Why did you not come visit us, Carrie?"

She had regained her composure and now looked alertly around the hall, as if for spies.

"I have been forbidden. I had a terrible row with my father when I got back and another last night. My mother was involved, too. That is why he's not here this evening."

Carrie leaned forward to say into Alathea's ear:

"He struck me last night."

Alathea staggered and pulled away, and then took Carrie's hand and led her to a side door in the big building. They went through it and stepped out into the bracing night air. The sounds from inside were muffled enough so they could hear the creaking of carriages and shifting of horses standing in the drive.

"Tell me," Alathea said.

"Across the face with an open hand," Carrie continued. "It didn't leave a terrible mark, but it's why I've sought the shadows tonight. He was drinking heavily, as he does from time to time, maybe as a protest to this great bloated event." She swept an arm back toward the hall. "And in truth I couldn't blame him for that. But when he drinks, there is a pattern. Without fail, he speaks of his hard work—no one has ever worked harder—and great successes, and of his making something out of nothing while others are born with everything given to them. If my mother is present, he damns her excesses, and if I am present, he resents my birth and my being, and that there will be no one to carry on his name or his affairs. And then last night he said I needed working, although I didn't know what that meant, and that I had failed even in school, and that women are only good for one thing— that's when he came at me and struck me. After that he set off for New York."

The two women, one in a red gown, the other in mauve, shivered together in the dark as Thanksgiving at last began to draw down.

"I cannot stay at Rose Hill," Carrie said in an echo of her summer lament. "But there is no place for me to go. Will you help me find one?"

"We will find something together," said my wife. "But we will have to be wary. Your father is a dangerous man, and danger must be respected."

They went back through the door and rejoined the ball. No one but I, and possibly my new friend, young Stocking, ever noticed that they had been gone.

## Chapter 5

*I* see by looking back over my account so far that there are several characters I have introduced but not quite explained, and by that I mean the servants employed both in my house and at Rose Hill. I fear that my descriptions to date would lead you to think of them as shadowy and insignificant figures, barely named, scurrying to and fro with calling cards, dusters and tea trays. But they are far more than that, as I'm sure you must know. In our house, although some of their work is no doubt menial in nature, I have always thought of them as a secondary set of arteries leading in and out of the same heart as our Kingsbury arteries do.

I have mentioned Abel. He was Arthur Abel, our butler and my valet, coming to us after having served in that capacity for my late father-in-law for some fifteen years. Abel was a compact, nearly bald, often dour Englishman blessed with the most remarkably hound-like acuity of hearing and smell—and also with great discretion, loyalty, and an ability to keep the household books. So great was his grasp of the house and its doings, and also the events in the town, that I don't know if I ever surprised him with a piece of intelligence, no matter how fresh I thought it to be. By the same token, he managed to surprise and even shock me on quite a number of occasions. He was thirty years my senior, with an excellent eye for propriety, so I had to suffer his mild disapproval on occasion. But we shared many laughs as well. In sum, he was not without his flaws, but, as Alathea and I put it to one another perhaps a thousand times or two, he was well named.

I have also noted briefly the presence of Georgiana Lewis in our midst. I called her a woman of all work because that is what she was when she first came to us, just after our marriage. In fact, she moved into our house on the same day we did. By the time of which I write, she should be more properly referred to as our housekeeper, although she did far more than that title implies, and still cooked or cleaned or sewed or hauled something from one end of the house to the other when the situation demanded. She was an ample-figured woman possessed of what a guest once called "stair-pounding energy." She perspired easily and smiled easily, too. She was a black woman from local stock. Like Abel, she was, as far as we could tell, determinedly single.

Beyond these two, who had been with us the longest and with whom we were most intimate, there were also a cook, a housemaid, a baby nurse named Mary Morris, and a groom who looked after our garden and property as well. Of these, I will say that our cooks came and went with alarming frequency, our governesses only slightly less so, and that our yard man took his direction chiefly not from me, but from my Yale fellow, devoted companion and frequent house guest Freddie Olmsted.

Meanwhile, across the street, Jane Welton had assembled a larger staff to answer the demands of fewer principal residents. Affairs at Rose Hill were administered chiefly by a housekeeper, Jerusha Steeves, who had survived, and in many ways managed, the transition of the house from the

Scovills to the Weltons. Alathea had known Steeves since childhood and admired her greatly.

Also employed beneath Rose Hill's steeply pitched roofs were a couple, Mr. and Mrs. George Platt—he the butler, she the cook—the aforementioned groom, Michael Walsh, Jane Welton's lady's maid, and two or three others lower down on the ladder. Until recently there had also been a young coachman named Archie Comstock, but he had been caught stealing money, jewelry and even a silver entrée dish from the main house. Once discovered (exposed by a jilted confederate), he was arrested, found guilty and sent off to prison in Wethersfield. His trial had been brief, but when he was given his say, he astonishingly tried to bring poor Mrs. Steeves into his circle of infamy—a ludicrous and incoherent gambit that found no favor in the court or anywhere else, but that caused great distress to the loyal housekeeper. Comstock's widely reported demise was the source of lively discussion, at times bordering on tumult, within our own servants' quarters, where everyone was intimately aware of all that went on across the street—and vice versa.

I go into such detail on this matter because it was Abel who came to me one night with news he felt compelled to share. On their Thursday afternoons off, he and Steeves occasionally liked to walk downtown together for tea at Brown's Hotel. Over their steaming cups they discussed old times mostly, but also the vagaries of their positions, the common problems that plagued them, and the personalities, both upstairs and down, who provided them with an endless stream of worries and gossip. And every once in a while, a real piece of information emerged.

"I wonder if I might have a word, sir," Abel said softly that evening after he'd returned from his outing.

I nodded my assent. I'd been reading through reports from Scovill's two top managers, Goss and Sperry, regarding the week's activity at the factory. Lamson had been gone for just over a year, and the new hierarchy at the plant was taking shape nicely, with all arrows headed in the right direction. Even so, I sensed urgency in Abel's request and was not displeased by the interruption.

"I have taken tea with Mrs. Steeves this afternoon, and in the course of our conversation she revealed something I thought you should know," said Abel.

He allowed me a look of forbearance.

"But we think it best if it comes directly from her. I have asked her to come in with me and she is just in the kitchen, waiting."

"Of course, Abel, if you think it the wisest course," I said. "You are aware of our, ah, tentative state with the master of Rose Hill."

"I am, sir. We have taken every precaution."

"Then go get Mrs. Steeves and bring her to me, but please fetch Mrs. Kingsbury as well."

"I didn't know if the details might be a little upsetting to her."

"Bring them both."

I folded up my notes and closed my ledgers and put them aside. I had a moment to consider what might be coming. Despite our best efforts, the servants were likely well aware of all that had transpired between the Weltons and the Kingsburys in the past twelve months, or at least the main part of it. Alathea and I were habitually circumspect regarding what we spoke of in front of our staff, especially the more transient ones. At times used words strategically with them when we wanted a certain outcome, but recognized that they did the same with us. It was a cat and mouse game that dated back to the days of the pharaohs, and likely beyond. But there was no telling what Carrie or her mother might be saying or doing across the street, or how loudly, or in what humor. Jane Welton could never be described as circumspect, and Carrie, as we knew, was prone to flights of careless behavior. As for Welton himself, he was not guarded at all in his words or actions, and indeed thought it a special right to lash out and loudly speak his opinions and act impulsively. At any rate, this matter, whatever it was, had to be of the highest concern for it to be taken outside the walls of Rose Hill.

As Alathea, Abel and Steeves came through the door one by one, I experienced an involuntary shiver, an excited one, at the sight of the four of us, different in so many ways—in circumstances, education, fortune—yet bound by the cosmos to arrive at this moment together. I saw that we were a committee, each member highly competent in his or her own way, gathering in my study to solve a problem. As they entered, I stood by the fire, absently poking a log I'd just thrown on. Alathea, having been taken by surprise and not liking it, spoke first.

"What is this all about, Frederick?" she asked impatiently. "I have not been summoned like this since the morning Willie stuck his toe in the kettle."

"I know as little as you do, my dear," I said. "I think it is Mrs. Steeves who would like to say something to us."

Steeves, who was still wearing her "day off" attire rather than her customary housekeeper's garb, drew herself up nervously. She was operating well outside her normal sphere, but our long familiarity with her was a great help.

"I know you both have a special interest in our Carrie," she began. She looked at both of us for reassurance, which we gave, and then plunged on. "She has had a most difficult time finding her way, especially since returning from the school in New Haven."

"She has been away for much of this new year, I believe," I said.

"She visited a cousin in Farmington," Steeves said, "but still, most of her days have been spent at home."

"We have seen her but only on the rarest occasion," said Alathea. "She has been kept away from us."

Steeves nodded.

"Carrie was overcome by a great melancholy in the days leading up to Christmas," she said nervously. "She rarely left her room, and in truth I am not certain where she would have gone had she left it."

"Oh, Frederick!" Alathea said to me with alarm, putting her hand upon mine. We had seen almost nothing of Carrie since the Thanksgiving Ball. After witnessing what her father was capable of doing, and after his direct threat to me, we feared for Carrie's safety if she were to be seen with us—and, as we noted to each other, we feared for her safety if we did not see her. Our role, our duty to Carrie, was impossible for us to determine.

"But in recent weeks she has found a sort of new companion within our walls," Steeves continued, "a young under housemaid, Carrie's age, somewhat forward in nature, but cheerful, named Polly. She took to Carrie in a simple, caring way, very slowly at first, and slowly Carrie returned the favor. They became friendly with each other. Genuinely friendly. I even forgave Polly some of her duties because I saw the good it was doing for Carrie."

"Her darkness lifted," I said as a way to help the story along.

My wife did not acknowledge my comment with so much as a glance in my direction. Both of us knew that this was not the end of Steeves' story—not by a mile.

Abel took a step into our impromptu circle. "Would it be permissible for Mrs. Steeves to sit?" he asked.

"Of course," I said. "We should all sit."

We moved to a corner of the room away from the fire. Alathea put herself next to Steeves on the Chesterfield sofa, so close their knees practically touched.

"Please go on," she said. "What was it that happened next?"

"It was all so sudden, ma'am," Steeves said. "Just a week ago—not even—the master came in late. He was loud and not happy, upset with something at work, as he so often is. When he's like that, you just step back and let him come through— and that's what the mistress does, too. Just let him go by. He poured out a glass and picked up the mail, and then as he stood there he heard it. Laughter from up the stair."

To my surprise, Steeves was a natural storyteller. As she continued her account, my imagination was able to render it as vividly as if I'd been there myself.

"'What's that?" he called up angrily. "Who's there?"

The landing went silent, then the sound of a door closing. He took the stairs two at a time and arrived at Carrie's door in a fury.

"Come out this instant!" he shouted, and pounded the door. "Who are you squealing with? Tell me or I am coming in!"

But of course he didn't wait. He flung the door open wide to find Carrie and a servant girl he did not know huddled together across the room. He gave Polly a hard look.

"Get out," he said through a clenched jaw.

The only way for Polly to leave the room was to pass by very near to where Welton was standing. It did not look like she could pass safely. Carrie held onto her.

"She will leave after you have left, father," Carrie said.

Welton bristled at this insolence. He moved slightly to give the girl a path.

"Get out," he repeated. "Out of this house."

Polly freed herself from Carrie's grasp and walked briskly past Welton to the door. She turned to look as he spoke again.

"You come right here, girl," he said fiercely to Carrie. "You have some explaining to do. Come over here now!"

"I won't. She is my friend, the only one who will have me. Surely you can permit that in your house."

"Be careful Carrie," said Polly from behind. "He will hit you again."

The terrible words hung in the air like smoke. Welton slowly turned back to face Polly.

"What has she told you?" he demanded with an even voice. He seemed calmer suddenly, but it was only the next level of anger. "What has my daughter said to you?"

But Polly was already running down the hall to the back stairway and up to her quarters on the third floor.

"I will attend to you later," Welton said to his daughter.

He left the room and walked methodically down the corridor where Polly had just fled. He climbed the stairs to the servants' quarters. He still had in his possession the day's mail. He made a weapon of the copy of *Scientific American* by rolling it up tight in his hand as he tried each door along the hallway. When he found Polly, she tried to keep him from entering, but it was no use. Once inside her tiny chamber, he began hitting her with the magazine—across her shoulders, face and head, repeatedly, on her back and thighs—as if to a misbehaving beast. However she writhed and turned, he found her. She covered her face with both arms and fell back onto the bed and still the grunting blows continued. Then he fell on top of her and with his face inches away from hers held the hard round edge of the magazine against her neck.

"How dare you befriend her?" he gasped, for he was quite out of breath. "She has not yet earned that pleasure, and she will not share her wild stories with the likes of you."

He put his rough hands on Polly's shoulders and looked her in the eye. His full weight was upon her.

"You have learned something, I think," he said. "What have you learned?"

But Polly was beyond speech, beyond even sound. She had never been so much as introduced to this man.

"That I am the master, and no other—that is your lesson. And if you have truly learned it, you may stay."

He lay atop her for another long moment, breathing heavily, reeking of onions and tobacco, and then got up, picked up his mail from the floor and returned down the back stair. Polly listened to his retreating footsteps until she could hear them no more. She remained face up on the bed. Her body shook uncontrollably, but she could not seem to summon tears.

Such was the state of affairs at Rose Hill that no one came forward during this entire episode either to witness or stop it. Jane Welton, once she saw how things were going to be, remained downstairs and well out of sight and hearing. Steeves and the rest of the staff listened keenly from familiar shadows, but of course dared not be seen. Carrie only shut her door and sat without expression on her bed.

"And this is a respected man in our community," I said, as Steeves came to the end of her account.

"Respected only for his wealth," said Alathea. "Nothing else." She turned to the housekeeper. "What has transpired since that night, Mrs. Steeves?" she asked.

"Polly has run off. We came to tend to her right away, but she was beyond our ability to fix her. She was a good girl. Her only sin was to be friendly and good-natured. She wasn't there in the morning and her room was cleared out, such as it was."

"Where could she go?" asked Alathea.

"She came in on the west wind," said Steeves, employing a fragment of downstairs poesy, "and that's what carried her out."

We were silent for a moment.

"And what of Carrie?" I asked.

"He never brought it up to her like he said. For Carrie it's worse than if he had. She feels like he could come back at any time."

"And what of her mood?" I asked.

"I fear she has retreated once again. She eats nothing, not even sweets. As I said to Mr. Abel, she's right—her father will come to her again. It could be tomorrow, it could be a month from now, but it will happen. It's just when that we don't know."

"And you suppose there is something we can do," I said to them both.

The two of them looked down and shifted uncomfortably, as if suddenly doubting the wisdom of having involved us at all.

"You were right to bring it to us," said Alathea reassuringly. "Your master is beyond our reach, Mrs. Steeves, but maybe Carrie isn't. We shall see."

And with that mildest and least committal of all the encouraging phrases, we once again tied ourselves to Carrie Welton's safety and well-being.

# *Chapter 6*

*I* would not blame you for wondering at this point about our policing and the pathways of justice in Waterbury. Looking back from our turn-of-the-century perch, we must keep in mind that Waterbury, in 1859, had been incorporated as a city for only six years. Before that time, when it quite happily operated as a borough—no more than a primitive country town, really—Waterbury's justice of the peace was the one public functionary to whom matters of conduct were referred, and most of the laws had more to do with cattle running amok than with dangerous or antisocial human behavior. There were penalties for riding horses or driving wagons on sidewalks, and for disturbing the peace with gunfire, fireworks or even insistent carousing, but in general the great realm of Satan went unaddressed.

With the charter of 1853 came all the fine modern amenities: new laws, constables, a city court and a prison. And soon after, as if by decree, there was enough crime to put the entire apparatus to vigorous daily use. Drunks who once were sent home or down to the river to sleep it off were now put in a prison cell. Thieves who once had to answer to family and associates, and might have had a chance at redemption, were now arrested and became publicly known

73

as thieves. We were a rapidly growing town, of course, and admittedly in need of a stricter hand over our more wayward residents, but many of us lived on with fond feelings for the earlier day.

In any case, under neither system was justice equal for those who lived up on the hill and those who lived below. Many of our friends and acquaintances in the big houses looked upon the constables as an additional layer of servants hired to assist and protect but never intrude—and the constables, without any exception that I knew of, lived up to those expectations. One of them coming to a house on official business was obliged to knock at the kitchen door, enter when invited to do so, and interview the butler or housekeeper, who would then pass the word up or down or nowhere at all. Better yet, the police simply did not come to the house unless specifically summoned.

"Recall what Alla and I have just told you about Rose Hill," I said to our dinner guests two days after our visitation from Abel and Steeves. "When the coachman Archie Comstock was discovered with silver and Jane Welton's gold earrings in his bedside drawer, the constabulary was called and he was taken away, never to be seen again. A few words from Joseph Welton to the police foreman was all it took."

Freddie Olmsted broadened the observation.

"But Welton's own offenses, although arguably much graver as you have described them tonight, are considered none of the police's, nor the public's, business," he said, pushing back from the table and his last bite of mincemeat pie. "It would not be thinkable for the servant girl Polly to go to the police and file a complaint."

"Nor would our friend Carrie think of doing such a thing against her own father," said Alathea.

"Never," I agreed. "Welton is the master of his house and household. He is the source of all laws, justice and punishment. The customs of the great country seats in England or the southern plantations are not as different from our own as we in Connecticut sometimes like to believe."

Then Olmsted took the discussion out even further.

"Well then, what is the difference between Polly and a southern slave?" he asked, looking around at the rest of us.

"When she runs away, she will not be hunted down like an animal," I said.

"Maybe not. But she has no real justice, no recourse to laws," returned Olmsted.

"She can be punished, but she cannot accuse," added Alathea. "She can be governed, but she cannot vote."

"It is not much of a life, I grant you, but she can't be bought and sold," I said. "If she wants to go work in a thread mill or open a business attaching feathers to hats, she is free to do so. Surely you see there is enough of a distinction that we are about to embark on a great war over it."

It was not a tactful conversation to hold in the presence of servants, and the four of us went politely silent as the plates were cleared. Alathea and I sat at the ends of the table, with Freddie and Mary Olmsted, the widow of his brother John, who had died two years previous, at the sides. They had arrived earlier in the day by rail from New York and surprised us by announcing they would be married in June and then settle, with her three young children, in Manhattan, where Fred and a partner had just won a competition to improve a great swath of greensward right in the middle of the island.

I don't know which event seemed more unlikely to me— that he would be married and have children to consider, or that he could settle down long enough to take on such a major assignment in New York City—a project with the name of Central Park, no less. As I mentioned earlier in passing, I had met him at Yale, where he dropped in on lectures and many undergraduate conversations and carousings while his brother and I were students there (later he was made an honorary member of the Class of 1847). While I dutifully kept my head down, studied law and made my way back to Waterbury, Freddie ranged for a decade from one enthusiasm to another. His brother compared him to a monkey swinging from limb to limb. Leaving the family home in Hartford, he worked in a New York dry-goods store and took a year-long voyage in the China Trade. He studied surveying, engineering and chemistry, but then, spurred by we know not, became enamored of farming. When he told me about this new love, and of his desire to experience it first hand, I set him up on a Waterbury farm on the west side of the Naugatuck River, where he labored hard but not for long. During his time there, he decided he wanted to be a "scientific farmer," and when his father bought him a piece of land on Staten Island a couple of years later, that's what he set out to do. But he couldn't be tied down to that, either. In 1850, he took an extended walking tour of Europe and the British Isles, during which he saw numerous parks and private estates, a well as scenic countryside, and then published his first book, *Walks and Talks of an American Farmer*, in England. Next, he went on two journeys through the American South as a reporter for *The New York Times*. Through his reportage, he opposed the westward expansion of slavery and argued for its outright abolition. From 1855 to 1857 he was partner in a publishing firm and managing editor of *Putnam's Monthly Magazine*.

I know of all this right down to the dates because throughout the entire period he and I exchanged copious correspondence. At times, it seemed he conveyed back to me every step he took and every thought that entered his head, but many of his letters were full of adventure and gave me a vicarious pleasure. Mine must have seemed terribly plodding by comparison, although perhaps they provided him with a needed anchoring to home.

Now here he was—by all appearances domesticated at last, all set to marry the dull but perfectly acceptable widow of his younger brother—accompanying me into my study for port and cigars. During our long and windy dinner conversation, the four of us had covered marriage, war and the Byzantine politics of Manhattan—and finally, with great mutual trust among all, I had turned to the myriad troubles at Rose Hill. As we now sat, glasses in hand, in a more commodious setting, Olmsted offered a thought regarding the last.

"The girl across the street, the daughter—have you thought of the Hartford Female Seminary at all for her?" he asked.

"Carrie would benefit greatly from surroundings like that," I responded. "But Welton would never go for it. He has no use for female advancement, and certainly never of the Beecher kind. He has banned his own father in-law, a most righteous man, from his house for his views on slavery."

"No way to whisk her away, I suppose."

"I don't see how."

He held his glass of port up to the fire.

"You mentioned, or Alathea did, that she might be a painter," he said, changing his tack.

"It's something that might hold her interest, yes. She's mentioned it more than once. I saw one of her canvases— more than passable talent for a beginner, I'd say."

"I've fallen in with a group of painters in New York who share my outlook on many things," Olmsted said. "A highly skilled Hartford man, Frederic Church, is chief among them. They produce enormous pictures—monumental scenes of nature, the same sort of pristine views and spiritual feelings we are hoping to create in our park. We engage in much excited talk about general betterment coming out of a shared wilderness experience. We can go for hours, and sometimes we do. Anyway, I know a few of them have formal studios and academies in the city. Perhaps your Carrie would find happiness in one of those."

"I like that idea, Fred," I said, "but Alathea will know best. Would you send me their particulars?"

Olmsted assured me he'd do so straight away upon returning to Manhattan. I then stood and raised my glass privately to him. As I did so, I thought of how long I had known him and how many times we had raised our glasses together. I thought of his dear dead brother, John, whom I had loved as a brother, and of John's children, who would now be under his care.

"I know this will not be the end of your restless travels," I said, "but I hold out hope it will be the beginning of your true happiness. To you and Mary."

Freddie lifted his glass in return and we tossed back our port.

A week later, Alathea sat stiffly in Jane Welton's sunny parlor. She had been let in and attended to by Platt and now could observe the room and its furnishings as Jane made her way down from the upstairs. She told me later that she thought it strange that her father had sat in this room—and not only sat in it, but had seen to its design and construction. She looked up at the high ceiling, then out the big windows to the porch and the town below. He never got to enjoy it, though—not really. He was taken away so quickly, so cruelly, just as he was ready to celebrate all he had accomplished in life and all he loved. She thought of that first Christmas here, with all the family gathered in this very room, and little Willie squalling in her arms. Where did you go in such a hurry, Papa? Where are you now? Those were questions that plagued her. She had posed them to Mr. Bushnell, her pastor, but he could offer only reluctant mutterings and familiar stories. She fluttered a hand briefly over her expanding middle. "You would be very proud to have another grandchild, a baby Scovill, on the way," she whispered to the room. Thinking of new life helped her as she waited.

Her eye returned once again to the ceiling and the ornate plaster moldings and gas chandelier. In each doorway, high up, across the upper portion, were fanciful cross-hatchings, nearly abstract patterns made of wood, perhaps echoing the twig work of rustic camps. They had been a Welton fillip, not part of the original design. Were they meant to take down the scale of the rooms? She thought they looked like spider webs —and then it occurred to her that Carrie might think so, too. What a horrible image for someone in her desperate position —an entangling web ready to drop down every time she passed through a doorway.

"These flowers are not throwing any light here in this dark hallway, Mrs. Steeves," Jane Welton called behind her as she entered the parlor. "Bring them out here where the sunlight can pick them up."

She turned and came across the room with both arms outstretched and that smile turned up to full magnitude.

"Alathea," she said, taking both her hands. "I think we may have spring in the air at last!"

"I noticed on the walk over that we both have forsythia just budding," said Alathea. "And our little line of purple crocuses is thriving with the warmth from our foundation stones."

"Such delightful harbingers!"

"I wish that many other things in life could be so reliable."

The two women went on cordially like this, speaking of their plantings and grounds, of neighbors and relevant gossip, of social doings in the town at large. They were not close friends, but they knew how to be friendly enough. Still, Alathea had requested this meeting, and Jane would know it wasn't to discuss the coming of spring—which is why she'd waited until her husband was away on business in Albany before sending the invitation across the street. After tea had been served and poppyseed cakes consumed, Alathea brushed a crumb from her lap and cleared her throat.

"We have spoken of my Willie and Mary, but not one word about your Carrie," she said brightly. "She is still with you, I gather."

Jane was accustomed to fielding this question, or ones like it, from her many social acquaintances.

"She has not been well, but she is feeling better now."

"Not something serious, I hope."

Jane now revealed more than Alathea had expected.

"More of a mood, dark spells, keeping to herself—that sort of thing. Gideon Platt came and spoke with her and examined her but could find no specific complaint. He concluded that some activity of the mind or spirit would benefit her greatly."

This was a new frankness. She would not have spoken so freely a year ago. Neither woman knew for certain how much the other knew. Both harbored secrets, or what they thought to be secrets, about Carrie.

"Is there a school that might interest her?" Alathea asked. "There are a number now for young—."

"Her father will not allow it," Jane interrupted. She started to say something more but held back. She sipped her tea instead.

"When I first met Carrie, she brought me a painting she had done of our house," Alathea said. "Is that a pastime she'd be able to pursue, or would like to?"

Jane put down her cup. She was silent for a long moment and then closed her eyes briefly, bracing herself before turning them to Alathea and answering boldly.

"Would you like to ask Carrie yourself?" she asked.

Alathea was nearly dumbstruck. Things at Rose Hill clearly had moved well off the center line. Jane's habitual parroting of her husband's views, so apparent always, before every audience both large and small, was gone. A break had occurred. Perhaps the final straw had been the same wild episode that had led her housekeeper to seek help from Abel.

"I'd greatly enjoy that opportunity if she is well enough," Alathea said.

Jane spoke in a confidential voice.

"She must leave this house, Alathea," she said. "I cannot say why, and you must keep this a secret between us, but it would be best for her to do so—best for all of us. I tell you only because I know of the affection you have for her, and it has long been obvious that she feels the same way about you."

"Does she know you feel that way?" Alathea asked.

"She might. We haven't spoken about it directly, but of course she knows that she must leave as well as I do. If only we could find the right place for her."

"I may have it, Jane. It is why I have come to see you today. Through a friendly connection, I may have just the place."

After hearing the outline of Alathea's plan, Jane Welton left the room to go find her daughter. The tea had gone cold, but Alathea finished it anyway. She wondered if she'd given Jane too little credit all these years. With the endless parties and other social engagements, random extravagances and silly utterances, it was hard not to. But underneath, and maybe only recently, she had been suffering and felt a need to confide. It was if she had gradually come to see that although Joseph Welton might pass as a husband of a certain kind, he would never do as a father, certainly not to a lone girl. And maybe Jane bore some guilt as the one who had produced a female and then no more—and then had stood so willingly with Welton as a hard, unloving obstacle in her young daughter's life, looming like a wall she could never climb.

Now she re-entered the parlor with her daughter in hand. Alathea smiled and stepped toward Carrie to take her hand and embrace her. It was so freeing to be able to make such a gesture in Rose Hill, and in the presence of her mother. Carrie did not look well, however. She was pale and her skin was broken out. Her hair was lank and lacked any sign of a caring hand. And she was thin, terribly thin.

"Carrie, we have not seen you out riding, as has always been your custom," Alathea said. "We have missed the sound of Knight's hoofs down the street."

"I'm not yet strong enough, I don't think," Carrie responded. She was trying to assess the purpose of this meeting, which was a surprise to her, and how much she could safely say. "I spend many hours with Knight down in the stable, and Michael will take him out the back gate and through town for a run."

"That's fine, but you need exercise, too," Alathea said with concern. She looked to Carrie's mother for corroboration, but Jane did not respond. She had closed back up again and now wore a disconnected look, as if bringing Carrie into the room was as far as she dared go on this day. Even Alathea could not escape the feeling that Joseph Welton was watching and would exact his punishment for this at a date and time, and in a manner, known only to him.

"I wonder if we might go visit Knight," Alathea said.

"Oh yes, let's!" Carrie brightened at the idea.

"Yes, go," said Jane, perhaps with relief. "I will leave you both to it. I have some notes to write."

The two women left the house arm-in-arm, walking slowly beneath the porte-cochere and down to the carriage house and stable. The late morning air was unseasonably warm and full of promise. The trees remained leafless, but their buds were reddening and getting ready to unfurl—the magnolia planted at Alathea's suggestion when Rose Hill was built would lead the way. A delegation of robins had arrived, possibly on this very morning, and were busily picking through the softening turf.

"You have been inside too much, Carrie," Alathea said, drawing the girl close.

"And you are expecting another child," said Carrie.

Alathea reflexively looked away. These were still the days of confinement for women in the last months of their pregnancies so that the public at large would not be subjected to the inelegancies of child bearing. She had not yet reached that late, distended stage, but her condition was evident. Jane had chosen not to mention the fact. Carrie couldn't wait to say something.

"You don't have to comment on everything you see or think," said Alathea with an indulgent smile.

"I meant it as a happy observation. When will it be born?"

"In June or July."

Carrie made a woeful face.

"I wish you well, but I will kill myself if I am still here then."

"But you will be," said Alathea. "If you won't even so much as leave your bedroom, how will you be anywhere but here when summer comes?"

"I know. I have given up," Carrie said. "My father will not allow me even the simplest of friendships."

"Why not?"

"You know the answer," she said matter-of-factly. "We have secrets and he is a brute. He wishes I were a boy. He hits me. But now he hits others, too."

Alathea feigned ignorance.

"What others?" she asked.

Carrie told the story of the servant Polly. Her account was very much as Steeves had told it. But Carrie ended with the thought she should have done something to save Polly. She said that she'd sat on her bed, listening and imagining, outraged at Polly's innocence in the matter, but unable to think of what she should do. Intercede? She said it would have been as futile as throwing herself in front of a cannon.

"And then Polly ran off, as if to show me how easy that would be to do," Carrie concluded. "But I didn't. I lost my strength and my will. I've despaired these last two weeks." She paused, then looked Alathea in the eye. "And now, very unexpectedly, you are here."

They had reached the stable, which was around the back of the carriage house and a level below. They entered through the darkened opening and could hear stirring inside. There were four horses in their stalls, but Knight was given primacy, with larger, more polished quarters. Carrie no doubt saw personally to his needs. The stallion capered playfully as they came near—midnight black, handsome and muscular, affectionate for Carrie—he was of a heroic bearing. She fed him a poppyseed cake she'd stolen from the parlor tray, then with the greatest care ran her palm up and down his forehead.

"You are the one I love most, aren't you?" she said softly to the horse. "You don't disappoint me, I don't disappoint you, and that's the way it must always be."

Knight nuzzled Carrie's neck and then ducked down to her pocket, where another cake was waiting. Carrie gave it to him and turned to Alathea.

"People are so... awful, don't you find?" she said. "They are forever complicating things that should be simple and clear, and they make beautiful things ugly. They can destroy with only a word or two."

"You have been doing some thinking up there in your room," Alathea said.

"Animals don't do that. They don't scheme and connive. They love you for who you are."

"Along those lines, your mother has surprised me," Alathea said. "She has been very brave to allow me to see you this way."

"Do you think so?" Carrie said.

"I think it goes against all her instincts for your safety, and for hers."

"For hers. Exactly. She cannot have me here any longer and still live the life she wishes to live for herself. My situation is too unpredictable, and after the episode with Polly she knows there is danger in it, too."

"Would your father be happy to know I was here with you?"

"Never."

"Then your mother must have some credit, and maybe more than you know."

"Why is that?"

They left the stable and began the walk back up to the house, their arms again linked.

"What if you were able to get far away from this place?" Alathea said. "What if you were to go to New York to paint and learn about the city and the wide world and meet entirely new people and put Rose Hill and Waterbury and everything else well behind you? How does that idea strike you?"

Carrie stopped walking and gave Alathea a disbelieving look, as if she were no longer a mere neighbor but rather an angel or an Arabian genie. Then, as racing clouds can suddenly pull apart and flood a spring pasture with sunshine, her face was overtaken by something at once radiant and fierce, and she embraced Alathea with all her might. Through a joyful rising of tears she told her that, yes—

yes, that sounded like it would be a very good idea, indeed, and thank you, thank you, oh thank you!

And so it was that a month later, six days after her eighteenth birthday, and following a long, difficult eighteen months by anyone's standards, Carrie mounted Knight (no, it would not be a train ride for Carrie, nor a stagecoach, carriage or wheeled conveyance of any kind) and began her journey from Rose Hill to New York City.

It is perhaps needless to say at this point that her father did not see her off, but he had finally agreed to the experiment, and Jane must get credit there, too, for prodding. At some level of his being, he must have known there was wisdom in getting Carrie out from under his roof. The most common way of doing this, of course, would be to marry her off, but he figured her as too odd a case, too wretched a soul, for that. He'd publically been heard to say as much. But in private he went further. Even if there were such a fool as wanted to marry their daughter, he'd told Jane, what sort of thoughts and secrets might they share? He could not afford to have stories and rumors and exaggerations upset his business dealings in town. He was adamant about that. He'd seen it happen with others, whether it was drinking or gambling or other renegade behavior, or in some cases all three of them in one unfortunate man. Even poor judgment—an outburst of temper or an ill-timed verbal attack—could be wrongly taken. And then word gets around and people pull back, and almost overnight everything you'd built up is gone, and others move in to take up the work as greedy as flies on a fish. All that hard labor for naught, all the years of scrambling and hustling. And all because you had made a simple mistake!

"What if she were to go off to New York, Joe?" his wife asked, as she later related to Alathea. They were in the middle of a conversation about Carrie, one Jane had insisted upon and that Welton had reluctantly agreed to. They stood (for he would not sit for such a thing) on Rose Hill's second-floor porch early one morning before he left for the pin shop.

"And do what there?" he wanted to know. "Certainly not a seminary. She is unfit for it and the harpies will only turn her more against us."

"There is an art school that will have her, friends of the Kingsburys—"

"Ah, the Kingsburys!" Welton snorted. "I should have guessed it."

"The painters are brothers, the Harts, and their sister is Mrs. Beers, a widow with two young daughters, who manages the academy," Jane continued quickly. "Carrie would have room and board and livery, she would learn to paint and assist in the running of the school and studio, and she would travel with Mrs. Beers if needed."

"How do we know she would not run wild through the streets of Manhattan as she has done here?"

"There is a Mrs. Olmsted who has promised to keep an eye on her, a woman much trusted by Fred Kingsbury."

Welton grunted but did not yet agree.

"Boys go off to college when they are Carrie's age," Jane continued. "She needs to get out of this house. No good can happen to her here—or to us with her here."

"Boys go off to become men. What would Carrie become?"

There was no answer to Welton's question, and Jane told Alathea she did not try to supply one. It was something she'd already wondered to herself, as did most everyone who had come into contact with her remarkable presence ever since she was a little girl—servants, shopkeepers, teachers, neighbors, the man who swept the street, the curate at St. John's Church. What would Carrie become, they wondered—or what would become of Carrie? Not quite the same thing? Maybe not, but in neither case could the answer be known.

Even so, two days later, Welton gave his blessing and put some money behind it, as he might with a wager. "She is a danger to us if she stays," were his only relevant words on the matter. Jane Welton told us of his decision, and we, through the Olmsteds, got the message to Mrs. Beers. Carrie, we were informed in return, would be welcome at any time. It was her idea, of course, to turn her trip to New York into an adventure. She sent her trunks of belongings ahead by train and then plotted out a four-day journey on horseback, with overnights at inns in New Haven, then Fairfield, then Greenwich, and finally into New York. The roads were in good condition and a lone young female on horseback was not unheard of at the time, at least in daylight, but putting up in a room over a tavern, as she originally planned, brought unnecessary risk into play. Instead, Alathea and I put my Yale network into play and arranged for Carrie to stay with friends of ours along the way—the Baldwins in New Haven, the Jennings in Fairfield, the Applewhites in Rye—making up an itinerary she agreed to. She would have agreed to just about anything, so happy she was to be leaving.

And now here she was, on this fine morning, all set to go. I put off going to the bank so I could see her off. Alathea, Willie, Cherry and I crossed the street and joined Jane at the top of the drive. By now, all the leaves and flowers were out and our hillside was resplendent with the colors and aromas of spring. Below us, the town sent up its dissonant song of couplings from the rail yard, hammering and pounding from new structures going up, and the insistent hum of factory works both near and far across the valley floor.

"Salem, Straitsville, Bethany, Woodbridge, New Haven," Carrie called her route down to me like a schoolgirl reciting her lesson. "And Elizabeth Baldwin is someone to learn a great deal from," she added with cheerful mockery, again repeating something I had advised her of earlier.

"Make light at your own risk," I teased her.

"I hope you will send us sketches of your new surroundings," Alathea said.

"They will have to teach me well, or you will not recognize a church spire from a mulberry tree," she answered.

Her mother raised a hand up to her. Carrie squeezed it without a word. She next took a step or two and leaned down to where Alathea and I stood.

"Thank you," she said quietly. "Thank you to both of you for listening to Steeves when she came to you, and acting upon her words. I thought you might, but I didn't dare hope. You did, though, and now I feel as if my life is beginning at last!"

With that, the truth was told. It was she who had sent Steeves to Abel for tea that Thursday afternoon and then watched from afar, as it were, as her scheme hatched out, step by step, finally into this morning of glorious freedom. Carrie had engineered her own escape! Once more she had left me foundering and speechless. I could only smile helplessly and wave back as she waved, turned away from us and, with Willie shouting his goodbyes and Cherry yapping at her stallion's hoofs, set out down the hill and onward to her great adventure.

# *Chapter 7*

*T*he following years were so filled with the clamor of war and upheavals in Waterbury and in the Kingsbury family that it is hard to account for them in any methodical way.

The war struck blow after terrible blow. The tensions built up all through 1860 and into the spring 1861, as violent episodes of one sort or another in the South and West threatened to ignite the larger conflagration. We read the breathless accounts in the newspapers and wondered not if, but when, the mortal struggle would begin. Like most other cities and towns in the North, Waterbury had outwardly seemed indifferent to the idea of going to war, and, in fact, the loudest voices had been the ones opposed to abolition and what turned out to be the Union cause. Then on April 11 the rebels attacked Fort Sumter in Charleston, and the powerful feelings of the quiet majority were at last aroused. It was as if a long dormant colossus had suddenly roared to life. Four days later, on April 15, President Lincoln called for troops. On April 20, Waterbury's Company D of the First Regiment, known to us as the City Guard, departed for New Haven, about eighty strong under the command of Col. John Lyman Chatfield. Before they left, they were made to take part in the ceremonies of what, in the way of these things, had been turned into a holiday. Their first assault as a unit came from the nine speakers who addressed them from the bandstand on the Green. They seemed to weather it well. Two bands next accompanied the men as they marched to the railroad station, their Sharpe's rifles and Springfield muskets on their shoulders. After they'd gone off to New Haven, and then on to Washington, money, some $10,000, was quickly raised at a town meeting for the care of their families.

In the weeks and months that followed, the exercise was repeated many times, as additional fighting units formed and left for the distant battle grounds—more than 900 men from Waterbury alone. It quickly became apparent that, despite the best of intentions, no subsequent leaving would match the enthusiasm of the first. And then, inevitably, as we followed the war through daily dispatches and letters from the front, the soldiers began trickling back home. They arrived in every which way—the sick, lame, lucky and dead forming a motley parade. The roll call in our town spared neither character nor class.

Henry Kingsbury, for example, the son of a cousin, had the bad luck to graduate from West Point in 1860. He was killed at the head of his column during the battle of Antietam while carrying the stone bridge at Harper's Ferry.

Hiram Upson, Jr., was said to have displayed courage and coolness at the first battle of Bull Run, but was mortally wounded in an assault upon the Confederate earthworks at James Island, S.C.

Even Col. Chatfield, who had marched off under such good auspices on that earliest day, was not spared. He died after heroically leading his men in the attack on Fort Wagner, S.C. He was wounded several times in the field but did not finally succumb to his wounds until he was back in Waterbury some three weeks later.

Not all deaths were so glorious, of course. Henry Peck's army life lasted only six months. He took part in one fight, the Battle of Fredericksburg, but was exposed to illness and died of typhoid pneumonia while hospitalized in Washington.

Perhaps saddest of all to Alathea and me was the news one day late in the war that Gilbert Stocking had died of illness while attached to Sherman's famous March. We would always think of him most fondly as the cheerful Yale freshman who dressed as a Prussian soldier and flirted with Carrie at the Welton's famous Thanksgiving Ball.

The slow tolling of bells and hanging of black crepe continued all through those years, in remembrance of these I've just mentioned and all the others who perished from wounds or disease in the war. Such was the constant state of mourning that even many of our newly constructed churches, public buildings and monuments took on a funereal caste in the form of a building material called brownstone. No one was in the mood for the shining marble, limestone or granite of former times.

As for my own service, I was drafted in 1863 at the age of 40 and struggled with my usefulness as a soldier of advanced years versus my role in helping to run one of the Union's vital manufacturing plants. At length, and after lively discussions with local elders and Alathea especially, I decided to buy my way out of active duty by paying $800 for a substitute, a strapping young local German named Drescher. In the years since, I have often thought about my decision and the privileges of my position at that time. I admit to having felt guilt over the matter. But my present-day acceptance of this wartime decision is no doubt greatly assuaged by the fact that Drescher served with honor and returned intact to Waterbury, where his family went on to establish a prominent standing of its own.

And I did indeed have a company to run, for the more the nation's outlook darkened in the 1860s, the more Waterbury's industries clanged and roared. Our fortunes had been rising in the decade leading up to the war, as I have earlier indicated, but when war finally came it seemed that nearly everything our factories produced was in high demand - and if you needed something new made, or invented, or produced in quantity, Waterbury could do that, too. Beneath the belching smokestacks, we turned out— among scores of other products—kettles and canteens, wagon wheel hubs, swords and scabbards, buckles, igniting wicks, stirrups and a torrent of buttons—so many buttons that Waterbury Button produced them for both Union and Confederate uniforms, making sure the latter paid with gold or Yankee currency and not their own peculiar notes. For some companies, it seemed, there was no taking sides on the shop floor, not if a dollar could be made.

As our own wartime fortunes rose at Scovill's, and our workforce grew from 150 to more than 500, I was obliged to take over the dual posts of treasurer and secretary for the company. New workers for our plant and others poured into the city, many of them recent arrivals from Ireland, Germany, French Canada, Lithuania and Russia. When I spoke to a group of our workers, I could never be sure that a single word of mine was understood. But they worked hard and took on any task we gave them, and they gave the city sinew and strength and, eventually, character. As demand for Scovill's products grew both near and far, so did our presence in the town. We built new plants along the Mad River and began to think of digging distant reservoirs to bring more water power into our operations. We felt satisfied with our role in the war effort, and spoke often of it reassuringly to one another during our monthly board meetings, but of course there was more to it than shiny altruism. Between my salaries (for the bank was booming with new depositors as well) and stock, and Alathea's substantial holdings, our financial lives had been made, even after an income tax instituted during the war (temporarily, as it turned out) had taken its share.

If only the accumulation of wealth was all there was to a life.

All our money and prestige and connections in society were not remotely enough to save our poor Willie when he was struck down by illness at the age of 10. On a morning in May, 1863, he awoke and complained of not feeling well and of having an ache all over. As the day wore on he became feverish and lethargic. We began to watch him anxiously. At dusk he complained of a severe pain at the base of his skull. We called upon Gideon Platt, our trusted family physician, known to both Alathea and me since we were children. He and his faithful sorrel horse came into our drive and he entered with black bag in hand, in every respect a picture of steadiness and accumulated wisdom. We followed him up the stairs and waited in the hallway as he examined the boy behind closed doors. After too short a time, he came back out to us.

"He is a brave boy," he told us as he removed his glasses, "and he will have to fight hard." He faced my wife, taking hold of her arm. "Alathea, I'm afraid he has a form of brain fever—meningitis—that the men have brought back from the South."

It was the worst news possible.

"What can we do? Is there a treatment?" she asked, her voice rising. "Can he be bled? Should we starve him?"

The doctor spoke calmly but there was no mistaking his message.

"There is nothing to do with this fever but try to keep him comfortable," he said. "He will survive it and recover, or he will take his leave of us."

Alathea's eyes widened. She put her hand up to her mouth in alarm and rushed off into Willie's room. I accompanied Dr. Platt down the stairs. He stopped just for a moment by the door.

"It's a very tough one, Kingsbury," he said. "The boy has so little in reserve."

Then he gave a nod and climbed up onto his carriage.

For the next three days, we sat by Willie's side and witnessed his terrible struggle. During the day, we opened his bedroom windows and let in as much light and fresh spring air as we could. At night, his lighted sickroom became the center of all things. We came and left and came again and spoke in hushed voices around his bed. Miss Lewis slept in a chair by the window; during those days I never saw her anywhere other than in or near Willie's room. But he did not improve. On the last day, as his fever raged, he fell in and out of delirium, nonsensically counting numbers and reciting the alphabet in his fragile high voice. He put his hands to the back of his head and cried and complained of the terrible pain. I sat by him and stroked his head and neck, whispering whatever prayers I could devise. After some little time, he looked up at me and said, "Thank you, Papa, I think that is all right." And then within thirty more minutes, and without a further word, he was gone.

It is one thing to lose a child at birth or in infancy. It was not an uncommon event in those days, or these, and we were in some part steeled against it, especially Alathea, who had been a party to it with her own siblings. But to have a good boy like our eldest—our dear Willie—die in your arms after you have shared his laughter and wiped his tears and proudly watched him as he began to take in the big world and show how he might make his way through it—well, that is nearly too much to bear. We could—and did—turn our attention to his sisters, now Mary, Alice and Edith, and the baby, Freddie, but the void that opened up upon Willie's death could never be bridged.

One thing Alathea and I did to help mend ourselves after our son's death was to resume our walks in the neighborhood. As summer came on that year, the weather held fine, and we took to retracing our old promenades. Above us on the hill, a couple of new streets had been laid out and a few new houses built, or were in the process. The wartime construction was, for the most part, modest. No one was building castles, even if they had the money to do so. The architectural exuberance shown during the 1850s, including our own, would not return for another fifteen or twenty years.

Although we regularly departed and re-entered using our front gate, we saw little of our neighbors across the street. Jane Welton continued her compulsive party-giving, although many of her galas were now held for the benefit of our soldiers, their families and the war effort in general. Separately, she also continued the tradition of the Thanksgiving Ball, even if none ever matched the excesses (or—and I will say it—the excitement) of the first one. Certainly, there would be no more pavilions built just for the occasion, Joseph Welton no doubt having made his feelings quite clear on that account. The most recent affair, in 1862, was not really a proper ball at all, but rather a very large dinner party. There was music but no dancing. The commodious rooms at Rose Hill filled up and the mood was quite pleasant and comfortable, but rightfully subdued. As we enjoyed our green turtle soup and goose with turnips, I could not help recalling the words Willard Spencer had uttered four years earlier, when he predicted that instead of marveling at actors painted up as Prussian soldiers hurrying off to battle, we'd be facing the horrors of the real thing. He had been proven correct, and now the pretenses of that far-off evening seemed impossibly vain and frivolous.

As to the Weltons themselves, Joseph remained a distant, dark, disapproving figure, busy in commerce but taking part in no civic, social or fraternal activities. Others in our circle regarded him with increasing wonder—not only was he unfriendly to the point of being unapproachable, but it was seen as a duty of successful men in our growing community to give some part of their time, however large or small, to the good of all, and he would have no part of that. When asked to participate in a local project, he'd claim that his factories were providing jobs and wages, and that should be enough. Needless to say, if every man in his position took such a stand, we would have no libraries or hospitals or public parks—in fact no civilization at all save for grasping hands and belching smokestacks. We'd heard a report or two of Welton's temperamental outbursts regarding wayward employees; on the other hand, our network of backstairs intelligence told of no further incidents, not major ones at least, with servants or anyone else in his household.

Meanwhile, Alathea and Jane had been together at any number of ladies-only luncheons and teas, and had on occasion spoken cordially if somewhat stiffly with each other. But there had been no invitations between them for intimate visits or one-on-one teas. Jane had memorably gone out of character at the last one—had for once risked her own well-being for her daughter's sake—and no doubt had little desire to revisit that brave moment. Alathea understood that this was the case, and felt Jane needed protection from her husband nearly as much as Carrie or that poor servant girl had. If that meant Jane would not be fraternizing with her Kingsbury neighbors, so be it. On several occasions at more general gatherings, however, Alathea heard Jane speaking to an assembled group about Carrie and her new life in New York.

"She is so obviously untruthful when she speaks of Carrie," Alathea said one day upon returning from a tea at Cornelia Benedict's. "She tells a carefree tale to all who will listen—you'd think Carrie had never had a problem in her life, and that she is the most sought-after young woman in New York. But her eyes, I think, tell another story, and she will never look my way."

I could tell Alathea had been particularly upset by something on this day.

"Well, no one else needs to know the truth as we know it, do they?" I asked.

"Of course not, but there's no need for fairy tales."

"And when it counted, she was instrumental in getting Carrie out of the house and to relative safety."

Alathea shot me a look.

"Following your lead," I added quickly.

"Yes. But sometimes I want the world to know what went on in that house, and what still might go on. Don't you?"

I repeated what I had already said many times—that I wished there were a way to hold Welton accountable for his behavior without further endangering or humiliating his wife and daughter. But my wife was not quite finished. She at last got to what was truly on her mind.

"When our own child lay pale and trembling in his bed, we would have given our own lives to save him if it were only possible," she said. "I would have bargained with the devil himself just to get another chance for Willie." Alathea gestured vaguely toward Rose Hill.

"And they have but one child and look what they've done," she continued, her voice quavering. "They've given her a life of nothing but misery and doubt—*doubt*, Frederick, this bright, magnificent girl never knows who she is or where she stands—and then they cast her out, feeling only relief, to distant streets and strangers. How could you do such a thing to a child who only wanted to love and be loved in return?"

She looked at me helplessly, for there was, again, no answer.

"We can only vow that we will never give our own children any reason to doubt their place in our care and affections," I said, and took Alathea in my arms, for she was now, at last, after all these weeks, sobbing uncontrollably in grief, and soon so was I, not for Carrie, but for our own terrible loss.

It remains remarkable to me today to think that even through the agony of war, turmoil and death of those days, even through the daily domestic eruptions of having four young children under one roof, and the unending pressures of my banking and manufacturing interests, the welfare of Carrie Welton was never very far from our uppermost thoughts. It had been about three years since she had cantered off on that spring morning. During that time, we had seen her but twice, briefly, in Waterbury (once for one of the Thanksgiving galas, once when Jane underwent a medical procedure); we had received intermittent reports from Mary Olmsted (all quite positive); and we had our own correspondence with her (almost entirely between Carrie and Alathea). At first, her letters came quite frequently. They were brief but contained the essentials. The very first one gives a good taste:

My Dear Mr. and Mrs. Kingsbury,

"Knight of the Forest" and I have only been here for two weeks, but already we are beginning to feel like natives. As you probably know, the studio is in the Dodsworth Building on Fifth Avenue at 26th Street, right across from Madison Square. Both Mrs. Olmsted and Mrs. Beers were here to greet me when I arrived. Mrs. Beers' two brothers, named Hart, have studios here, and so does she! She is not the usual item at all. There is no Mr. Beers evident and she is raising her young daughters, Martha and Emily, here. They run free and are often quite covered in paint! Knight and I have been exploring our environs in wider and wider circles, and I can tell you most assuredly that nothing in Waterbury can match it. Well, one thing does. Would you ever guess that the name of our neighborhood here is Rose Hill? It is always good to have a constant reminder of home, I say, and all the happy days I spent there. I must go now, but I do want to thank you both once again for all your efforts on my behalf. You would be pleased to see the color in my cheeks, Alathea (Do I <u>dare</u> call you that?). And I managed it without standing on my head, as Mother once told me to do just before guests arrived!

Affectionately,
Carrie

The letters that followed slowed in number and differed in their particulars, but Carrie's enthusiasm and sense of discovery in the city remained undiminished. For our part, we were happy to hear from her, but thought of her now as a friend who had gone away and was busily making a new life for herself. The particulars would come in due time. We spoke often of going to New York for pleasure and taking Carrie out to dinner and letting her show us her environs, but the disruptions of wartime life and commerce always seemed to get in the way.

And then one very warm evening in late July, as Alathea and I strolled down Prospect Street toward the Green with Edith and Alice, we saw Carrie riding up the hill in a livery cab. I hailed her with a shout, and she ordered the conveyance to stop and let her down, and then sent it on to Rose Hill with her belongings.

She never looked better, or seemed more genuinely outgoing. There was an easy grace in her stride as she crossed the street. She wore a summer dress, brown and white striped, with ruffled sleeves. Her hair was long but swept up, with just a few curls straying onto her perspiring brow. She smiled broadly as she approached.

"I was hoping you wouldn't be away," she said, and made a special hello to the children.

"Where could we go with our disorganized clan?" said Alathea. "It would take us so long to get anywhere, we'd just have to turn right around and head back home."

The two women laughed and embraced and I held Carrie by both hands and drew her close. Her eyes were clear and untroubled.

"What brings you back to Waterbury?" I asked. "I don't think your mother is at home."

"She is away with her sister at Momauguin and my father is off for at least a week to Worcester and Boston. I can sneak into the house and use it as a safe haven."

"Haven from what?" Alathea asked.

"Let's not speak on this dusty street," I interrupted. "Please come up with us to our house for a glass of lemonade, Carrie. We can sit in our new outdoor room and hear all about your adventures in New York."

Ten minutes later, with the children otherwise occupied, we were seated in impromptu fashion in our porch, a recent addition to Henry Austin's original creation. Many of the finer houses were putting porches on, with the perhaps exaggerated notion that sitting out in the air, but with comfort, would lead in due course to better health and improved overall happiness. Whether this was true or not, it was too soon to tell, and very likely the matter would never be the subject of scientific study.

However, our porch possessed something that was, as far as I knew, unique. At Scovill's we had not long ago taken an order from the War Department for 7,000 camp sieves, but because of a miscalculation on our part we'd produced far more of the fine wire mesh than was needed for the job. In a moment of sublime inspiration, one of the men at the shop put up a length of the uncut mesh across a couple of windows in his department to keep out the mosquitoes that sometimes swarmed up from the river in summertime. After applauding his ingenuity and ordering more of the same for certain other factory windows, I realized the wire barrier might do just as well for our new outdoor living room, then under construction. And so, after a few quick design changes, it had. Although our views down the hill and out across the city were to a slight degree darkened and impeded, the flies, mosquitoes, moths and other flying pests were kept in their own realm, and we in ours. Before long, of course, these coverings, significantly refined, would be called "screens" and many houses and businesses would employ them (although, oddly, our company would never manufacture them).

After I had finished telling Carrie the overlong porch-and-screen story, Alathea with an air of some impatience returned to what she considered to be the real subject at hand.

"You spoke on the street of seeking a safe haven, Carrie," she said. "What are you running from?"

Carrie took a sip of lemonade.

"As you probably are aware, New York has gone mad," she said.

"We have been reading about the riots—draft riots, they call them," I said. "Terrible reports, almost as harrowing as the war itself, it seems. Have they involved you in any way?"

"They involve everyone in some way. There have been roving, violent Irish mobs in the streets, and sounds of running and shouting through the night and the smell of smoke in the air. They burned down the Colored Orphan Asylum just to the north of us. They grab people on the street and beat them. There's such a sense of dread and danger."

"Are bodies hanging from lampposts?" asked Alathea, who had followed the reports with me.

"They have hanged blacks and drowned them. It is very dangerous to be a sympathizer or even someone who looks well-off enough so that he might have paid the deference fee."

I hoped Carrie did not see the color rise from my collar.

"And then another danger swept into the city," she continued.

"What is that?" I asked.

"In Madison Square, directly across the street from where we live, they are now tenting thousands of troops sent to quell the rioting."

"And they are as bad as the rioters," I offered.

"For me, worse. They are a nightmarish presence—just a sea of stupid, filthy boys. I cannot leave the house or look out a window without their catcalls and confident talk. Their numbers give them courage. Even now, after the rioting has eased, the troops remain and made it impossible for me to stay any longer."

"At least you are able to come back home," said Alathea.

"My mother wrote and just in passing mentioned the house would be empty and then typically wondered how the servants would abuse the situation. It never occurred to her that I might abuse it, too." She raised a hand and then continued. "I have realized I haven't spoken to you since your dear Willie's death."

"You wrote a very fine letter," said Alathea. "It meant a great deal to us."

"I shall never forget hoisting him on my knee to 'Ride a Cock-Horse,' and how his laughter made me laugh, too."

There was a long silent moment as my wife refilled the glasses. A June bug bounced loudly but haplessly against our wire barrier.

"Have you become a painter at all, Carrie?" I asked.

"I am closer to Mrs. Beers' children in talent than I am to her, I'm afraid," she said, relieved to have a change of subject. "I continue to sketch and paint, and I enjoy it, but it's easy to see that I lack real talent. Anyway, I have gradually become less a student and more what they call an *au pair*—a useful member of the household who isn't paid."

"Do you have specific duties that you must perform?" asked Alathea.

"I am more a helper, but I am far from a governess. I also attend parties and openings with the Harts and am encouraged to take part when visitors call on us."

"Other painters?"

"Often."

"And what are they like?"

Carrie laughed. "A singular breed."

"How so?"

My wife, with a window opening onto a forbidden world of sorts, had turned into an avid questioner.

"They don't necessarily hold to what we might call 'Waterbury conventions'," Carrie said. "You would think them unkempt and uncouth, and they are often penniless. Some are dashing, others only desperate. The gatherings are very rarely dull."

"As opposed to teas at Rose Hill," Alathea said.

Carrie nodded and gestured toward the house across the street.

"I am out of Rose Hill, that is one thing. I am away from the heavy hand of my parents, and my father's endless disapproval in particular. But New York offers many temptations and I have fallen prey to some of them. I am open to risk and I don't know if I am a good judge of character. I lack experience, even now. The people I meet seem to know so much more of the world than I do. Men always seem one step ahead of me, and it's usually a step I don't want to take."

"Men always want to lead the dance," said Alathea.

"That doesn't get them far with me. I am quite sensitive to the extra degree of pressure and the steering smile."

Then she tried just such a smile of her own.

"Anyway, when Mrs. Beers travels to paint with her group of ladies, as she has done these past two summers, I am invited to come along," she continued. "In fact, from here I am traveling to Saratoga Springs to meet her and her traveling group."

"Who makes up this group?" Alathea asked brightly, although she was disappointed in the fresh tack. She also gave me a look that I read to say Carrie would only reveal so much while in my presence.

"Well-to-do New York women," said Carrie. "It's a new thing she is trying. For a fee, Mrs. Beers leads them out of the city to a boarding house run by a Mrs. Jensen and from there to lovely retreats in the country where they can observe and paint, as well as dine and converse together. I gather the idea is based on similar exercises in Europe, especially in Italy."

"And what will your role be there?" Alathea asked.

"Mostly to watch her children. They are still only small and could not by any means be left behind in the city. I will take them on outings and picnics and present them to the ladies at opportune moments."

"Be careful, Carrie," I teased. "I hear from local touts that they've just opened a new horse racing oval at Saratoga this summer. Your allowance will be in danger."

"I would love to see the horses run!" Carrie said. "But we will more likely keep ourselves to the spring-water tonics and sketchbooks."

Our conversation then turned to more local matters—changes in the neighborhood in the three years since she'd left, the tragic, seemingly endless course of the war (although the recent news from Gettysburg seemed promising), and our diminished contact with her parents. At length, we could hear the various signals of our own household calling out to us, and we had to let Carrie go. We promised to see more of each other in the few days ahead before she was to depart for upstate New York.

It shouldn't come as a surprise that Alathea saw Carrie the very next day, in a spur-of-the-moment reprise of their first tea together. It was probably no shock, either, that, despite her great affection for, and trust in, Alathea and me, Carrie had not told us—could not find a way to tell us with me present—the whole truth about what she had come to Waterbury to escape. Had the draft riots, the Irish renegades and sudden infestation of hectoring federal troops in her Manhattan neighborhood been a nightmare? No doubt they had. But there was something else at work as well. Amidst all the various social groups that made up her life in the city during these three years—the Harts and all the rest of the brash young painters, the parties, the Olmsteds' fascinating circle, the high-flying business hustlers who also swam in those waters—there was in addition a repetitive discordant note for Carrie, as teased out by Alathea. She was desired by men and did not know how to respond to them. This had been true nearly from the day of her arrival, but as her circle widened, so had the number of men who wanted to squire her, romance her, be with her, take her arm, show off in front of her and even fight over her. The men, many of them, were young, ambitious and highly competitive—the very stuff and marrow of a bold, aggressive city. Carrie understood that she was supposed to be pleased by the attention, but she did not always feel that way. In truth, she didn't know precisely how she felt. In some respects, she enjoyed being in the company of men, with their forthright conversations, low humor and dares. She could ride with them, run with them, enter through any forbidden doorway with them. But at the same time, she had her reasons—most intimate ones anchored in her thoughts of her own domineering father, and of dear Polly, and more—for not trusting men and for being wary of the strong grip on her arm, and for resenting their superior position in society. And now, with some of them, especially the ones who seemed to want to possess her, she'd felt a growing sense of unease.

As much as anything, she said to my wife, she'd sought a few summer nights' refuge in an empty Rose Hill to see if she could escape, or at least sensibly consider, those feelings. And then in a matter of days there would follow the long, careless respite in Saratoga Springs. As she'd lain in bed the night before, Carrie had tried to imagine those sun-dappled lawns and found a little peace, but it was not lasting. For her, she said, Rose Hill was haunted, not only by her former days in Waterbury, but also by the thought (as she soon after wrote in one of her increasingly rare letters to Alathea) "that happiness—true, lasting happiness with another person— might be nothing more than a ghostly dream as well, an elusive, unknowable presence forever hovering just beyond my grasp. And one more troubling thought: Even if I were somehow to find that love, mightn't it turn out to be just another room in the house that already holds me, and another obstacle thrown up against me to keep me from ever truly breaking free?"

# Part 2

## Chapter 8

".Notice the light, Carrie. See how it washes across the side of that big limestone façade. That purplish pink! We could be in Greece or Capri!"

It was so tiresomely repetitive for a painter to notice the light and enthuse over its virtues, thought Carrie. It was an early evening in late September, 1864 in Manhattan—not that September was a uniquely superior time for natural light; painters found equal pleasure, and felt free to express it, in the colors of February and May and every other month as well. And no, she thought further, we could not just as easily be in Capri. We are on Fifth Avenue, the lower part, our carriage bumping along on new cobblestones through the pungent odors of manure and offal toward Tenth Street, where many more painters, poets, writers and actors, all gathered for tonight's gala, would no doubt be held equally in thrall by the sun's fading display.

The painter sharing the carriage with Carrie as a sort of chaperone was James McDougal Hart. He was a raffish fellow of 35 years, happily married, rather short, with long curls and a drooping mustache beneath a slouch hat that he wore at a raked angle. He wished no one to miss the fact that he was an artist. As indeed he was—one of three talented Harts to whom Carrie had grown attached during her time in New York. James' older brother William was a landscape painter of increasing renown, and their sister, Julie Hart Beers, was the woman with whom Carrie lived and whose children she watched, with, she could readily admit after four years, diminishing interest.

Which was much the way she now regarded the slowly passing limestone façade.

"Do they have limestone on Capri?" was all she could think to ask.

"I couldn't tell you," admitted Hart. "I've never been there —only seen it on canvas. But I believe limestone is common to the Mediterranean."

The conversation could not proceed from there, and it didn't. Such was their friendship, however, that Carrie felt no need to fill in the long pause that followed—not her strong suit even on the best of days. She listened to the clop of hooves and looked out upon Fifth Avenue, wondering anxiously how she would be received that evening and whom she would see. As she worried over the color in her cheeks and lips, Hart continued to observe the light and mumble approbations. The carriage ride was only a short one, from Dodsworth's Building on 26th Street, where Carrie lived and Hart had his studio, to the so-called Studio Building on 10th Street, where the "Artists' Reception" was being held—a handsome three-story building in the middle of the block, a place designed and built specifically for painters, illustrators and architects to live and work, and the exciting new hub of New York's art world.

Hart jumped down from the carriage and held Carrie's hand as she stepped onto the pavement. She took in the scene at a glance. Clustered around the Studio Building's entrance were animated groups of young men and women, mostly men, conversing, smoking cigars and trying to see and, at the same time, be seen. They were gotten up in every manner of dress. Carrie spotted a fez, two scarlet-lined capes, and no shortage of cunningly customized walking sticks, some being raised into the air or jabbed recklessly for punctuation.Several of the men spotted Carrie as well. She was by now a known entity at these affairs and it was with satisfaction that she heard her name whispered as she and Hart walked through the crowd. She had been far from unmindful of her own attire on this evening—her daring, loose-fitting, uncrinolined white dress had been modeled, as many in this group would surely notice, after Whistler's picture *The White Girl*, which had caused much talk at the previous year's scandalous *Salon des Refusés* in Paris. Her long hair, while not quite "wild" à la Whistler, showed an exciting nonchalance that did not escape attention. Carrie could not deny that in some ways she was very much her mother's daughter. She wondered, too, if her mother ever felt as inwardly self-conscious with so many eyes cast upon her.

James Hart sensed the attention as well, and a new source of pleasing light, this time radiating from right by his side. During the carriage ride down, he had failed to see Carrie as others were now seeing her. He'd noted only that she seemed a little bored and impatient sitting beside him, and he hadn't noticed her gown at all. He still tended to think of her as the rather quiet and moody 18-year-old who one day had appeared at the door of his sister's academy and then gradually, in her very singular way, made herself a part of the household. Now on this crowded city sidewalk, with so many men taking notice, he saw her true for who she had become, and it made him want to linger a bit before going in. He steered her toward a familiar prominence.

"Is this the woman in white?" Freddie Olmsted asked, smiling broadly and extending both his arms in greeting. Not being a painter, but a man of many parts, he had seen Wilkie Collins rather than Whistler.

"I hope not," Carrie said with an answering smile. "I have not read the book, but doesn't she end up in an asylum?"

"I was speaking only of your attire, my dear," Olmsted said. "You will steal attention from the paintings."

Olmsted then turned to Hart.

"And you, Hart, are doing well for an old married cove."

The two men laughed, and their eyes met briefly as they did so. They were each reveling in that special excitement of being right at the center of things and knowing it— and of being the focus of others' attention even in a self-regarding crowd. To men of ambition, it felt as good as standing naked under a warm island waterfall. And there was the added sense on this evening, the beginning of a new social season, that New York itself had emerged fully as the American capital of the arts. Boston and Philadelphia, though certainly worthy, could no longer make that claim; each year, more talent from those places was coming to Manhattan for the studios, the collegiality, the publicity and the patronage. Even in this little group on the sidewalk one could find proof: Olmsted was from Hartford, Hart from Albany, and two others, Jervis McEntee, a painter, and Richard Morris Hunt, the architect of this very 10th Street building, had found their way to Manhattan from upstate Kingston and Vermont respectively.

"I didn't expect to see you in New York," said Hart to Olmsted. "I thought your business was in California these days."

"Mary and I were indeed at Clark's Ranch for the summer. An extraordinary place. I must tell you some time about our hike in to see the stands of giant Sequoias. But my attention now must go back to the park. Things are moving quickly there."

"I have been riding up and down its trails," Carrie said to Olmsted. "It is truly a marvel. There are new things to see every time we go."

"Somehow we will have planted 20,000 additional trees and shrubs by the end of the year," he said back. "Not to mention the boat landings and archways and fountains and endless statuary. People keep giving us statues. There's really no place for them all. Do you need a statue, McEntee?"

"I create them. My wife would say we have enough."

"At least until you can sell one," said Hunt.

"She would suggest that it be more than one."

The men laughed again. There was an inside aspect to the banter because McEntee's wife was the sister of Olmsted's design partner in the Central Park venture, Calvert Vaux. Additionally, Olmsted and Hunt had recently clashed publicly over the design of the gates that would ring the park, with Olmsted's simpler design having won the day. They had since made up over drinks and oysters at the Union League Club. Now Olmsted raised a hand for attention.

"But this surfeit of statues is not our greatest problem at the moment," he said. "You will never name what is."

No one ventured a guess.

"What is your problem, then?" Carrie asked at last.

"It is almost unimaginable, Carrie, and I hesitate to say it now that I remember you are here in our group." He paused only a moment. "We are receiving dead animals through the post."

Carrie recoiled. If anything had been true of her development over the past four years it was that she had become an ever stronger advocate for creatures of every stripe and size. Her love for her own Knight, and the companionship with him that had helped her through many a difficult spell at Rose Hill, had by now prompted her to look at all beasts—but especially those falling ill and injured under the hand of man, evident everywhere in New York—as worthy of special care and attention. Her face reddened. Olmsted had struck a very tender spot.

"That's horrible!" she exclaimed. "What can you possibly mean by that?"

"Well, I don't mean they're sent dead, but that's the way they arrive. People intend them for the park or for what now seems will become a zoological garden there, but they die in the shipping, especially during the recent hot spell. This week alone we've received a red fox, a pair of peccaries and flamingos and a raccoon—all dead."

"This can't have been your idea to ask people at large for donations of animals," Hunt said.

"Of course not," said Olmsted. "There was a newspaper story some months ago that described our overall efforts in the park. Along the way, it mentioned our extraordinary variety of flora and wondered, without my knowledge or approval, what it might be like to have a similar range of fauna in the middle of New York. And then the story was picked up and repeated everywhere, even Europe. That began the deluge, which it now appears must run its natural course."

"The curse of telegraphy," said Hunt.

"Can't you similarly put out a message asking them to stop?" asked McEntee.

"We went to the same reporter, but he refused to do that. He and his editor seemed to think it was much more amusing this way. What a reprehensible class of people they are."

"Well it's not amusing at all for the poor animals," Carrie said heatedly. "Imagine them crated up on those trains or carriages, struggling for a breath, probably with no one feeding them or giving them even a drop of water."

"Dear girl, no one wants this to stop as much as I do," said Olmsted. "If you can think of a way, I'd be most grateful."

Hart interceded.

"Whatever the outcome, this is hardly appropriate talk for a young woman in a beautiful white dress on a lovely evening in September, and it's not at all what we came for," he said. "Shall we go in, Carrie?"


Carrie was glad to be taken off the street and out of the conversation. Once indoors, Hart's duties ceased and she easily separated herself from him. She managed to regain her composure as she strolled through the crowded hall. The building had been designed specifically for events like this. Most of its sprawling interior was taken up by artists' apartments, which included living quarters and studio space. At the center of the hive was this large, open room, with a domed ceiling and big windows in rows on each end. It was meant for receptions and exhibits, preferably showcasing work by those who toiled elsewhere in the building, or who were at least members of the National Academy.

These artists' receptions traced their origins back five or six years to Carrie's own Dodsworth's Building, and a period when it was first determined that a certain critical mass of talent had settled in New York. It would have been hard to imagine another American city where Frederic Church could have turned the exhibition of one of his paintings, "Heart of the Andes," into a stunning spectacle, as he had in 1859 right here in this Studio Building. The exotic canvas, displayed with the greatest possible sense of drama in the spring of that year, drew swooning crowds—in the course of a month, some 12,000 people stood in line to pay twenty-five cents to see it.

After that seminal show, the art scene seemed to explode. Receptions were scheduled regularly during the season, as were "art conversazioni" attended not only by painters and other artistic types, but also by judges, city officials and clergy. It was written in the somewhat breathless city arts periodical *The Crayon* that the crowded events featured "men worth knowing and women worth seeing." By 1864, some observers would go further to say that the art had become secondary to the beauty and fashion—and youth—on display, and that some young artists were earning "reception reputations" for attending only in order to bathe in praise from the attractive women in attendance. Carrie could certainly be found somewhere within these ranks. Right now, as she ruminated on exactly what her place might be, she sought the familiar young faces of what had become her social circle—not an easy task in this swirling crowd.

Tonight was the first reception since spring. Many of the painters in attendance had only recently returned from their sketching trips, summer retreats or other far-flung travels, and there was a steady echo of backslapping and laughter in the big room. The season was opening with the display of three new paintings by "Studio men," each with the war as its subject. As she walked, Carrie saw the featured works only from a distance and through a sea of bobbing top hats. Each glowed in its place of prominence—Eastman Johnson's "Union Soldiers Accepting a Drink," Edward Lamson Henry's "Presentation of Colors" and Winslow Homer's "Home Sweet Home"—but for now she was content not to fight her way up to see them close. As she walked she felt herself drawing the interest of many in the crowd. Her loose-fitting dress gave her the sensation of floating, as if she had just wafted down from a canvas to mingle and twine with the rabble. "Is this what they called aloofness?" she wondered to herself. "Does it show on my face?" She decided that it did and that it had to. For her to appear any more open would only invite the hand on the arm and the unwelcome comment. Although most of the men were harmless and well meaning, the thought repulsed her. And yet, she thought, she had worn the white dress. Why had she done that if not to attract that same attention?

"Carrie!" a young woman's voice called out to her. It was Elsie Bentley, one of her new friends, the daughter of a painter, who had taken to riding with her on Sunday afternoons in Central Park. With a smile, Carrie walked over to where Elsie stood with several others of roughly the same age.

"We were all just commenting on your gown as you approached," Elsie said. "Covington said you looked like the figurehead of a ship."

"I meant that as a compliment," said Earl Covington, a talented painter whose reputation had not yet been made. "A thing of great presence and beauty, but you had a searching look in your eye."

"As if you were looking for your ship," added another young painter, Haimish Sutro, to general laughter.

Carrie took a cup of ale from Covington and joined in the amusement. Here, with a dozen or so others, was the companionable society that she had finally discovered in New York—the young people, all in their twenties, whose company she enjoyed and who had accepted her and her moods and occasional dark spells with what she felt was artistic understanding. Over the last couple of years, they had managed to find one another at receptions like this one; they had just naturally fallen together, and now, as a group, they were suddenly a presence in the Lower Broadway art scene. They had talent within their ranks, and opinions on things that were sometimes picked up in the local press. They seemed to represent a bright ray of promise within their own war-torn generation. People were beginning to know who they were.

"Speaking of appearance, Haimish, you are dressed pretty plain for an ambitious young painter named Haimish Sutro who wants a mention in *The Crayon*," Carrie said. "You show the same flair for color as our President Lincoln."

She enjoyed the male game of give and take, and she could more than hold her own. Certainly, Haimish did not pose much of a threat. Meanwhile, Elsie could not take her eyes off of Carrie's dress.

"You look like the subject of a painting rather than a viewer in the gallery," she said a bit defensively. She was wearing a far more traditional stiff, crinolined affair in blue and gold, and felt outdone.

"It is Whistler's notorious woman, is it not?" offered Covington.

Carrie smiled in assent.

"Next you will be giving us a Manet picnic!" he continued, laughing. "Let me know when and where, and I will bring the wine."

The room hummed around them. As the evening light faded in the big windows, the people inside came into sharper relief within the soft pools of artificial light. Carrie could pick out James Hart in the distance, and the Van Dyke beard of his brother William, and the bushy sideboards of Frederic Church, like Olmsted a Hartford man, and now, also like Olmsted, a leading light in the great city. Carrie had met Church at an Olmsted soirée and somehow ended up describing to him her horseback ride from Waterbury to New York, a tale he enjoyed immensely while readily admitting it was a trip he'd never have the nerve to try.

As Carrie looked into the crowd, another pair joined their circle, having entered the hall from one of its adjacent studios. One was the diminutive, wild-haired young man named Aaron Polk, a student at Richard Hunt's nascent architecture school, which was also located in the building. He was one of the Tennessee Polks, and had somehow found his way to New York despite the raging war and all its confinements and restrictions. This, and his soft accent, gave him an exotic air that endeared him to all he met. He liked to describe how he'd come to Gotham via the Underground Railroad, which of course wasn't true. Still, Carrie was drawn to his appetite for risk.

She did not recognize the extraordinary man who had arrived with Polk. He was tall, with a wispy mustache and thick sideboards, and dressed like... Carrie could not say with any precision. He wore knee-length black boots, buff trousers, a spectacular green cutaway with red embroidered cuffs and collar, and a soft hat, a cap really, pulled down hard, that had the look of—could it be?—a jockey's headgear.

All this Carrie took in greedily. A dandy, she thought. A dude.

"This is John Hawkins—or 'Hawk,' as he likes to be called," Polk said to the group. "He has just arrived from Bermuda. I found him slouching on my street corner this very afternoon and learned that he is a painter looking for a place to plant his easel."

Those in the circle feasted their eyes upon this latest addition, but no one could think of a word to say. Finally, Covington raised his cup and spoke.

"Please do tell us, how did your horse finish?" he asked, and laughter broke the ice.

The group spent the next hour getting to know the new man. When it was Carrie's turn, she decided she could not bring herself to call him "Hawk," and that "John" would have to do. She stood with him and Aaron Polk by the refreshment table. Polk produced a hip flask of gin with which he fortified the contents of their mugs.

"This is what they call a dog's nose—ale and gin," Polk said as he poured the liquor. "Although I'm not sure why it would be called that."

Carrie abstained. She drank very little alcohol, only enough not to seem a priss. She had learned her lesson not long after first coming to New York, when a friend of the Harts had fed her cup after cup of sherry flip at a Christmas party until she sat down on the floor in the center of the room and began to cry. After Julie Hart had helped her to her feet and taken her to her room, she asked Carrie what had made her so sad. She'd blurted that she had no "real" home that she could go to for the holidays, which made Julie, who had also drunk one cup too many, start crying, too. Carrie did end up going home to Rose Hill for Christmas that year, but her feeling held. She'd felt welcome for only a day or two, and then her presence became inconvenient. In any case, she vowed not to drink so much ever again.

Now John Hawkins was telling the story of his life on a fabled isle and his perilous voyage to New York.

"We are from Yorkshire originally," he said, with what Carrie gathered to be a Yorkshire accent as thick as the pudding. "My dad was a blacksmith and farrier on a large estate and saw a notice one day, I think in the newspaper, that called for Englishmen to come find work in Bermuda. Apparently, they wanted to populate the island with more white workers and families. My father being of a wandering disposition, we were soon, the four of us, on a ship headed west which somehow found that tiny dot in the middle of the Atlantic."

He was enjoying the story-telling but paused to take a sip from his mug.

"I have heard of Bermuda," said Polk. "Is it anywhere near Barbados or Jamaica, or any of the great rum islands?"

"It is quite isolated, much closer to us, but still with palm trees and banana plants and stands of cedar," said Hawkins. "The blue of the water alone, or the multiple blues, would make anyone want to come and paint there. But, alas, I was not happy. I was not old enough to have stayed in England by myself, but I was too old to adapt and become an islander. I yearned for the city—always had. In Yorkshire, I'd set my eyes on London; in Bermuda, with all its shipping ties to the States, my goal became New York."

"Those are pretty high hopes for a blacksmith's boy," said Polk, revealing his patrician roots and maybe the first signals of inebriation. "Do you have any schooling?"

"Only the village school in Yorkshire, and then whatever I've been able to read or overhear."

"And so you are with us tonight in your fancy embroidered jacket, risking all," Carrie interjected, not sure of where Polk was headed.

"After three long years in Bermuda and a horrendous ocean voyage through island reefs, high winds and even the very eye of what the crew called a genuine hurricano, yes, I am here, a fresh stick of chalk, ready to begin once again from the very start."

He had a fragile air, Carrie thought as he went on. His speech was colorful and friendly, but there was a vulnerability there, too. She noted that as he spoke, however confidently, his eyes searched hers and Polk's for approval. If his father had been a typical blacksmith, they couldn't have shared much in common, and the society of a small island would not have embraced his flamboyance. He had arrived from afar, like a windblown frigate bird, she decided, and she quickly felt drawn to him as one misplaced soul to another.

Now she thought both men were showing the effects of drink. Polk was asking Hawkins what he knew of New York. The latter listed a few common things, but soon gave in.

"My knowledge of the place is woeful," he admitted, "but that is why I've come—to see and study and learn what I can, and to become a part of it. Isn't that why everyone comes?"

"If you are to paint here, you must learn the ins and outs of the city," said Polk in a sort of sloppy, half-patronizing way. "As an architect, I study the buildings. As a painter, you must study the life."

"I want to do that, that is my whole purpose, but I've only just arrived," said Hawkins. "Here's what I will do: I will start tomorrow."

"Why not start tonight?"

Carrie and Hawkins became most attentive to what Polk would say next.

"Let's leave now, the three of us. Set out for the other New York."

"What do you mean by that?" asked Carrie.

"The Tenderloin. Hell's Hundred Acres. Five Points. Why don't we show Hawk here the muck of it?"

"The real New York," Hawkins offered.

"Yes," said Polk. "Exactly. Anything but this genteel, painterly tea party. Do you have the nerve for it?"

"Did I not just leave behind everything I knew?"

Polk turned to Carrie.

"And you, Carrie? Are you game?"

He threw down the challenge in a way that thrilled her. She was familiar with the areas Polk named. Everyone was. They made up the part of the city that was lawless, dangerous, shot through with illness and desperately poor. It was the home turf of the Bowery Boys, who had just run wild during the draft riots, the murderous Daybreak Boys, and any number of other gangs and lone hoodlums. She had ridden Knight through the fetid streets on several occasions —right down Mulberry Street in fact—not quite by accident and always ready to turn and gallop. Nothing untoward had happened. Was she ready to be so lucky once again, this time without a gallant black stallion to give her protection?

"I don't think you realize how dangerous it can be down there, John," she said to Hawkins.

"You forget about London, Carrie," he said back to her. "I guess you've never seen the blood and smoke of The Old Nichol, as I have, or passed through the shadows of Spitalfields none the worse for wear, as I also have done."

Carrie felt a flush overtake her face and then a secondary surge of recklessness.

"We are absurdly dressed for such an outing," she said, still trying to appear cautious and sensible. "And I certainly don't trust that we will know the best way to go around the worst parts."

Before Polk could counter, another voice was heard.

"I can do that," it said.

They turned to find the boy who was tending to the ale and punch. Up until now he had been invisible, simply proffering his refreshments; now he was anything but. He was a young, thin, smiling Irish boy, the kind with pale skin and dark hair and a thick brow that could brood or brighten depending upon his mood and the phase of the moon. As they eyed him, he spoke again:

"That's where I live, in the muck, as I heard you say. I've just been told to turn in my apron for the night, so if you like I can take you down there myself."

"Where do you live?" Polk asked him.

"Oh, right in the thick of it," the boy said, smiling. "Based upon your present conversation, I'm sure you would approve. I mean, the dead babies alone are prodigious in number."

Here's yet another specimen, thought Carrie. They are coming out of the very walls tonight. She wondered how much bitterness was hidden behind that smile—or could this truly be his outlook? Was it possible to be so cheerfully resigned, even on the subject of infant mortality? Maybe the Irish could be. Or was that a terrible thought? Wouldn't they mourn, just as the Kingsburys had done?

"What is your name?" Polk asked the boy.

125

"Hugh Lyons, but they call me Faker. I'm leaving now, if you'd like to come."

Polk looked at the other two.

"Let's," said Carrie.

"Yes, let's," said John Hawkins.

And with that, they slipped through a side door in the Studio Building and into the New York night.

As the odd quartet made its way across to Fourth Avenue, Carrie began to worry over the possible consequences. James Hart was supposed to take her back home when the reception ended, and he would worry terribly when she couldn't be found. And then he would have to tell his sister and she would worry, too, and no doubt become angry. She felt a pang in her stomach. But at what point would she ever be free to make her own decisions? If she had told Hart of her plan, he certainly wouldn't have allowed it. Once again, she occupied a middle space, not quite a dependent of Julie Hart and her family but not fully on her own. Then she heard Polk and Hawkins erupt in laughter, and the intoxicating excitement of the adventure at hand, a feeling she had not experienced in a very long time, surged within her and swept away her misgivings.

Out ahead, Faker Lyons led the way. As they arrived at Fourth Avenue, he called back to them over his shoulder.

"Normally, I'd get home on my own shoe leather," he said, "but I think you'd sooner hop the bobtail, would you not?"

"We would," said Polk, "and here's your fare. Consider it a sign of good faith."

The horsecar tracks ran down Fourth Avenue, then joined Bowery around 4th Street and finished up at City Hall Park, although this group would not go that far. They found room on a bench in the back of the car and instantly created a theatrical presence there. They spoke a little too loudly, as if on a stage, and took too much pleasure in their own patter. They were well aware that other passengers were regarding them with a kind of amazement—at their clothing, their open gaiety and general antic strangeness. Faker Lyons made an effort to blend with both groups.

"Where will the others think we have gone?" Polk asked, seemingly to the entire car. "Surely, if they were to form a search party they would not set off in this direction."

"Chances are that they will not miss us quite that much," said Carrie.

"Well, I hope they do, although I don't know who you are talking about," said Hawkins. "I like the idea of a search party and our eluding it. I wonder if we are leaving clues behind."

"Oh, you are," said Faker softly, but the others didn't hear him.

"Maybe if we sang a song," said Polk. "That would help us leave a trail."

He searched for something that would be especially memorable, but Hawkins beat him to the punch.

"Among our ancient mountains," he sang slowly,

"And from our lovely vales,

"Oh, let the prayer re-echo,

"God bless the Prince of Wales."

Now the amazement on the part of others on the car was augmented by anger, at least on some faces, and a rumble of disapproval. Faker jumped to his feet and put his face six inches away from Hawkins'.

"Mister, you are in the wrong neck of the woods, and certainly all wrong in general, to sing that verse out loud," he said. "Do you realize that you may as well be in the darkest part of Ireland right now?"

Hawkins blanched and rose halfway to his feet.

"I am sorry," he shouted past Faker's rigid form. "It was the first thing that came into my mind. It has no meaning to me. It's the only song I know the words to. Please forgive, I beg you."

Depending upon the make-up of his fellow passengers, this blurted apology, with its thumping Yorkshire cadence, might have made matters better or worse. In this case, all seemed willing to overlook the offense, albeit not happily, as the ravings of an evident fool.

As the horsecar approached Canal Street, Faker motioned for them to disembark. As she did so, Carrie first noticed they were now in a part of the city where cobblestones had not yet replaced the mud and manure. She absently thought that her shoes would be the first victims of this foray.

"Stick by me and we should be fine," Faker said, not that they needed to be told. Once the car moved off, the darkness was nearly complete, broken only here and there by the dim, unsteady pools of kerosene lamps or open cooking fires. Sounds came as if in a fever: cries, rough laughter, a burst of song, voices raised in anger, children squalling as they raced by, pigs and chickens rummaging and rooting nearby, and always the murmuring undercurrent of people convening out of doors. From above came the warning shout of a tenant unleashing the contents of a chamber pot onto the street below, "night soil" as Carrie had once heard it called. Another did not have the courtesy to shout.

"Do you know the word 'stygian'?" Polk whispered out of the side of his mouth to Carrie as they walked.

"Something to do with hell, isn't it?"

"Much like this very infernal darkness, I'd say."

Neither wanted to talk for fear of attracting attention from the shadows. Carrie thought of how her white dress had sent a signal of one thing at the artists' reception and quite another thing here. As they left Canal Street for Mott, they passed through a relatively well-lit area, and she felt eyes upon her, as she had uptown, and whispers, too, but not of her name.

And then John Hawkins was on the ground, flailing, with someone on top of him. Carrie let out a cry. Polk jumped ineffectually atop the assailant. Faker ran back to them, cupped his hands around his mouth and called out in a high-pitched voice.

"Whyyy-oooo!" he cried, and then repeated it several times in rapid succession. "Whyyy-oooo!"

Almost immediately, his cry was echoed by others who came running in from all directions. Within a matter of mere seconds, the attacker had been pulled off Hawkins, hustled off into an alley and, by the sound of it, thoroughly beaten. Still more arrived and stood protectively around Carrie and the others. One in particular, a dashing figure wearing a long dustcoat and a stovepipe, strode in and took a long look around, resting particularly on Carrie, before addressing Faker angrily.

"I should have guessed it would be you," he said.

"They're artists who wanted to go on a slum," said Faker. "I thought I'd show 'em the sights and then finish off at my den."

"So they'll be lifting you out of your sorry station then? Is that the game?"

Polk interceded before Faker had a chance to respond.

"Excuse me," he said, gesturing to all those in the sudden gathering. "Before you go any further, can you tell me what just happened?"

"Your friend here was jumped by an independent slugger," said the dustcoat. "But young Hugh Lyons knew what to do. He gave the call and the Whyos came runnin'."

There were sounds of approval from the others.

"The Whyos? Who are you?" Polk asked.

"We take care of our own, first, and if anyone is goin' to rob and plunder, it's goin' to be us," he said. He took a step back and then took Carrie's hand and seemed to address her exclusively, almost soothingly. "You now are free to move along safely. We will keep an eye. But should you return on your own one day, I give no such assurances. And you," he turned to Hawkins, "if you come back dressed like a fuckin' grasshopper again, I'll kill you myself."

With a wave of dark laughter, the Whyos retreated back into the shadows once again and Faker, like a tour leader among the Greek antiquities, gestured for the group to gather themselves and keep moving. Hawkins had been a little roughed up but unhurt. He'd managed to hold onto his wallet. Carrie tried to clean off the back of his waistcoat, but his trousers were hopelessly muddied. He smiled and strutted forward, not at all diminished by the incident. Carrie felt somewhat emboldened to speak up now that she knew her welfare was in able hands. She had been quite taken by the handsome man in the dustcoat.

"Hugh," she called forward, again not wanting to use a nickname, "I would not have taken you for a member of this —would I call it a gang? And the leader seemed to have some special regard for you."

"Special regard, indeed. That's my big brother, Dan," Faker said. "He's a murderous fellow, true, but not where I'm concerned—at least not yet. I wouldn't test him too hard, though. The Whyos control Five Points and they had to fight all the way to the top. They're always on the ready for blood."

They turned onto Park Street and soon stopped in front of a sagging tenement, one in a long row of nearly identical dilapidated hulks. It was four stories high, with rickety porches attached to one side all the way up. There was the unsteady glow of candles coming from inside several of the rooms and a feeling of foreboding peculiar to side streets. But Faker was home now, and he bounced up the front stoop. He opened the door and turned.

"Welcome," he said with a slight bow. "Come inside, please."

The group climbed the steps slowly but not at all surely. After all they had already seen and heard, what sorts of sights were they in for now? Could it be a trick or a trap of some kind? Still, they had come too far to protest.

"In for a penny, in for a pound," said Hawk under his breath, speaking for all.

They plunged forward behind the young Irishman down a dark hallway to a door at the end. He put his hand on the knob, but spoke again before he turned it.

"As you come in, you will see why I have led you on this merry chase, and why I volunteered to do so," he said.

He opened the door and quickly moved inside, where he put a match to a lamp and started lighting candles. As the light came up, the others advanced. Because of the flickering illumination, the darkness at the edges and the almost complete lack of furnishings, Carrie at first thought the room had a barren, grotto-like appearance. But as her eyes adjusted to the dancing shadows, she began to make out other things. She turned slowly to take it all in. The walls, the ceiling, even the floor were covered, every inch, it appeared, with the most extraordinary painting—great strokes and splotches of color in broad patterns and shapes—curlicues, zigzags, slashes and ribbons. Next she saw there were canvases as well along the walls—or, more properly, rectangles of nailed boards—with figures painted on them, robed men and women, treeless landscapes and twisting roads. The three visitors moved in and out, back and forth, silently, until Polk managed a word.

"You find us greatly surprised, Lyons," he said. "I don't know what we thought you were leading us to, but I'm sure this was not it."

Faker stood just apart from the group, his hands folded in front of him. He looked at once shy and triumphant, like a baker called out by a king for special recognition. But words of praise were not the first to rise to Carrie's lips.

"Please tell us what we are looking at," she said.

"It's the holy path," Faker responded as if it should be plain to see.

"The path to what?"

"Christ's path to the cross. The stations, they call them. Only I'm not done yet." He went over to the first painting. "Here's the demon Pontius Pilate, and here's Jesus fitted for his cross, here he falls, here he meets Mary his mother, then Simon, then Veronica, then he falls again. He's only halfway there."

The scenes were as jagged and crude as the boards they were painted on— powerful in their own way, like a child's untutored effort, yet almost certainly possessed by madness.

"And what's all this swirling paint on the walls and ceiling and floor?" Polk asked.

"That's the outer universe," said Faker. "The water and dirt and blood and all the stars beyond. I thought you painterly people would fall right to it."

He paused.

"I want to be in that crowd I saw tonight," he said. "I would give anything for that."

As the others continued to speak, Carrie fixed her gaze upon a fiery orb and tried to contemplate her present circumstances. Only a trip to China and a subsequent kidnapping by bandits might have taken her more completely away from the stiff propriety of Rose Hill and Waterbury's society. Yet she felt oddly at ease in this dim tenement room, standing with this gaudy trio of outcasts. Of course she was an outcast herself, having literally been cast out from her home, so there was an unstated kinship in the ranks. These were not the type of young men who would try to take advantage of her. They were, each in his turn, too affable, too delicate and too preoccupied to think of her in that way—so that was another layer of comfort. She took a long breath and prepared to rejoin the conversation. She felt far more than several hours away from her carriage ride with James Hart and his declaration of love for the limestone façade.

"You don't know when you'll feel the touch," Faker Lyons was saying with an air of grave authority. "I was just walking along the sidewalk when a voice told me to find some paint and get busy."

"Was it Jesus?" asked Polk.

"Well, one of the three at least."

"So that's what started you?"

"I cadged my supplies with the help of some Whyos and went to work, yes. I began in that corner with the Biblical void."

John Hawkins was moving along the room's periphery.

"And you live here, too?" he asked.

Faker nodded.

"You don't ask for much in the way of comforts, do you?"

"I have a place to sleep and a source of water. I keep my supplies in a closet with my clothes. What else do I need when all I do is paint?"

"And what do you do for food?" Hawkins asked.

But before the boy could answer, there was a rapid knock at the door. Carrie, Polk and Hawkins jumped at the noise. They looked at each other nervously as Faker went to answer. He opened the door a crack, spoke briefly, then turned to them.

"There's a cab out in front," he said. "Courtesy of my brother, who will be happy when he knows you have gone. You should probably leave right now."

The unspoken problem of how to get back home had been solved, and on this piece of very welcome and unexpected news the three made their way to the door. Carrie paused to shake Faker's hand.

"Thank you for your company tonight, and for all of... this," she said, sweeping her hand around the room. "Surely, there has never been anything like it."

"I hope you will come back when I am done," he said. "In the meantime, I am friendly with a purveyor of ale and beer, so maybe you'll find me working the taps at future receptions," he said. "But you must know I'd rather be on the other side of the serving table."

"Perhaps one day you will be," said Carrie in her kindest possible voice, although she could not possibly offer more than that.

After all the goodbyes, they boarded the cab, with Carrie seated between the other two. At first, there was a palpable release of tension, an explosion of talk and laughter, and a quick revisiting of what they had just experienced—the attack on Hawk, the arrival of the Whyos, Faker Lyons' astounding parlor and his conversations with the deity. But as the carriage was still only just making its way back up the Bowery, they abruptly fell silent, staring dazedly straight out ahead, as if at last fully under the spell of the evening, and of New York.

As for Carrie, she knew she liked having this excitement— these unusual people with their strange thoughts and experiences and visions—as a part of her life now. She realized it was what she had ridden out in search of with Knight all those years ago in Waterbury, when she would call up to the moon and get nothing but silence in return. Now the moon had answered her back, and it was thrilling. She didn't want to run away from the Harts or the Olmsteds or the Kingsburys—it wasn't that. She wanted them, too. Was that too much, she wondered—to have everything you wanted and nothing of what you didn't want? On this night, it seemed possible. Anything seemed possible. But as she began to contemplate what "anything" might mean, and why the strangeness and danger of their outing appealed to her so much, she suddenly felt very tired. She yawned and smiled sleepily and threw her arms across the shoulders of her two friends and began to softly hum the forbidden tune that John Hawkins had earlier sung. And then they were all humming it, their high, sweet voices barely audible over the sound of the horse's hoofs as the cab rattled its way up Madison Avenue toward home.

## Chapter 9

"'The down-town streets, the jobbers' houses of business,'" Elsie Bentley read, "'the houses of business of the ship-merchants and money-brokers, the river-streets.'"

"'Immigrants arriving, fifteen or twenty thousand in a week,'" said Carrie, picking up the verse.

Elsie had the next line:

"'The carts hauling goods, the manly race of drivers of horses...'"

"Manly!" interjected Carrie with a giggle.

"'... and brown-faced sailors,'" Elsie finished with exaggerated gravity.

"'The summer air, the bright sun shining, and the sailing clouds aloft,'" read Carrie.

"'The winter snows, the sleigh-bells, the broken ice in the river, passing along up or down with the flood-tide or ebb-tide.'"

It was Earl Covington who had presented them with the book of poems the night before, telling them they should expect to be scandalized. Now they lay side by side, the book between them, in a warming pool of May sunlight on Carrie's bed in their shared bedroom. They were reading the first verse they had turned to, called *Mannahatta*.

"'The mechanics of the city, the masters, well-form'd, beautiful-faced, looking you straight in the eyes,'" Elsie continued.

"'Trottoirs throng'd, vehicles, Broadway, the women, the shops and shows.'"

"'Trottoirs throng'd,'" repeated Carrie in a high aristocratic voice.

"Trottoirs!" said Elsie with a snort.

"What is a trottoir, do you suppose?" Carrie wondered. "Could it be a ring for horses?"

"How could it be thronged then?" Elsie asked. "Thronged with trotting horses?"

"We'll have to ask Covington," Carrie decided. "Perhaps it has a hidden, rude, French meaning that only he will know."

"'A million people—manners free and superb—,'" Elsie continued, "'open voices—hospitality—the most courageous and friendly young men.'"

"'City of hurried and sparkling waters! City of spires and masts! City nested in bays!'"

Carrie paused and looked over at her friend, who took the cue.

"'My city!'"

They both read the final two words loudly and dramatically, and then, laughing, fell away from each other and onto their backs.

"I don't feel very scandalized, I must say, but I can't dispute what he calls 'courageous and friendly young men,'" said Elsie after a moment, looking up at the ceiling. "Often a little too courageous if you ask me."

"Which they don't usually do," Carrie said.

"What?"

"Ask you."

Elsie laughed yet again.

"No, that would not be their strong point," she allowed.

They were enjoying themselves and being a little silly, and yet the poet's words had made it through—all those images of the New York they knew so well washing over and through them like a warm tide. 'My city,' indeed, Carrie thought to herself, and a little indignantly. It's mine, too. As much mine as anyone's. As open to me as to anyone.

She and Elsie had discovered a wonderful sense of ease with each other. They'd been living in these rooms for two months, since late March, in an arrangement that could have been considered a bit unusual even by New York standards—two young single women rooming together with no visible means of support. However, because the apartment was located within the familiar confines of Dodsworth's Building and nearly encircled by known families and faces, including that of Mrs. Beers, the word had been passed back up to Waterbury that the situation would be proper enough, and sustaining funds continued to flow.

It had been Mrs. Beers who had suggested the move, the conversation coming on New Year's Eve, as 1864 turned into 1865. One of the artists in the building, watercolorist Albert Bellows, had been hosting an open house in his studio and rooms. At one point still rather early in the evening, Julie Beers cornered Carrie by a jumble of easels, tables and chairs that had hastily been taken out of harm's way and piled into an alcove. Carrie sensed a rehearsed moment coming on.

"You are dear to me, Carrie, and to Martha and Emily, as I'm sure you know," said Mrs. Beers.

Carrie nodded pleasantly and tilted her head slightly.

"And because of your kind attention to us all and your many exertions, I have been able to make something of a life as a painter and instructor," she went on, "and I will always be grateful for that. But—if I may say it in the most unvarnished manner—I think you may have outgrown your role as a mother's helper and are ready for a new situation. In fact, I think you are well along in the transformation."

It was true. In the months following the memorable visit to Five Points, Carrie and her circle of friends had spent much time testing the boundaries not only of Manhattan, which always seemed to be shifting, but also of just how much they could experience together in the name of novelty and excitement. Carrie had been careful never again to overstep the bounds of her responsibilities as she had on that night in September (she had endured a heated lecture the next morning and made an abject apology to James Hart), but in her interests and activities she had clearly moved on. And for that matter, the Beers children had reached an age when regular vigilance was no longer required.

"I am grateful for your patience," Carrie said, "and I agree that I am ready for something else. I'm just not sure of what it is, or even could be. There are so few possibilities open to me, and I could never go back home."

"I have been thinking about it and speaking to others about it, Carrie. There are rooms vacant in this very building. If you can find someone for company and get the approval of your parents, you'd be able to keep your own hours and carry on and entertain as you wish, within certain limits, of course."

Carrie sensed that her comings and goings of late had tried the patience of even this tolerant, unconventional woman, and perhaps might have done some careless harm to the household she was trying her best to help oversee.

"I'd still want you to assist with the children from time to time," Mrs. Beers continued. "And of course you'd always be welcome to come along on our summer excursions."

Carrie was gently being cut loose. In a few months she would be 24 and thoroughly without a destination in the traditional sense—not into the arms of a promising young man, nor to a career as a teacher, secretary or shop clerk, nor to a useful position, including room and board, with relatives or friends, nor even to a quiet upstairs room in her childhood home (and onto the lips of local gossips). As she briefly considered her plight, she realized that one obvious model for who she might become one day was Julie Hart Beers, the forthright woman standing right in front of her. But the older woman's painting was a true talent, and she had brothers and other family who looked out for her, as she did for them. Carrie did not have any of that. In fact she wondered if she had a talent for anything at all. Did a kind heart and a quick wit count for anything? She felt so undeveloped, so unfinished.

"It won't be long before you don't need me at all," she said to Mrs. Beers.

"Our door will always be open to you, Carrie."

"Very well then, I will consider your plan for me."

She thought immediately of Elsie Bentley as the person who might be able to come join her. She was the daughter of the painter, Joseph Bentley, and Coral Fillmore Bentley, both from Massachusetts families of substantial means. Elsie was the youngest of three—an older sister was married to a professor of Greek and Latin and living in New Haven, her brother was a young war correspondent for the *Boston Daily Advertiser*. Elsie herself was a quite properly spoiled youngest child, a couple of years younger than Carrie, with blonde, bright good looks and an even disposition. She had become Carrie's particular friend in the mostly male world of young artists that they frequented, and they had gone on memorable jaunts, ranging from viewing President Lincoln's funeral train, to riding on horseback to see an actual Chinese man selling cigars on Park Row, to stepping together into the roiling ocean waves under a full moon at Coney Island. Although it had not yet been announced in any way, it had become quite clear to Carrie that Elsie and Earl Covington had fallen in love. She'd noted it with a small inner shock one evening at the conclusion of a soirée, a lecture, really, in a Lower Broadway drawing room. When Elsie got up to leave and absently left her shawl on the arm of her chair, Covington sprang to his feet to return it to her—and just before calling out to her to hand it back he put it up, very briefly, to his face. It had been a simple, nearly invisible gesture, one probably lost on everyone else in the room, but Carrie had noted it truly. Earl loved Elsie. He wanted to gather away to himself the very scent of her, like he would a lock of her hair, and certainly Elsie would return his love. The match was perfection itself. One day in the not too distant future, perhaps when Covington had made his inevitable breakthrough with his own paintings, the two would be wed and they they'd live together happily and bring into the world children who would be known widely for their handsome looks and good luck. But for the time being, Carrie had a companion and a kind friend.

All during that spring and into the beginnings of summer, the group of young companions made its colorful way through New York's busy downtown social scene, leaving a bright trail of newspaper notices and gossip in its wake. Rarely did an opening or reception go unattended by at least some of them, or a recital, or, for that matter, a boxing match. When no special events required their attendance, they could often be found at Charlie Pfaff's beer cellar on Broadway, where art, beer and witty conversation commingled in a smoky subterranean vault. Chief among its denizens was Henry Clapp, the so-called King of Bohemia, an editor and publisher who'd brought the louche café life back from Paris to New York, and who presided nightly at the head of a raucous wits' table.

Nothing could have been more appealing to the young painters than Pfaff's. It was a retreat where their long hair and Van Dyke beards did not feel out of place, and where they could chew their cigars, drink from tankards of ale, tell a story, strum a guitar or sketch madly as the evening took colorful shape around them. And although Pfaff's was not much of a place for women, Carrie found it stimulating and even, in its own peculiar way, sheltering. She'd gone on a number of occasions (it was there that Covington had presented her with the book of poems by Whitman, who before the war had himself been a Pfaff's regular) but always within the safety of the group. Although she could never feel quite fully at ease in the surroundings, Carrie admired and perhaps even envied the men's leisurely camaraderie. She observed that although she was adept at a certain amount of give-and-take, she could never mount the cynicism and savage, uncaring wit required for a seat at Clapp's table. She was generally content to take in the proceedings while nursing a small cup with one or two others in her group. She was approached many times by men, often emboldened by drink, with their offers of a good seat at the opera, or tea the next day, or far more. But very rarely did she enter such conversations. It was daring enough just to be present at Pfaff's.

One night, Carrie sat in a dim corner with Elsie and a couple of young men— boys, really—who'd only just arrived in town. They were going block-by-block up Broadway, describing all the wonders to be found there, when Aaron Polk appeared before them with a pair of women in tow.

"Carrie, Elsie, young gentlemen—you find before you the delegation from South Carolina," he announced with a broad smile and an accent somewhat deepened for the occasion. "This great beauty to my left is Ada Clare, the writer, actor and Queen of Bohemia, of whom you no doubt have heard. And accompanying her, perhaps just for this evening, is the great voice, The Diva, Clara Louise Kellogg, lately of the European stage. Can we find room for them, and for me, with you at this table?"

The group shifted noisily until all were accommodated. Polk called for Champagne punch and fresh glasses. Ada Clare effortlessly seized the table's center of attention, as if illumined by a hidden source of light. She was clothed all in black, setting off her perfect ivory complexion, pansy blue eyes, fine features and fair, wavy hair, which she kept cut short and parted on the side, occasionally tossing back a stray forelock with a boyish, impatient flip. She looked around at the others and spoke with a rapid Charleston drawl.

"You boys look like you just fell off an onion wagon," she said cheerfully to the newcomers to the city, whose expressions were now striking the perfect balance between awe and panic. "Where were you a week ago?"

Each looked at the other, not wanting to be the one to blurt out something regrettable. Finally, the one with the wispy beginnings of a beard on his chin responded.

"Chagrin Falls, Ohio, ma'am," he said. "Out by Cleveland."

The table had a laugh at the town's name.

"You are visibly chagrined just to mention the name," Ada Clare returned with a sweet bat of her eyelashes. "And by the way, no one will answer to 'ma'am' in this place. I'm Ada, she's Clara— although her first name is so close to my last that while we are all here in Pfaff's you should probably call her 'Diva,' which she would enjoy, or even 'Marguerite,' for the character she sang in *Faust* and that has made her lasting fame."

Clara Kellogg bathed in the words of her friend and smiled in turn to everyone seated at the table. She raised her glass.

"To Chagrin Falls," she toasted. "Which sounds like the setting for an American opera."

"Or at least the home of an American mountebank," said Polk to general laughter.

The party drank up and continued their banter. Carrie managed a few words but was content to at last observe the infamous Bohemian Queen close up. She had heard of her, of course, and seen her from afar at Pfaff's. Everyone knew her irresistibly sensational story. At age 20, Ada Clare had gone from South Carolina directly to Paris following the deaths of her parents, who had left her a little money. Once in that great city, she created a presence that was, as one would later write, "easy, sunny, free and loose," and in any case determinedly emancipated. She dallied with, among quite a list of notable others, the doe-eyed pianist, composer and seducer Louis Moreau Gottschalk, who was most likely the father of her son, Aubrey. Arriving in New York a year or so after the birth of the child and her abandonment by Gottschalk, she refused to be ruined by her circumstances. She famously referred to herself as "Miss Ada Clare & Son," spoke approvingly of free love, welcomed New York's Bohemians, under the name of the West 42nd Street Coterie, into her home for Sunday night receptions, and used her affair with Gottschalk as material for her own poems and works of fiction. And here at Pfaff's she was the organizer, the unofficial hostess, the source of vital energy and the guiding spirit—in short, the Queen. She was a trend-setting Bohemian, which she'd once defined as "a cosmopolite, with a general sympathy for the fine arts, and for all things above and beyond convention."

Now she was good-naturedly trying to add a delightful new dimension to this evening at Pfaff's by goading Clara Kellogg into song.

"Clara doesn't come out very often; her mother won't allow it in order to save her voice—and her soul—from being lost to the likes of us," she announced to the table as Kellogg cast her eyes downward and blushed. "But if we've been bestowed with a gift such as the one she possesses, we must use it as freely and openly as it was given. Can we not all agree on that?"

"Oh, yes, please do give us just one song," Elsie urged. "These old cellar walls could stand to hear a real voice for once."

Clara softened and put both her palms down on the table before her.

"I think that the Champagne has taken hold," she said. "What would you have me sing?"

"I confess that I am not overly familiar with the opera," said Polk. "But there is a popular song, 'Beautiful Dreamer,' that has been very much in my heart of late."

"Yes, I'd love to hear 'Beautiful Dreamer'!" said Carrie, who had heard it sung at a memorial service earlier in the year and had been struck by its mournful melody.

And so, without further encouragement, Clara Louise Kellogg began, softly at first and then commanding the room with her powerful soprano:

Beautiful dreamer, wake unto me,
Starlight and dewdrops are waiting for thee;
Sounds of a rude world, heard in the day,
Lull'd by the moonlight have all pass'd away!

All conversation stopped as The Diva rode out the verse. For all their posing and sharp talk, the men at Pfaff's recognized greatness when it was present and were happy to fall under its spell.

Beautiful dreamer, queen of my song,
List while I woo thee with soft melody;
Gone are the cares of life's busy throng,
Beautiful dreamer, awake unto me!
Beautiful dreamer, awake unto me!

There was respectful silence for a long moment and then the tapping of Henry Clapp's tankard upon the tabletop, and then of others, and then warm huzzahs all around. Once it became clear that another song would not be forthcoming, someone in a smoky corner raised his voice.

"To our American prima donna!" he called out.

The room repeated his cry, and drank lustily, and then filled the air with reinvigorated talk and laughter.

"I have noticed you here before," said Ada Clare to Carrie as Polk refilled their glasses with punch. "Although you could not know it, you have a presence, a simple elegance, that would not seem out of place in the Bois de Boulogne. How old are you, my dear, and what is your name?" She put her hand on Carrie's forearm. "Tell me all about yourself!"

Carrie looked around a little self-consciously, but the others at the table were already involved in their own conversations. She could not recall when she'd been faced with such a blunt approach on the part of someone she'd just met. She blurted out a few particulars about her origins, but then gradually found her balance and ultimately retained the presence of mind to drop the names of Olmsted and Church before she was done. Ada's eyes widened perceptibly at the mention of those two stalwarts.

"Unlike us, Carrie, they are probably both fast asleep right now, with visions of what they will achieve tomorrow dancing through their dreams," she said. "We may make the city a little more interesting with all our smart talk, but they are truly transforming it. They are making great things, those two. They are at a different level than we are here in this cave, except for Whitman, who I must have you meet someday."

She took a long drink from her glass. Carrie felt she had in some way entered into the middle of a conversation rather than its beginning, or perhaps into one of those talks one sometimes has with strangers—one in which confidences are unexpectedly revealed and candor given free reign. She thought Ada seemed a little reflective and sad, an unexpected thing to see in such a public place and from one generally known for her high spirits. In any event, the two established an instant rapport.

"I wonder if it would be possible for me to meet them at some point?" Ada asked after she had put her glass down.

Carrie smiled politely as she tried to imagine how Mary Olmsted or Isabel Church would greet the sudden presence of renowned temptress Ada Clare in their midst. Both were quite conventional women by comparison, although by no means unfamiliar with eccentric behavior among those in their own circles. Still, Carrie thought, it would be a mighty stretch to bring the Bohemians, or at least this one, an actual Jezebel, into the parlor for tea with either woman.

Ada watched closely as Carrie went through her machinations.

"Never mind about that," she said, leaning over to speak directly into Carrie's ear over the noise in the room. "If our paths cross, they cross. It's just that right now I am seeking inspiration. I thought I loved acting and was good at it until I tried it in San Francisco last year and was nearly run off the stage. Then I thought I might write a novel, but I am in the middle of it now, fighting it every day and finding it does not come to me at all like a gift. Here is my problem, sweetheart. No one knows it, but today I have turned 30, and all day I have been wondering what lucky channel might carry me forward from here. One pestering thought has come to me very clear over and over again: I need to make arrangements."

The five words were, on their own, innocent enough, but for these two women, at this moment, they were urgent and fraught. "I need to make arrangements." The sentence carried on its simple frame no less than all the weight of the future, the burden peculiar to the unmarried woman of a certain intelligence and standing, and even the whiff of distant unknown shores of pain and loneliness. Carrie and Ada exchanged a glance that slid beneath the noise in the room.

"If you find that lucky channel, let me know," said Carrie, who now felt free to give life to some thoughts of her own. "My pestering thought is that I see the men all around us in this room and wonder at their self-assuredness, no matter how unwarranted it might be. Is that something they are born with, or can it be learned?"

"Well, I like to look back to our origins and our upbringing. What is your father like?"

Carrie blanched and looked away. The mention of his mere existence, she thought. His eyes. His hands.

"He wishes I were someone else," she finally managed.

Ada saw a conversation she could not possibly pursue in a crowded beer hall. She took a tactful shortcut instead.

"That is just the problem," she said. "Men, your father perhaps among them, do not like a confident woman, not really, and they are the ones who decide what is the acceptable level of confidence. A true talent like Clara can perhaps manage it, but not someone like me who is in the end only the product of gossip and publicity. I was writing in my journal just this morning that as I turn over a new year and decade I find I have arrived at an unenviable place: I have found notoriety rather than fame, and I excite curiosity rather than genuine interest. It may be the best I can do."

She caught something over Carrie's shoulder and rose quickly to exchange cheerful good wishes with a departing group—exaggerated and false good wishes, as it now appeared to Carrie. Then the Queen of Bohemia resumed her humble throne.

"I am scaring you, or at least boring you," she said, pushing back that blonde forelock. "I am just in a mood tonight."

"Not at all," said Carrie, and then she went on, choosing her words carefully. "But I wonder what advice you might have for one not unlike you, a runaway, too, five years your junior, daring but also afraid, not given to convention...."

Carrie's voice trailed off. But just as Ada might have given an answer, she was suddenly engulfed by a circle of young men who with shouts of birthday greetings raised her up off her chair and into the air and carried her over to the bar on their shoulders. She had been found out and now would be thoroughly celebrated. As she rose, however, Ada did something that endured. Even as she seemed to smile for her admirers, she kept her gaze dead evenly upon Carrie and slowly shook her head in a way that was not merely solemn but seemed truly foreboding, especially amidst all the surrounding gaiety. It was an image that would stay with Carrie for the rest of her life. "No, there is no advice for women like us," the pale face warned as it receded back into the throng. "We are alone in this world and we must make our way through it as we come upon it. There is no other choice for the likes of us."

## Chapter 10

By the end of June, everyone had made plans for the summer ahead. In mid-July, Elsie would go to her mother's family place in Manchester-by-the-Sea north of Boston, where her father liked to spend the days sketching and painting, and her siblings would arrive to help renew the family's many pleasant seaside rituals. Not by coincidence, Earl Covington had found a shack in the nearby fishing village of Rockport, where he and Haimish Sutro, roommates in the city, would live together, and sketch, too, and also try to devise ways to picnic and walk the sands with Elsie and her summer friends. With the war over, Aaron Polk had planned on taking a trip back to Nashville, but the entreaties he sent to his family found no welcome at all in the terse letters he received back. "If your own mother considers you to be a traitor, then there's no point in ever going back home again," he said matter-of-factly to his friends. Instead, he, like many others in their set, would travel north in sketching parties that would go to Tuckerman's Ravine in New Hampshire, Mount Mansfield in Massachusetts, and across to Bear Mountain in New York "in search of any purple twilight scene or group of cows that will pay my bills," as he put it.

As for Carrie, in August she would go once again to Saratoga Springs with Julie Hart Beers and her children. She hoped to tack on an additional week or so to travel north into the Adirondacks, where she had never been, for she had seen sketches and paintings and had spoken with those who had marveled at its untouched valleys and sumptuous views. She would go by herself, she decided, perhaps even on horseback, making camp along the way. She'd been thinking for some time of getting away from the city with only Knight as a companion, a reprise of her journey to New York seven years earlier. She regretted that the still-vigorous stallion had become a jaded Manhattanite, spending much of his time munching idly on straw and peppermints in a Cottage Terrace mews, by now thoroughly used to the cacophony of the city and the jostling of its increasingly crowded byways. He also had become familiar with every low, sooty growth of clover in Central Park, where his mistress liked to ride as often as she could, usually, but not always, in the company of a young friend or two. Knight needed an invigorating jaunt up into the mountains as much as Carrie did.

During the intervening days, Carrie and Elsie continued their explorations together. With so many of the resident artists and their families headed for the hills, Dodsworth's Building had become as empty and echoing as a summertime schoolhouse, and with so few eyes upon them the young ladies felt free from whatever minor obligations held them in check during busier periods of the year. Until it was time for them to pack up and leave, they determined that they should get out to the far corners of New York and find a cool breeze wherever they could. They were mindful that there were parts of the city forbidden to them, owing to outbreaks of smallpox or cholera, or where gangs still ruled the neighborhoods. But the long daylight hours allowed them to stretch their travels into places they'd never been before.

They rode out dusty Bloomingdale Road and up into the heights north of Central Park. One hot morning, they took the ferry ride past Elysian Fields to look in at Hoboken and Jersey City and then back again to 23rd Street. They made it a game to tag the various gates of Central Park—Miners, Warriors, Hunters, Girls, Mariners, All Saints and the rest— until they had seen and touched them all. Upon hearing that there was a place called Spuyten Duyvil, they made it a point to get there on horseback, admire its views of the Hudson, and hurry back to town in time for a show—featuring an opera singer and a tightrope walker—at Niblo's Garden on Broadway.

It was in just this spirit of simple, girlish fun that Carrie and Elsie rode into a day and night of multiple, unimaginable horrors.

In that year, July 13 dawned into a perishing hot spell, a blaze of heat that had begun on Independence Day and only gotten worse since. New York shimmered and swayed unsteadily with the mounting temperatures by day and gave back almost nothing of them at night. Work could not be done. Those stuck in the city spent as much of their time as they could out of doors, in shade, and, if at all possible, by the water. They thronged the parks and whatever lakes and reservoirs could be found there, or flung themselves desperately into the cooling but treacherous rivers that circled the island. Many drowned or were lost. At night they slept on rooftops, fire escapes and piers, occasionally, it was reported, rolling off to their doom. As Carrie and Elsie knew from their French lessons, July 14 was Bastille Day, and in recognition of both the next day's anniversary and the continuing heat, they'd decided to make a trip to one of

Manhattan's old fortifications. The Battery and Castle Garden were located at the confluence of the North and East rivers—at the very southern tip of the island—a spot they hoped might bring a stray breeze off the harbor. In any event, there was a park there, and a seaward prospect, and perhaps enough green to carve out a suitable place for several languid hours.

They did not make an early start, or at least not as early as they had planned. First, the pears and plums were no longer good, and substitutes had to be found. And then there was a discussion about the best way to travel. Having heard that horses were dying by the score due to the heat, neither Carrie nor Elsie wanted to ride her own. They felt much the same way about taking a taxi and being at least in some part responsible for the horses' discomfort. Walking was out of the question. Finally, with some growing feeling of urgency, they decided that a four-horse car on rails would not put too much of a burden upon any particular animal. They gathered their things and set out, only a little before noon, through the suffocating heat to the Sixth Avenue line.

Once aboard, it was in the area around Canal Street that they first smelled smoke and noticed people running south on Broadway. By the time they got to Park Place, the car was forced to a halt by what had become a shouting, unruly mob moving east across the tracks. They learned from the shouts all around them that Barnum's enormous American Museum on the corner of Broadway and Ann had caught fire, was fully engaged in flame, and now was in danger of collapsing. "The poor animals!" Carrie shouted. She took Elsie by the elbow and they plunged into the chaos, moving with the crowd toward the increasingly searing heat and swirling smoke.

Everyone in New York save the most stubbornly lazy and ill-informed had been to Barnum's astonishing museum at least once. Carrie had gone with Alathea Kingsbury, when the latter had accompanied her husband to the city on a one-day business trip almost exactly a year earlier. It had been the rarest of occasions, and after catching up during morning tea (children thriving; things quiet and shuttered for summer at Rose Hill; Archie Comstock, the thieving coachman, dead in a prison stabbing) Alathea remarked that she longed to see something she'd never see in Waterbury.

They spent the rest of the day eagerly taking in Barnum's teeming maze of wonders—the lolling hippopotami and Labrador whales in their enormous basement tanks, the fortune teller, the learned seal and the renowned giantess Miss Swan. There were live snakes and monkeys, alligators and electric eels, a one-armed, one-legged Civil War soldier, a stuffed sacred cow, rare coins and an exhibit called "Happy Family" in which cats, canaries, dogs, snakes and monkeys appeared to live together in remarkable harmony. There were popular peepholes revealing a king's palace, Venetian canals and a Revolutionary War battlefield. And there was a gallery of brilliantly accurate waxen figures, including Napoleon, Queen Victoria, Tom Thumb, and Chang and Eng, the Siamese twins.

And now, before a wild, agitated, oddly celebratory throng numbering in the many thousands, it was all burning to the ground. The extent of the carnage was difficult to register in the encompassing smoke, but wild rumors swirled and spread. Had the whales actually been roasted alive after their tanks were emptied out to help battle the flames? Could it be that the snake cage had been overturned? One certainty was that a replica of Jefferson Davis dressed in petticoats had been thrown out of an upper window, scooped up by the mob and promptly hanged from the nearest lamppost. Firemen worked the blaze hard, pouring on as much water as they could get to the scene, but they were also spotted carrying certain treasures—exotic coins, exquisite porcelain and jade, a mummy—out of the smoke and into waiting, assaying hands.

In the hectic surrounding streets, pickpocketing, thievery and looting were general. The crowd moved as one brainless organism—often with rising shouts and screams—away from a tumbling wall, or toward the sight of the fat lady and the towering Miss Swan, prows forward like tugs pressing through river ice, escaping up Broadway to their rooms. There was panicking and a scattering in all directions when someone cried out, "The snakes are loose!" Dozens of spectators were crushed or otherwise injured and the air was filled with their cries. Many, many men lost their hats; boys were wandering through the crowd with half-a-dozen balanced on their heads. One man was seen escaping from Knox's hattery, one of the nearby compromised retailers, with a dozen Panamas in hand.

Early on, when the picnic basket was ripped from Elsie's arm by a pair of marauding 12-year-olds who quickly melted back into the crowd, the two young women realized Barnum's animals weren't the only ones in danger.

"We have to go!" cried Elsie, and Carrie agreed. But the pressing crowd made it impossible for them to reverse their course. Instead, they found refuge on the front steps of St. Paul's Chapel, just across Broadway from the blaze. There, beneath the generous portico, they were a little protected from the mob, and were just high up enough to observe it. From that spot of relative safety, they viewed horror upon horror. The worst for Carrie was when, through a break in the smoke, she saw a poor terrified ape leap from a museum window only to be chased down and shot by a city policeman.

Then the entire front of the building collapsed, sending out a great wave of smoke and dust. Only a single upright spire of brick remained standing. All had been lost. Carrie and Elsie had been nearly speechless during the extended height of the clamor, communicating mostly with alarmed looks and much pointing, but now, after more than an hour, the smoke and heat at last seemed to carry into another quarter and the crowd's fervor eased just a bit. Carrie turned to her friend, whose trembling hand, she discovered with a feeling of the most pleasing comfort, she was holding.

"Did you hear them shout that a lion had escaped?" she asked quite loudly. "That's when I felt the most fear, even though I don't think there ever was a lion, not a real one anyway, in the museum."

Elsie nodded absently. As a very dutiful child at heart, her thoughts escaped to a safer place, and one closer to home.

"I will regret losing that basket," she said. "It's been in our family since I was a little girl. My mother must never find out."

They were silent again for an extended period. The crowd, with the exception of tirelessly antic boys, had begun re-forming into conversational clusters with loud recountings of what they had just seen. The police for the most part had regained control of the adjacent streets and sidewalks. Still, the day seemed to have lost very little of its terrible momentum, and what appeared to be thunderheads now billowed high in the far western sky.

"Carrie, you have streaks of soot running down your face," said Elsie, offering a handkerchief from her sleeve. "In fact, now that I look I see that we are covered with dust and grime from head to toe. I don't think we can continue on our way, can we?"

It was a question posed by someone who was in a state of shock, or close to it.

"Well, we've lost our food and plates and the dear little yellow picnic blanket that traveled with me when I rode to this city from Connecticut," Carrie said. "I unfurled it every day at lunchtime during that trip."

"I think we can only proceed on foot from here," Elsie said. "The carriage traffic is all in a snarl."

"Well, let's leave right now before Barnum starts charging admission to see his smoking ruins."

They stepped gingerly out from under the portico and through the scattered debris and thinning crowd toward a westbound sidewalk. Looking back upon this day in later years, Carrie would wonder that she had been so unable to take in the enormity of what she had just witnessed. The spectacle had been terrible and the danger very real, but the loss of life and property, all the costs of the tragedy, had not truly registered with her. She should have been in tears, or at least in a daze like Elsie, immobilized by the all the chaos and death, and in particular the suffering animals and the indifference of the mob. She later wondered if she'd merely been too full of youthful bravado to yet appreciate the preciousness of life and its stingy parcel of days. Or could it be that she'd been hardened by the enormous toll—the daily menu of death, brutality and destruction, the epic demolishing of years and generations—of the recently concluded war? Or maybe she actually was in shock, too, and just didn't recognize it, like so many of the young men she'd heard about who'd been in battle. From a very early age she'd known how to put on a good front. Now, after seeing Barnum's great creation cascading down right before her, Carrie once again moved with purpose. She and Elsie shifted their focus to making a safe escape.

They did not know that the tumultuous events of the day had barely begun.

The fire and its attendant lawlessness had put a charge into the city, especially its lower precincts. The streets and alleys were animated with movement and sound, and permeated with the acrid, occasionally choking smells of the fire. Carrie and Elsie, brave though they thought themselves, did not feel entirely safe amidst all the freewheeling. Their knowledge of the city told them that they could not drift without purpose, not in a place where even the youngest of children would be testing one another's daring. They determined that if they walked up Broadway and then across Chambers Street to the river, they would find the pier for the Erie Railway Ferry, which they knew from prior outings would take them across to Jersey City and then back again further north to 23rd Street. They lifted their skirts slightly, lowered their gaze and hurried along in silence.

When they arrived at the pier, the immediate shock of the fire had worn off a bit and they were happy to see the *Pavonia* just pulling in. They also saw that alarmingly dark clouds in the west were throwing lightning down onto New Jersey and would soon be over the Hudson. Finally, they saw a familiar, awkward shape running toward them and calling out their names. Judging by the thick black layer upon his shirt and derby, John Hawkins had evidently been in close vicinity to the fire as well. Now he joined them, out of breath and quite boyish in his delight at seeing them. Under one arm he was carrying a stuffed armadillo.

"Did you see it?" he shouted. "Was there ever anything like it?"

"You look like a chimney sweep, John," said Carrie. "I hope we don't look quite as bad as you do."

"I was inside, Carrie!" he continued. "You could hear the horrible suffering beasts! Everyone was carrying things out." He remembered his prize and held it out. "I got this and some coins and medals. I saw the poor porcupines in their cage—no one could figure out how to reach in and rescue them!"

As Hawkins ranged on, Carrie wondered what else, ill-gotten, might be in his pockets, and whether the derby on his head might have just been pulled out through a broken shop window. Even under the soot it looked rather new. She had known for some time now—everyone knew—that he wasn't a painter and never had been, and that parts of his great introductory story, his deliverance from Bermuda, had been fabricated; he'd been caught mixing up major details in various tellings. The verdict among her crowd seemed to be that eccentricity could be forgiven, and perhaps welcomed, if accompanied by real talent. Even innocent eccentricity of a certain type could be brooked. But Hawkins' sort of calculating behavior, cloaked beneath an ill-fitting, false rascality, set him quite apart—and not in the best of ways.

After their adventure to Five Points, when Carrie's opinion of him as a vulnerable, likeable, one-of-a-kind *artiste* was at its height, they'd enjoyed some time together in what she thought of as a further introduction into the city for him. She made sure he was included in all the group outings, and one day walked with him all the way around the rim of the Croton Reservoir. They became quite friendly, and once, after a Saturday afternoon session at Pfaff's, even entered into a rambling and difficult conversation about their fathers. They were walking uptown toward home when they witnessed the horror of a man whipping a boy on a public street corner.

"Now that's how you toughen a lad up," Hawkins said facetiously as the boy pulled himself away and ran into an alley, and the man fell in a drunken stupor against a lamppost. "A good pounding is sure to change his ways."

"Spoken from experience, I take it?" said Carrie.

"When he was drunk, my dad called me 'Daisy,'" Hawkins said. "He told me he couldn't use the name he gave me originally because I didn't measure up to it. He thought I had to toughen up and earn it, so he set a whole stream of tasks before me. I was eight or nine and he had me take cold dunkings in the cattle trough to begin the day. Sometimes I had to clear the ice off the top first. There were mornings I just wanted to go under and stay there. And then I was to put up my little fists and box some of the local Yorkshire lugs – bigger boys who put me straight to the ground."

Carrie was surprised by the similarities to her own story.

"Your father thought you not man enough," she said. "Mine attacked me for not being a man at all."

They found a park bench and recounted dark episodes from their childhoods, each topping the other with stories that still burned in the memory. Carrie told of the time her father struck her before the Thanksgiving Ball, of his mistreatment of the servant Polly, and of the times he threatened to sell off Knight as punishment for her stubbornness or insolence, or even just her melancholy. But however much each revealed that long afternoon, and it was plenty, Carrie did not go as deep into her resentments as she could have, and she suspected John Hawkins held something in reserve as well. She noticed that although they spoke of intimate events, they sat literally at arms-length from each other. Full trust had not been established, and would not be.

For it wasn't long after that conversation that Hawkins was found out. Suspicions among the other men in the group had deepened after he had blithely walked out on several bar tabs and then had been seen running in the company of a known grifter named McFadden. Clearly, he required a second look. The men went so far as to convene and speak frankly among themselves about Hawkins, his scrambled tales and all the rest of it. They quickly established that no one had ever been asked to his rooms and studio on Amity Street. Subsequently, it was there that Haimish Sutro (who'd drawn the short stick) surprised him one day with a visit and discovered a tiny room barely large enough for a mattress and chair, and no studio or evidence of painting materials at all. Instead of expressing contrition at having misled everyone, or offering an explanation, Hawkins became indignant, called Sutro "a spy" and "a prying fuck" and then fell away from the social circle that had once embraced him so warmly.

And yet he hadn't fallen away entirely. He remained a recognizable figure on the periphery of the art scene, although now revealed in a new light. With his artistic pretensions stripped away, they saw him now as little more than a common hustler – his fast patter and sidelong glances evidence of a larcenous heart rather than a compelling biography. The men spoke more freely, and with little friendliness or amusement, about Hawkins' effeminate speech and manner, and offered much dark speculation about exactly how he grubbed his meager earnings. It was well known that there were several establishments where the unlamented Hawk might turn a quick dollar or two on a Saturday night. Even knowing his fuller story, Carrie retained some sympathy for the boy. She even worried that her harder feelings – and those of the group – might be rooted in the fact that Hawkins was never one of them. From the beginning, he was an unpolished creature, and his lack of means, schooling and attendant refinements meant the estrangement was predestined and, in its own way, cruel.

Now, as she, Elsie and Hawkins boarded the *Pavonia* together, and it pulled away from the pier, Carrie's thoughts turned away from the past and toward the immediate question of their getting on and off the river alive. As they crossed uneasily toward Jersey City, fitful gusts from the approaching storm began to froth and roil the current. Carrie heard nervous laughter from among the boat's crew and thought she saw fear in even their expert eyes as they looked up at the blackening sky—now so agitated and bruised that it showed purple and even a kind of dirty green in places. The first, westward crossing was managed ably but with a mounting sense of doom. A boy was pitiably seasick, a sudden gust carrying his spew onto his shoes and stockings. A small dog escaped its owner's grasp and threatened to leap overboard before being saved at the last by a one-armed young man wearing his Union cap. The ferry made a difficult landing at the Erie Railway pier and the Jersey-bound passengers hurried to shore. The first enormous drops of rain began to fall.

"Will the boat continue on?" Elsie shouted over the sound of thunder. "Should we get off here?"

"And do what?" Carrie answered. "Get on the train to Buffalo?"

Elsie pointed to a tin shack at the end of the pier.

"We could wait out the storm there and take a later ferry."

But before they had a chance to consider that possibility, the *Pavonia*, ever mindful of its timetable, lurched away from the pier and back onto the river. Within moments the storm was fully upon them. The afternoon darkened further, as if under a full eclipse of the sun, the wind grew loud and steady, the thunder and lightning nearly incessant, and the rain arrived in earnest in thick horizontal sheets, a brutal deafening assault that pounded the vessel and churned the river with a stupefying redundancy. The *Pavonia's* little universe – up, down and sideways – was all water upon water. Yet the craft cut patiently through – lanterns ablaze, bravely shouldering the swell – as if hers were the last human cargo on earth.

Carrie, Elsie, Hawkins and the others had early on sought the shelter of the ferry's enclosed salon. There they all stood unsteadily, three dozen of them, in absolute silence, each left to his or her own prayers and mortal thoughts as the boat rose, fell and pitched in every which way. It was here that poor Elsie lost her nerve. Perhaps her breakdown was caused by the immediate danger presented by the storm, or maybe it was the accumulating events of the day, but she finally could take no more. She put her face into Carrie's shoulder and began to cry. She didn't say a word. Carrie didn't cry in return; she bent and softened to take Elsie in, and then, rare for her—for she was not devout—addressed a private appeal to the deity. It began by asking for delivery from her own fear, but then turned into an escalating plea for every manner of blessing—for her dear Elsie and their wonderful, sustaining friendship, and then for awkward, struggling Hawkins, and for all the innocent animals lately trapped and burned to death in Barnum's museum, and the careening, hopeless lost souls rioting through the city streets, and then the brave young soldier in the Union cap who had already likely endured more than enough horror for several lifetimes, and even for the terrified little dog who could only think to jump into the swirling river. As Carrie and Elsie held each other close, others in the packed salon began to cry out as well as the storm reached its height. Who were they crying out for? What thoughts and dear images came rushing in for them as the *Pavonia* slid sideways deep into a trough and threatened to founder? John Hawkins couldn't have answered those questions, and certainly such thoughts never occurred to him, but he did use the confusion and tight, jostling quarters to expertly gain possession of a billfold and a silver pocket watch, even while keeping the grinning, most lifelike armadillo securely under one arm.

By the time they arrived at 23$^{rd}$ Street, the howling front edge of the storm had passed somewhat off to the east, but the trailing rain came down hard and the thunder continued with ferocious, echoing cracks. The three scrambled onto the pier and had no choice but to make a run for it. As they did, the falling torrent turned the soot from the museum fire into a gray, dripping sludge on their clothing and skin, and then washed it away altogether. They continued to run half-blindly even after they were entirely soaked through. And then John Hawkins shouted.

"Let's stop here!" He indicated a nondescript doorway. "We can dry off and wait out the storm!"

They followed him without hesitation.

The building's outer door gave way to a tile-floored vestibule, a heavy oak inner door and then, to the right off the entry hall, a handsome square sitting room fitted out with three leather chairs, a glass-fronted bookcase, ferns standing in ceramic planters, a scattering of Persian rugs, a couple of brass cuspidors and hanging portraits of what seemed to be Far Eastern sages. Hawkins gestured for Carrie and Elsie to sit and then parted a dark curtain and hurried through. But even though they were by now exhausted, the women felt too soaking wet to sit. Instead, they stood, shivering a bit, and took in their surroundings. Carrie tried to make out the title of some of the books in the case, but a reflection of light upon the glass prevented her from doing so. She fiddled with one of the doors in an effort to open it. They could still hear the rain pounding against the front of the building.

"What is that sweet smell?" asked Elsie, almost imperceptibly raising her nose into the air. "Do you smell something?"

"I was just wondering the same thing," said Carrie. "It reminds me of syrup."

"That's it—maple syrup!" declared Elsie. She considered the aroma for another moment and then sighed deeply. "I'm really quite hungry. We haven't eaten since I don't know when."

"Maybe John is getting us griddle cakes," said Carrie with a smile.

"Yes, with butter and strong coffee."

Instead, he came back through the curtain trailed by a large, high-cheeked woman, about 50 years old, dressed in flowing scarlet and saffron-colored robes. Her long, graying hair was pulled back into a single braid running down her back and she wore soft black shoes—slippers, really—that whispered beneath her robes as she crossed the room. All in all, she was an exotic bloom for this part of the world.

"Please say hello to Mrs. Cobb," said Hawkins. "This is her place. She'd like to show you her set-up here."

Carrie thought she saw the woman shoot John a disapproving look for his choice of words, but then in the next moment she was smiling broadly and acknowledging both Carrie and Elsie by name and with a slight bow.

"Right now, let's get all of you dry and comfortable," she said. "Does that sound like a good idea?"

There was something in the way she put forth the offer that made it seem like a first step, but where it might lead Carrie could not guess. There was also a patronizing tone that did not encourage trust. And of course Hawkins' involvement raised a sizable warning signal. But they were soaked, and it was still a long way home in the rain. Part of her wanted to find out what more this day could possibly hold for them. She nodded her assent and turned to see Elsie do the same.

Rather theatrically, Mrs. Cobb clapped her hands twice and two more robed figures, much younger and somewhat thinner, came through the curtain. They smiled politely, and then there was an awkward moment of silence and a quick exchange of anxious glances all around before Mrs. Cobb gestured toward the newcomers and spoke.

"These are my daughters," she said, "Carolina, who is the elder, and Pearl Louise. They will take you in hand."

Both the girls, who appeared to be in their late teens or early 20s, struck Carrie more as employees working a job than family members. Their smiles were dutiful and their welcoming words and gestures would never be mistaken for spontaneous. Still, it was easy to fall under their spell. Most unusually, both girls had painted their lips with a deep brownish shade of red. Carrie had known this to be done, but had never seen it before. Carolina took Elsie by the elbow, gave her an encouraging tug and led her through the curtain.

Next it was the younger sister's turn to take Carrie through.

"There's a bath and dry towels for you," Pearl Louise said, moving her red lips close to Carrie's ear. Her voice was languid and dreamy. Carrie felt quite relaxed. The clamorous events of the day were already moving behind her.

"What sort of place is this?" Carrie asked.

"A place of many wonders," replied Mrs. Cobb, touching Carrie lightly on the shoulder as she moved by. Carrie smiled and tried to acknowledge Hawkins as she left the room, but he was hidden behind Mrs. Cobb's substantial bosom and she saw only the top of his head and a rain-soaked trouser knee.

The other side of the curtain revealed a long, high-ceilinged corridor lined with doors and, at the end, an archway leading into what appeared to be a large room. The lighting was low but not unpleasantly so. Carrie saw the trailing end of Elsie's "summer sheer" as she disappeared into one of the rooms along the side whose door was then promptly closed. The syrupy aroma was much stronger here, and Carrie noticed it now seemed to be joined in a heady mix with burning tobacco.

"You are wet right through," said her escort, opening a door across from the one Elsie had entered. "Come in here with me and we'll see what we can do."

The room was about the same size as the sitting room they'd just left, except that it was lined on the floor and all four walls with green and white tiles. There was a wooden bench holding a neat pile of towels along one wall and a deep sink with a large mirror above it on another; in one corner was an armchair and side table perched on a smallish Asian rug. Tea for one had been set out on the table. But the centerpiece of the room was an enormous white porcelain tub, broad and long, set up on claw feet and filled nearly to the top. Carrie noted the dim reflection of the overhead gas globe bending and jittering on the water's surface and welcoming tendrils of steam rising into the room.

"Is that really for me?" she asked. Nothing—no feather bed, rose-strewn bower or mossy summer glade—could have looked more inviting at that moment.

"Until an hour ago, we had our baths filled with tepid water because people wanted to cool off," said Pearl. "But the storm has broken the heat wave. We heated up the water so you might escape coming down with a chill. Have some of this ginger tea and we will help take your things off and get them dry."

Carrie felt like Queen Victoria, or a privileged visitor to Baden-Baden, which she had heard the Churches speak of and whose nursery rhyme name had stuck in her memory. She took the strong, sugary tea sitting in the armchair as Pearl removed her shoes, and then she stood so that the back of her dress could be unbuttoned, peeled away from her damp shoulders and pulled down to her feet. As she stepped out of the dress and onto the cool tile floor, as she stood before this perfect stranger dressed only in her cotton chemise and drawers, Carrie easily could have questioned her circumstances and demanded an answer as to where in the world Hawkins had brought her. She could have called for her clothes and walked back out onto 23rd Street and hurried home. But the soft light, the waiting tub, the comforting sound of water running in the pipes to and from the other rooms, and Pearl's attentive hands made her want to stay. She felt peaceful and submissive. Maybe this was yet another gift of the many that New York would bestow upon her. Certainly there was nothing threatening about a hot bath.

"If you allow it, Carrie, I will take your chemise now and you can climb into the tub," said Pearl. "Or if you prefer, I will leave the room."

"Oh no, please attend to me," Carrie laughed softly. "Nothing could be better."

In a moment she was standing naked, but with a complete sense of calm, before another person. It was something she had never done before as an adult, not even in her rooms with Elsie, where they were both rather furtive about dressing and undressing. For that matter, she could not recall doing it as a child. But now, in this half-light, she simply stood and did not move as Pearl smiled, took her hand and helped her over the side of the tub and into the perfectly hot and immensely soothing water. As she slid down, she felt Pearl's strong hands on her neck, kneading it up and down, and then, too, on her shoulders. Then she felt her head being lowered gently onto the curving surface of the tub.

"Don't stop!" Carrie said as Pearl rose to leave.

"I have other things to attend to," she answered. "You are not the only one here, you know."

"No, I don't know," said Carrie. "I don't even know where I am."

Pearl put her finger to her painted lips.

"Just enjoy your soak," she said. "I'll be back before long."

She lowered the gas until the room was nearly dark, then left through a back door. Carrie slowly raised her knees and then lowered them again, stirring up the heat in the water. She felt it ripple up to her neck. Beads of perspiration began to form on her brow and upper lip. I'm still naked, she thought. Anyone could walk in and find me like this. And what could I do if they did? My clothes have been taken, I have been separated from my friends—I would be helpless. She dismissed the thought and closed her eyes. Time seemed to waver and then slow down. Several times she heard the creaking of footsteps coming and going in the corridor outside, then a short burst of female laughter in the distance that could have been Elsie's, then only the slow plinking drip of water from the faucet into the tub. She had never felt so listless and without purpose. She wanted to open her eyes but she couldn't even do that, or only just a tiny bit—and now, suddenly, she needed to, because Alathea Kingsbury, her voice loud and clear, was saying how beautiful something was. Carrie smiled and asked her to describe it, and Alathea took her by the forearm and said, "It's completely empty, Carrie. I've never seen anything so empty." Now Carrie could just make out that they were in Rose Hill. Her father was sweeping the bare parlor floor with a broom. "Your timing is impeccable, as always," he said to her with a broad, welcoming smile. "The tea and pancakes will help you see." And indeed now there was a light swinging above her and she was very slowly rising to her feet with some sense of bustling activity around her, and then she was steered, no longer naked, through a series of images that floated by like the lighted windows of a creeping passenger train: a strange, rodent-like animal watching her from a chair, Hawkins arguing with Mrs. Cobb in an office and then stopping and eyeing her warily until they passed, a sunken-cheeked man rushing by, and then an arching tunnel and a big room with small burning campfires everywhere and people speaking very low or sleeping on shelves, all turned away from her, and then someone provided a place for her to lie down, too. After the briefest moment of dislocation she relaxed and felt herself breathing slowly and evenly again, and then the vision spread across her as obvious as daylight: If she could only climb up and away, she thought, to some very high place, just to see the big view one time, to take in the whole picture—isn't that all anyone really wants, to see scenes of the past and the future arrayed all around like sun-struck mountains in one of those paintings, and the places you've been, and the people you love, all right there for you to see and study and put meaning to and make sense of? Isn't that really all that anyone wants—to have everything come into view at once like that in perfect clarity, like a magic trick explained, for one blessed, unforgettable moment?

The path rose up before her. She took one step and then another. And then for Carrie there was nothing at all.

# Chapter 11

Carrie opened her eyes to see her mother's familiar profile no more than three feet away. She closed her eyes again and made an assessment that was somewhat hampered by an unpleasant swimming sensation. She was lying on her back in a bed. She was covered with only a sheet and her head was resting on a pillow. The room she'd seen in that brief moment was bright with sunlight. She felt a breeze from an open window and heard the sounds of the city: boat whistles, river traffic. Nearer to hand, she heard voices amplified by a slight institutional echo. "Doctor Childs is wanted in the operating theater," someone called out. Carrie opened her eyes again, and this time her mother caught her.

"She has come to," Jane Welton said with excitement, turning to speak to someone behind her. She turned back to Carrie and stared into her face. "At last," she said with relief but also with the air of someone who had just endured a great deal. "We almost lost you."

An apron-clad nurse suddenly loomed on the other side of the bed. She put her palm on Carrie's forehead and made a satisfied sound.

"Are you ready to rejoin us, Carrie?" she asked. Carrie nodded as well as she could. The nurse put her right arm under the pillow and drew Carrie up to a more upright position. With her left hand she offered a glass of water. "Drink this," she said. "You have gotten yourself very dried out."

Carrie did so. The cool water felt good running across her parched tongue and down her throat. She turned again to her mother.

"Where are we?" she asked. "My brain is very much in a muddle."

Jane's manner had switched from relief to disapproval.

"We are in Bellevue Hospital, third floor," she said. "You have been under the care of the city's finest physicians and they have pulled you through."

"But what is wrong with me?" Carrie asked.

"Some would say that a great deal is wrong with you," her mother answered, "but we must save that conversation for another day. Most immediately, it seems you have been poisoned."

The nurse fixed the pillow behind Carrie so she could sit up on her own. Parts of the epic day now came back to her—the fire, the storm, Elsie, John Hawkins. And then the place Hawkins had taken them. She looked around the hospital room and noticed Aaron Polk sitting in a chair in the corner.

"Your friend is very devoted to you," said Jane. "He rescued you and brought you here. You very likely owe your life to him."

Polk rose and Jane gave up her bedside chair to him, declaring that she was going for tea elsewhere on the floor. The nurse said she would go order a tray of broth and toast.

"Your mother exaggerates," said Polk, taking a seat beside Carrie, "and her devotion greatly exceeds mine."

He put a hand lightly on Carrie's shoulder and smiled as he took a long look at her.

"One of the doctors said you were young and strong, and as soon as I heard that I knew you would weather the storm," he said. His honeyed Tennessee drawl was most welcome, thought Carrie.

"Please tell me what happened," she said.

"That scoundrel Hawkins brought you to an opium parlor," he said. "But the first thing you must know is that Elsie escaped and ran to my studio for help, and then we went for the police. By the time we got to you, you were pretty far gone."

"Why would they have poisoned me?"

"We think it was accidental. Elsie said she was offered tea, but it didn't taste right so she turned it down. The doctors think it was dosed with opium—too much opium. The police said it was a misguided attempt on the part of the proprietress and Hawkins, who she paid as an occasional factotum, to bring in new business."

"How did Elsie get out?"

"She said the young woman she was with tried to undress her and put her into a tub but that she didn't want to. The mother came in and tried to convince her, and, Elsie said, actually attempted to restrain her. But she broke free and ran out. She said she called for you but thought it better to get out and find help."

Carrie recoiled with shame at her own undressing—it was coming back to her now—and the girl eyeing her and putting her hands on her—in short, her willingness to drink in the tea and whatever came with it. She remembered Elsie's voice in the corridor and realized now that it was a cry rather than laughter. And the big room—that must have been what Polk called the opium parlor.

"I've heard of places where people take opium," she said, "but I thought they were run by Chinamen."

"They are but for this one, run by Mrs. Cobb and her daughters. It is thought to give a more refined experience than the lowly dens downtown." Carrie's friend paused for a moment. "I have learned a great deal in the last two days," he continued. "I have even learned that as long as Mrs. Cobb pays a hundred dollars a week to certain among the police, she will never be put out of business. Reprimanded, maybe, but never shut down."

"And what of Hawkins?" Carrie asked.

"He hasn't been seen, and it's good for him that he hasn't. He may have left New York altogether."

An attendant appeared in the doorway with the tray of food, but Polk held her back with a raised hand. He drew closer to Carrie.

"There's one more thing that you must know," he said.

Carrie looked at him expectantly.

"Elsie's parents have come down and taken her back to Boston."

"Well, I can't blame them for that," Carrie said. "She was about to leave for the shore anyway."

"No, you don't understand. They moved her out."

"Never to return?"

"Never to return," said Polk. "And there's more. They said they don't want you to contact her in any way, in person or by letter. They think you have influenced her in ways that are not healthy."

"But surely—" Carrie began, but Polk cut her off.

"They didn't ask my opinion or anyone else's. It was clear that their minds had been made up during the train ride down from Massachusetts, maybe even before."

The food tray was now in the hands of the nurse, who brought it forward.

"We had to empty your stomach, Carrie, so it's time you put something back in," she said. "Can you manage it yourself?"

Carrie spooned in some broth and took a bite of toast. Polk got up and walked over to the window and its view onto the East River.

"How long am I expected to stay here?" Carrie asked the nurse.

"That's for the doctor to say," the nurse replied. "But I would guess another two nights at least."

Carrie wondered if this would be the end of New York for her. She didn't want to leave, but she couldn't really think of a good argument for staying, not after all this. She took another taste of soup and absently held the spoon upside down in her mouth as she stared at the wall opposite her bed. But if I must leave New York, she wondered, is going back to Waterbury my only alternative? The mere thought was a horror to her. She saw her room in Rose Hill, and her child's desk there, and the endless procession of days. She would have to do some fast planning, but now was not the time. She was ready to sleep again.

"I thought you were traveling north, Aaron," she called weakly over to Polk. It was an effort to say the words.

"I leave for White River Junction in two days," he said.

"We were lucky you hadn't left yet."

"You mean you were lucky."

"Yes, I was lucky," said Carrie. "Thank you, Aaron."

Polk came back away from the window, two or three steps toward Carrie.

"I have to say that while I enjoy a good adventure as much as anyone, I don't understand at all what you were doing in this instance, or why you would take such enormous, unaccompanied risks," he said. "Elsie at least had the good sense to get out and find help. Why couldn't you have done the same?"

But Carrie's eyes were already closed. She took the question with her into a deeper realm. She turned it over once or twice but could not find an answer.

It wasn't until several days later that Carrie truly felt up to her old self. By then she had been moved out of Bellevue and into a suite of rooms her mother had taken at the Fifth Avenue Hotel. Jane Welton had chosen the hotel for several reasons: It was by far the most luxurious and fashionable in New York; it had been recommended by one of Carrie's physicians, Dr. John Franklin Gray, the famous homeopath, who lived there; and it was located just across Madison Square from Carrie's now forlornly empty rooms in Dodsworth's Building. As Carrie recovered, she appreciated several of the hotel's extraordinary offerings, such as the private bath (each room had one) and the "vertical screw railway," a miraculous small compartment that carried her from her home on the fifth floor down to the lobby and back up again. In general, she passed the days agreeably.

One thing she tried to do during the many idle hours of her recuperation was to chart a course for her own future—one that would most likely lead her away from New York. Some time before, probably beginning with her run-in at Pfaff's with the despairing Ada Clare, she had come to the conclusion that the city was no longer the best place for her, and the episode at Mrs. Cobb's sealed it. If she had possessed a specific occupation or singular talent that could flourish in Manhattan, that would have been one thing. If she were married to someone who wished to call New York home, or had to, that would be another. But for her, now, the city seemed to be a place of diminishing opportunities and too many temptations. The fact that Elsie was now gone, whether by her own decision or not, only heightened those feelings in Carrie.

Such thoughts flowed easily as she rested and reviewed her situation. It was far more difficult to produce useful ideas for what to do—and where to go—next.

Carrie's convalescence also allowed her the opportunity to begin to see her mother in a wholly new light. Instead of the shrill, hectoring presence Carrie had feared, Jane Welton turned out to be, for the most part, patient and caring. She'd made her anger and disappointment known, of course, and quite clearly, but it hadn't come across as scolding. It was more like one woman speaking to another, seriously but also with some understanding. Carrie wondered if their being away from Waterbury and Rose Hill had anything to do with it—and it made her now wish that she had been allowed to accompany her mother for a summer or two at Watch Hill, or on jaunts to visit her Porter relatives in Philadelphia and Baltimore. They may never have become close friends, as some mothers and daughters do, but there might not have been those strong feelings of enmity that had so soured her youth.

Then one afternoon, out of the blue, came the truly unexpected turn. As the two women half-reclined in their corner salon and took in the breezes that flitted sporadically across the room from one open window to another, Jane abruptly changed the mood in the room.

"Your father sends his wishes for a quick recovery," she said.

Carrie did not respond. It seemed such an obvious falsehood.

"He genuinely is concerned about you, Carrie," Jane continued.

Another silence, but Carrie couldn't hold her tongue for long.

"If he cares so much, why isn't he here?" she asked angrily.

"He did express an interest in coming—" Jane began.

"He would never!" Carrie interrupted. "Why would you even say such a thing?"

They sat again in silence for some time. Then Jane spoke.

"I know what kind of man he is, more than anyone," she said. "I know how angry he can be, and how careless in his treatment of others."

"Careless? He is a monster."

There. Carrie had said it out loud to her mother. She felt her cheeks flush and tears coming to her eyes. The forbidden closet had been opened and now the contents would come spilling out.

"He is more than that, but he has been very unfair to you, Carrie," Jane said.

"Oh, it goes far beyond being unfair, Mother, as you well know. Maybe you'd like a list of the things he's done. I've counted them up many times. He's scolded and bullied me relentlessly, hit me, menaced me in any number of ways— and never once do I remember a loving word or kind gesture. Never once!" Now Carrie was struggling through tears. "Do you know how difficult it's been for me to make my way, first as a little girl and even now, all these years later? How brave and uncaring I've had to make myself seem? How I've had to fight off thoughts of being stupid and worthless? And during all that time, what did you do for your daughter and only child? How did you help her? You conspired. You did nothing. You stood by and allowed it to happen!"

Jane did not rise to challenge this outburst.

"I chose not to see," she said at last. "I thought that somehow he would change, but that was a vain hope."

Carrie continued to sob. Never before had she dared say so much. Nor had her mother.

"I saw to it that you could get away to New York," Jane said.

"That was my doing more than yours."

"I was the one who convinced your father. And I provided you with the funds that allowed you to stay."

"I do thank you for that."

A fire wagon noisily hurried by on the avenue below. They waited until it clattered into the distance.

"For better or worse, I have made my life in Waterbury with your father," Jane said with a shift in her tone. "But as I have watched over you during these last few days, I've considered who we've been to each other, and where I've fallen terribly short—and I've done a great deal of thinking. You must not come back. Maybe someday you will be able to, but not now."

"But I don't think I can stay in New York," said Carrie, regaining her composure. "I no longer feel comfortable here. I'm not sure that my friends are still my friends."

"I don't know about that. I think the young man who took you out of that awful place is certainly your friend. But I agree that you should leave. I went over to your old building and had a long conversation with Julie Hart Beers. She knows everything that has transpired in recent days. She likes you very much, Carrie, and wants you to join her in Saratoga Springs as you originally planned. We both think it would be the best thing for you."

"So do I," said Carrie.

"That will take care of the summer," said her mother. "After that, we shall just have to see. Things will happen that we cannot anticipate now."

Jane now stood and walked over to where Carrie was seated.

"Now you must rest some more," she said. "These wild emotions are not helpful to your recovery."

"On the contrary, I think they're very good," said Carrie as she stood, too. "You can't imagine how much more clearly I see things right now."

Jane awkwardly reached her arms out to her daughter.

"Will you hold me, please, Carrie?" she asked, knowing her daughter had every reason not to. And when Carrie did, Jane smiled—not the theatrical smile that had made her reputation back in Waterbury, but a smaller, truer smile that seemed to come quite naturally—and found herself saying, "I've been thinking of this moment since I first saw you lying there so helpless in the hospital. I hope we can give ourselves a second life together."

As Carrie held her mother, she saw their reflection in a full-length mirror across the room and wondered if something had actually changed in her own feelings or if she was just being a dutiful daughter. After all, how much could one explosive hour on a warm summer afternoon erase of twenty-five years of terrible hurt and injustice? But it did seem a hopeful beginning, she decided, one that at least for now was not worth dissecting into a thousand pieces, like the workings of a clock.

It is amusing that anyone could think of Saratoga Springs, in August 1865, as an escape from the temptations of New York City—from the urban summer heat and atmospheric miasma, perhaps, but not from sin and dissolution. In the fifty or so years since Gideon Putnam first laid out the upstate village and foresaw the drawing power of its restorative spring waters, Saratoga had grown into a warm-weather resort that could rival Newport to the east and Long Branch on the New Jersey shore. And now that the war had ended, the town seemed determined to find its ultimate identity as a place where the idle rich, and those who preyed upon them, could spend their days and nights eating, drinking, fornicating and, especially, gambling.

Saratoga was the place to reliably find "the wealthiest men, the handsomest women, the finest horses, the most costly equipages, the grandest dresses and the best living." At the same time, the gaming crowd, no matter how crass, could find a warm welcome at John Morrissey's gambling establishment on Matilda Street, where faro, whist, roulette and other games were always open to newcomers, as long as they were not female, not local residents, and used cash to play. Even more famously, there was now a six-day horse racing season at a stunning new track that could accommodate 7,500 spectators, as well as other racing dates for trotters, more action at the Saratoga County Fair, and even, on one day that August, a half-mile race featuring a field of one-legged Civil War veterans. At times it seemed that any moving thing, from birds on a tree limb to the rising sun, could attract a crowd of eager bettors and scheming odds-makers.

Most of Saratoga's temptations were known, by reputation, to Carrie as she stepped off the train with Julie Hart Beers and her two daughters. As they rode to their familiar digs on Spring Street, she once again admired the broad avenues and summer sunlight as it filtered through the limbs of the graceful elms. Broadway was busier than she'd remembered it from the year before: a lively tableau of horses and shiny new conveyances; pedestrians in ones, twos and bunches; and noise and gaiety spilling out of shops, dining establishments, and boarding houses, but especially from the mammoth Union Hotel, originally Gideon Putnam's modest boarding house and tavern, now owned by the Leland Brothers and turned into a sprawling, lavish destination. As they rode by, Julie indicated a Greek-inspired building to the north of the hotel.

"That's the new opera house—so-called, although I'm not sure how much opera will ever be performed there," she said. "I received a picture card of its interior from my brother James. Spectacular. General Grant himself was present for the Fourth of July grand opening gala."

"Will we be able to go?" asked Martha, who, at age 11, was just beginning to flutter at any mention of a "gala."

"August is full of concerts, hops and garden parties," Carrie said, as the girl's official caretaker. "I am sure we'll be able to dress up and attend some of them."

But in reality Carrie would have very few such obligations. Mrs. Jensen, the proprietor of the boarding house, had found a cheerful, maternal 17-year-old to look after the children while Julie was either instructing her art students or traveling with them to nearby sites for outdoor painting sessions. Carrie would be on call for special circumstances, or she could take the girls out from time to time, but for the most part she would be free to do as she pleased, whether that meant reading on Mrs. Jensen's big front porch, tagging along on one of Julie's art-class jaunts, or exploring some of the diversions now offered in town.

For the last, she would need her own companion, and here, again, Mrs. Jensen had come to the rescue, this time with her own daughter. Genevieve Jensen was a couple of years younger than Carrie, quiet but impish, and a remarkable knitting prodigy whose sweaters and throws, Julie said, were sold up and down the East Coast and even in Europe. Genevieve perfectly suited Carrie's purposes— she was eager to experience new sights and sounds, and she knew Saratoga Springs inside out, including ways to get into restricted areas and events to which they had not been invited. Inevitably, the person at the gate or door was someone she had gone to school with, or whose sister or brother she knew—for other than in summer, Saratoga Springs was a very small town indeed.

The horses that year were scheduled to run on six days, from August 7th to the 12th. Each day featured only two or three races, so the week was filled with many other things to do as well. Each of the large hotels planned a grand ball. The local theater was drawing what the press called "promiscuous crowds" with offerings such as *Married Life* and the notorious *Aurora Floyd*, based on the novel by Mary Elizabeth Braddon. There was a concert company, Negro minstrels, serenaders, and what was described as "a variety of nocturnal amusements." There were also the pool sales every evening at White's and Underwood's, where the odds were set for the next day's races and bets thrown down.

As to the track itself, one New York newspaper described a typical day:

There was a large concourse of people on the track. There were several Major-Generals present, philosophers, poets, politicians (an unlimited number) and a very large number of ladies. There were also several of the clerical profession on the grand stand, who seemed to be much interested in the proceedings—indeed, every class and profession in life was represented. The fact that ten thousand people, from all parts of the world, can mingle together for one whole week, in the greatest harmony, and that, too, surrounded by the excitement of racing, is one worth recording.

Such was the scene, more or less, on August 7, when Carrie and Genevieve attended Opening Day at the oval. Carrie feared they'd be relegated to the Field Stand, some distance from the main action, but Genevieve called the boy at the ticket window by name, and soon they were seated just to the rear of the owners' area in the Grand Stand, with a perfect view of the racing and all its attendant activities. As they sat beneath parasols, very much seeing and being seen in their finest cotton print confections, a lone portly gentleman huffed up and lifted his gray crush hat to them.

"I spotted you from several rows down in front," he said in a friendly manner. "'Percy,' I thought to myself upon seeing you, 'here are two ladies in distress.' I could not help but think that you might be in need of some guidance regarding the horses, the riders, the races and all the rest of it—in short, the entire panoply."

"It is our first time, or at least it's mine," said Carrie, peeking innocently out from beneath her parasol, but at the same time recalling Frederick Kingsbury's warning from two summers ago that she keep her wits about her in the vicinity of a race track. She quickly sized up the new stranger. Her judgment in such matters was not perfect, far from it, but she confidently rated him as being completely harmless.

"Very well," said the man, who was perspiring quite freely. "Introductions first. I am Percy Bush of Wilmington. I have a horse running in the second race, but until then I am simply trying to enjoy this delightful if rather warm afternoon. Do you have a connection to one of the mounts today?"

Carrie and Genevieve introduced themselves and admitted that they were mere spectators with no special rooting interest.

"Then please cheer for Fleetwing when his time comes. He will be up against the great Kentucky, but maybe he will find inspiration if he hears your voices."

Carrie said that of course they would, and then the horses for the first race began their parade before the Grand Stand. Bush took on a professorial manner.

"This is the Travers Sweepstakes for 3-year-olds, a mile and three-quarters," he explained. "Last year, William Travers' own Kentucky, who I've already mentioned, won. Not quite sporting to win your own cup, I don't think. In any case, over there is the favorite, Gilda, ridden by the top jockey Gilpatrick, and here is Oliata with Abe aboard. Abe was only recently given his freedom by his Louisiana master, and now he and Gilpatrick have tremendous duels on the very best horses. And here," he went on, pointing, "is Maiden, with my boy Sewell riding. He looks like Jim Crow, even more raggedy maybe, but he's one of the best—so good that there have been several instances of rivals trying to take him out. A shot from a man who did not wish him to appear on the track took his right eye out, and one of his legs was damaged under similar circumstances."

Carrie and Genevieve were suitably scandalized and watched closely as the lineup passed by.

"I didn't realize this was such a dangerous sport," said Genevieve.

"Those dangers are nothing compared with riding in a close pack of galloping horses as the track turns toward home," said Bush with a knowing frown. "You have to watch the ground ahead, the other horses, and the whip hand of the jockey beside you who may decide to give you a quick lashing or two. A gunshot is nothing to it. Many of the boys end up with broken bones, or laid out for the rest of their lives, or even dead."

Meanwhile, Carrie had caught a whiff of manure and her thoughts flew elsewhere.

"This is such a place for horses," she said wonderingly. "The avenues, the tracks, the sheds, the open fields—you see them everywhere. They are like royalty here. If I could have my own Knight with me I think I could be very happy in Saratoga Springs."

"Keep in mind it's only for these few days, and the winters are long," cautioned Bush. "By this time next week, most of the horses and their owners will have gone scattering off to find riches elsewhere. Some are headed to Montreal, others to Riverside or Lincoln. I will stop in Hoboken and Paterson on my way back home to Delaware in time to see the fall come in."

Just then the race commenced. It was a fair start, and as the horses gained their speed, the crowd remained hushed and expectant, every eye and thought centered upon the pack of six horses, waiting for a significant separation to occur. After more than a mile, the race at last emerged as a contest between Oliata and Maiden, and the voices of support in the crowd rose into a perfect crescendo. Within a hundred or so yards of the judges' stand, Sewell applied the brutal gad and Maiden passed under the rope half-a-length ahead. The crowd was by now standing and cheering, and as the horses thundered past the finish and the outcome became known, Bush gave each of his new friends a quite passionate embrace, actually lifting Genevieve off the ground.

"My jock has won it!" he shouted, beaming. "Do you think he might do the same for me? I think he will!"

He fairly danced as he went on, but as the crowd quieted, a lone voice could be heard calling in their direction.

"Percy! Percy!" The sound was high-pitched and insistent. Bush turned to Carrie and Genevieve.

"That would be Mrs. Bush," he said sheepishly. "She has spotted me at last. I have the feeling that it's time for me to go join the other owners for the next race. If you ever want to place a bet, let me do it for you. Women are not allowed, you know."

He shook hands warmly with both of them, seemed to want to say something more but didn't, and went off to join his wife and the others. Once he was gone, Carrie and Genevieve looked at each other and burst out laughing. "That would be Mrs. Bush," Genevieve mimicked, and they both laughed again, but with affection. However, not far beneath the laughter, Carrie saw again and again the frantic whipping and driving of the spur into the flank of the winning animal and its wild eyes as it crossed the line.

Despite growing mixed feelings on Carrie's part, racing week passed most pleasantly and good-naturedly. The fine August weather held and grew even warmer. Mr. Bush's horse did not win that opening day (Kentucky did), but his Lexicon and Satinstone gave him first-place finishes as the meet progressed. Genevieve brought Carrie to take the waters at the Congress, Columbian, High Rock and Empire springs, although neither felt particularly reinvigorated after having done so. They spent much time at Mrs. Jensen's place on Spring Street, where Genevieve tended to her copious knitting and Carrie, with some degree of restlessness, played on the wide lawn with the girls while their mother helped coax life into her students' canvases.

In all, Carrie soon felt she had "done" the town, with the lone exception of John Morrissey's gambling establishment. The fact that it was considered strictly off-limits to her for any number of reasons made it even more interesting. She never tried to enter, but she did make sure as often as she could that her evening strolls, normally taken with Genevieve, Julie and the two girls, included Matilda Street and a turn by Morrissey's. Sometimes when she was idle she would find an excuse to go by the place alone. She could not account for the fascination the gambling house held for her, or exactly what it was that drew her to it. She was not a card player herself and did not see the point of putting up her own money where an unlucky turn could lose it all. Perhaps, as with Pfaff's in New York, it was the clubbiness of the place, the camaraderie, that attracted her. She saw it as she strolled by—the men at leisure on the broad porch, smoking and talking. They were not, for the most part, laudable types; indeed, she sometimes thought she could hear the scheming in their voices, the tightness in their laughter, even when they were away from the tables. So what was the magnetic pull? Well, why did Eve take the forbidden apple from the tree?

Such were the thoughts playing in her imagination one warm evening as she wandered off Division Street, onto Matilda and past Morrissey's. She walked slowly, taking it all in with sidelong glances while not appearing to turn her head, when she noticed a figure slouched against the side of the building, smoking a small cigar. Her eyes widened with a tremor of recognition; it was a familiar figure from her past, minor but quite unforgettable. She turned her head to see him plain. And then she crossed the street and walked straight toward him until at last he looked up, saw her, and straightened.

"You can't enter, miss," he said with a hint amusement in his voice. "No women allowed."

As he spoke, Carrie knew for certain the handsome face, the dark eyes and the easy authority in his manner. She paused just a moment, enjoying the fact that she knew him and he did not know her back, at least not yet. Finally she spoke.

"You've come a long way from Mott Street," she said with what she hoped was disarming directness, "since you came to my rescue one night."

Dan Lyons was visibly taken aback. He was not wearing the high hat and dustcoat he'd worn nearly a year before, when he and his Whyo associates materialized out of thin air to save Carrie, Polk and John Hawkins from a thug's assault on a dark street in Five Points. Now he was dressed conventionally for a summer evening in the country, clearly an employee of the house rather than one of the gaming members. A wave passed across his face.

"You were with my brother," he said. "You were dressed in white, like a ghost of some other world passing through our dingy quarter."

"My name is Carrie Welton," said Carrie, somewhat surprised at the speed of the man's recovery and the colorful nature of his speech.

"Mine is Dan Lyons."

They shook hands almost with the warm feeling of reestablishing an old friendship.

"I am glad to meet you," said Carrie. "I never got the opportunity to thank you for coming to our aid on that night, and for seeing we got home safely."

"All part of the service," said Lyons, his swagger fully restored. "You were swimming in deep water that night." He looked at Carrie fully face-to-face. She saw that his eyes were, of all things, a disconcerting dark shade of violet. "What brings you up here to the Spa?" he asked.

Carrie described her recent circumstances, leaving out many of the major points, especially those having to do with her misadventure at Mrs. Cobb's, else he would think she did nothing but get in and out of trouble. She concluded with a full description of the episode at the track with Genevieve and Mr. Bush, his nagging wife and overfriendly hugs.

"Percy Bush is one of our best customers," said Dan with a laugh, indicating the building at his back. "I think his roulette losses here paid for the rebuilding and repainting of this porch last spring. We'd like to figure out a way of getting him to stay a little longer in town."

They continued to stand a little awkwardly, but Dan saw there might be quite a bit more to the conversation. He excused himself and came back with two chairs from the porch. He set them down beneath a rose arbor in the back yard and asked Carrie to join him there.

"My duties are done for the day," he said, "but I'm in no hurry to leave."

Carrie removed her wide, beribboned straw hat and sat down.

"There's your face out of the shadows at last," Dan said. "Lovely."

Carrie looked down and blushed. The word was common enough, but his soulful Irish way of saying it found its way straight to her heart. She felt that if she didn't say something right away she might not say anything ever again.

"And what duties might those be that are done for the day?" she managed at last. "You seem to have come a million miles from where I last saw you."

"It's not as far as you think," he said, taking the seat beside her. "Have you ever heard of a man named John Morrissey?"

"I've heard that name many times since I've been up here," she said. "This is his establishment, is it not?"

"'Tis that. He's also responsible for the race track being here, and many of the improvements in Congress Park and elsewhere. He's been a colossus to me, and his story has been a lesson. He had nothing to begin with. His Ma died drunk in a ditch, so not surprisingly he was a regular troublemaker as a lad, a thief and a thug. But he always kept an eye on the ball. He knew how to fight, so that's what he did, and eventually he became a champion boxer who beat Yankee Sullivan in 37 rounds in front of thousands. And in the city he was head of the Dead Rabbits, the gang that controlled the Five Points in the 1850s when I was only a nipper."

"Did you know him then?" Carrie asked.

"Oh no, I was much too young—just scrappin' for food for me Ma at that point," Dan replied. He seemed to become more Irish as his words flowed.

"How did you meet him, then?"

"Well, at some point he decided he'd go straight—or maybe he always knew he would. He taught himself how to read, the same way as I have. He married a ship captain's daughter. And then, for his service to the party through the

Dead Rabbits, keeping the polling places in line and such, Tammany Hall cleared the way for him to open a gambling house in New York without police interference. That eventually led him upstate—he was from Troy to begin with —and to the very establishment we see before us. And then he put up most of the money for the new racetrack, even though Travers and the others get most of the credit. Now, with his fame, his boxing belt and his connections, he's thinking about running for the U.S. Congress next year. Tell me that ain't a tale to top Abe Lincoln's."

Carrie was smiling broadly at both the story and Dan's natural excitement as he told it. He effortlessly drew her in. She wanted to be drawn in. She could see how John Morrissey would want him on his side.

"You still haven't said how you met him," she said.

"I put the Whyos in a position to do some favors for Tammany Hall, just like the Dead Rabbits had done— knocking a few heads, keeping the peace on Election Day, that sort of thing. I guess my ways of doing things got noticed. One day last March a barouche pulled up beside me on Mulberry Street, the driver motioned me inside, and there he was, Old Smoke, wanting to talk to me. He asked me some easy questions about my talents and my background, but I could tell he was just sizing me up. Before I got back down to the street again, he'd asked me to come work for him. And so here I am, moving chairs on and off the porch on Matilda Street!"

"What is it you do, other than that?"

"All manner of things. I might go behind the bar to make sure the drinks are being poured proper. I see to it that important people like your friend Mr. Bush are personally well taken care of. There might be a matter at the track that needs my attention. It's a big business and all needs to be run correct. I am always on call."

"I remember you saying something like that when you were in the Whyos."

"A leopard doesn't change his spots."

"But I can see this one has climbed pretty far up into the tree," said Carrie.

The conversation had reached a natural pause. The late-day shadows around them had gathered into dusk, and gaslight was now glowing from every window in Morrissey's establishment. The raspy notes of katydids could be heard all around them, signaling that the first frost was a mere six weeks away.

"We have a piece of the United States Hotel," said Dan. "I'd be honored if I could take you to dinner there."

Carrie wanted to go with him. She had made a decision to herself about Dan Lyons. He was the man who would put an end to her wandering curiosity. There was something strong yet sweet about him, a native intelligence, a transparent ambition, but without pretense. He was so different from the other men she had known. And he was so handsome—seen in the light from the house, his dark hair and features, his straight nose and firm chin, his broad shoulders—his capable, protective air—made Carrie want to fall straight into his arms. But not on this night. She didn't see how it could happen tonight. She wasn't even sure it could happen at all. It was such a new feeling to her. She felt she needed to consider it just a bit. She had made so many careless mistakes, and now would not be a good time for another.

"I am sure I am wanted back at Mrs. Jensen's," Carrie said. "I went out for a walk and here it is two hours later."

"Well, I would like to see you again," said Dan. "Maybe you would like a tour of the track and stables."

"I would love that more than anything!" said Carrie. "Can I send you a note through the house here?"

"Do that, please," Dan said.

He took her hand and assisted her as she rose from the chair and handed over her straw hat. And then, no doubt encouraged by the dancing shadows on the lawn and the pulse of the summer night, he kissed her—a natural, sweet kiss on the lips—and just long enough for her to kiss back.

"I'm glad you crossed the street tonight, Carrie," he said.

"I am, too," she replied. "Now please let me go. I am missed at home."

Carrie took several steps away and then turned to face Dan once again.

"By the way, whatever became of your brother—Mucker, was it?

"Faker."

"What became of Faker and his painting?"

"The worst thing," said Dan. He spread his arms just a bit and opened his palms toward Carrie as he spoke. "His block of tenements burned down in January, the coldest night of the winter. We were watching it together, enormous flames, and then he ran inside. Just like that—one moment he's with me and the next he's gone, trying to rip his stations off the wall and save them, I guess, or maybe just be with them at the end. I tried to go in after him, but it was impossible. No one could. It was an inferno. There was no trace of a body to be found in the morning—only his poor bones."

Carrie wished she hadn't asked the question. She saw again Faker's otherworldly gaze as he spoke to her of his inspiration and his wish to be considered a legitimate painter, but she could think of nothing to say. She turned toward home a second time, walking slowly, breathing evenly, until Dan Lyons once again resumed his rightful place in the forefront of her thoughts.

Carrie let a whole day slip by. She was in something of a paralyzed state. She thought of Dan all the time, and of their kiss on Matilda Street. She dizzily partook in the events at the boarding house—meals, turns at watching the girls, even an afternoon horseback ride with Genevieve down to Ballston Spa and back. As their horses drank from a stream during their ride home, Carrie unburdened herself to the girl, telling of her chance meeting and all that followed.

"You sound pretty well stung," was Genevieve's homespun response. "I don't know much about it, but this seems like all you could hope for."

"It's not love, I don't think," Carrie said. "At least it's not that pure, high-minded, eternal, up-in-the-clouds sort of things you read about in books. I feel like it's much lower to the ground."

They sat still for a moment.

"But I do hear his voice right now in the water moving over the rocks," Carrie said.

When they got back home, there was a letter with a Massachusetts postmark waiting for Carrie. The handwriting on the envelope was warmly familiar.

My Dear Carrie,

I write to you from the big porch of our summer house at Smith's Point. From here on this sunny morning I can look out over a wide expanse of bright green lawn, then a tangled growth of beach plums, bayberry and poverty grass, and, beyond all, the deep blue of the ocean. Just now a sail is moving at good speed left to right across our opening. How I wish you could be here to share the fresh sea air with me as we've shared so many things before. I am writing to tell you the happy news that Earl and I will be married at Christmastime. Although we never spoke of it, I suspect you knew of our deep affection for one another, and now he has asked for my hand! Father, who adores Earl and is convinced of his future as a painter of note, granted permission in record time—so here we are, counting down the days! Now for the delicate part, my dear Carrie. My parents—wrongly!—put much of the blame upon you for what happened last month in New York. I have shed tears trying to convince them otherwise, but they simply will not hear it. Perhaps someday, with the help of Earl, I can make them understand, but for now I cannot put you on our wedding list. I think even this letter would be forbidden, but it is my small act of defiance to send it anyway. My parents, whom I love, can be quite unreasonable at times, but for now I am under their roof and therefore under their aegis. What they are unable to control, however, are my memories of our adventures together in New York. Already, I must admit, it all feels somewhere in the past to me—a completed chapter—but with thrills and laughter and so much genuine affection between the two of us. It will always be a part of me, Carrie, and it is my ardent hope that one day we can get together to recount it all in person. Until then I remain your most devoted, loving friend,

Elsie

Carrie read it through three times before deciding it was a goodbye letter. Despite several passages to the contrary, she saw a finality in it, and an underlying wish, a plea even, not to engage their friendship any longer. Elsie had, as she put it, completed a chapter, and now, in her conventionally well-organized, obedient way, felt it was time to start a new one. Carrie was hurt—how could she not be?—but she wasn't angry or anything like vengeful. Elsie could not be anything other than Elsie, and here she was at her essence—loving and sweet, if perhaps withholding a large truth or two. Carrie thought she would always remember Elsie as the girl laughing in the morning sunlight as they read lines from Whitman back and forth. A delightful friend. Leave it at that.

What Carrie also took from the letter was that a new chapter had opened up for her, too. She'd thought dimly of it in recent weeks, and had spoken of it with her mother and Julie Beers, but now she knew it for certain. The realization, the pull of the unknown future, gave her courage. She took paper from a desk drawer and wrote a note of her own, but it wasn't to Elsie. Instead, she plainly asked Dan Lyons if it was not now time to go explore the track and stables together. She paid a neighbor boy to drop the note at Morrissey's gambling house and within hours had her answer. Dan would come by and pick her up just after sunrise the very next morning, the last day of the racing season.

They decided to travel on foot rather than ride in the one-horse rig Lyons had waiting in the street. He dismissed the driver and they walked together along Nelson Street, just skirting the southern end of the settled part of town, and then turned down Union Avenue to the track. The sun was just barely up, and the morning held within its mists the very first hints of the season to come—a fragile mid-August chill that would warm and disappear within the hour. As they walked, nearly touching elbows but not, Carrie again told Dan of her day at the track with Genevieve. Perhaps not to allow a silence to fall between them, she spoke in greater detail this time, recalling exactly who wore what, how the jockeys were arrayed, even the melodies that drifted out from the bandstand. Lyons listened attentively, or gave the appearance of doing so. His mind was to some degree also engaged upon the busy day ahead and his place in it, but he did enjoy listening to Carrie as she enthusiastically retraced the events of five days earlier. At strategic intervals, he asked a question or two. He had intuited at a remarkably young age that conversation, attentive conversation in any form, was the quickest route into a woman's heart.

"Do any others in your New York circle spend time up here?" he asked, as Carrie at last wound down her account. "I'd think they'd be attracted to scenes at the track—to draw and paint them, I mean—and then the society and the gambling would seem to be right up their alley, too, at least for some."

"I don't think it's quite been discovered," answered Carrie. "I noticed a painter I've met, Winslow Homer, sketching the opening-day crowd, but most of the others have long-established summer haunts that they cling to. I expect this place will grow in favor, however."

Next followed a silence that Carrie thought might become excruciating until Dan gently took her hand and led her through a gate and onto the Saratoga oval.

"Here is where the great fortunes are made and lost," he said with a note of false drama in his voice. "But actually, for some, that's true. They say a man lost $10,000 betting on Arcola on Wednesday."

201

Carrie gasped but said nothing in reply. Dan had not let her hand go, even after they'd passed through the gate. They walked along the outer edge of the track in a clockwise direction. Along the way, men were making adjustments to wooden structures on the turf—jumps for the horses to clear as they raced.

"Today there'll be three hurdle races to cap off the meet," Dan said as they passed a work crew just finishing up. "It's called a steeplechase in the program."

"Steeplechase! What a lovely poetical name that is," Carrie said with a smile.

"It's Irish, of course," said Dan with a note of pride. "They used to race horses from village to village, across streams, over hedges and stone walls and the like, and the only way to find your way to the next town was to look for, and then chase down, the local church steeple."

He turned to Carrie for a reaction but she continued to look straight ahead.

"Anyway, it's certainly a popular type of racing with the patrons," he said. "And because it's also the last day and a Saturday—and a sunny Saturday at that—there will be throngs out here today."

Now the morning was silent save the song of birds on the wing and the distant echo of a hammer as the last crew finished up work on the last hurdle. Carrie looked across the track and its infield to the great empty grandstands, still now mostly in shadow. All is in readiness, she thought with a nervous inward smile—truly all.

As they drew closer to the stables at the southeast corner of the grounds, they could begin to hear the sound of the horses—the nickering and whinnying, an impatient hoof banging twice against a stall door—and catch their aroma.

"Shall we enter? Dan asked, and Carrie nodded. She felt she was in familiar territory here.

As they got to the entrance, however, a portly man in somewhat disarrayed evening dress came hurrying out. He attempted to brush by them with a downward look and a hurried tip of the hat, but Carrie couldn't let him go.

"Mr. Bush!" she exclaimed, and of course Dan knew him as well. "Mr. Bush," she repeated, "you are a most devoted owner to sleep with your horses!"

Bush drew to a halt, surveyed Carrie and Dan, and smiled sheepishly at having been exposed.

"I have found that this is the hour above all others to be here, before the day begins in earnest," he explained, a little out of breath. "I love to look the creatures over and confide in them—although I admit I ain't normally dressed like this to do so. I was unusually late leaving the gambling house, where Dan here often attends to me. I was on a prodigious winning streak but couldn't leave well enough alone."

There was a pause as all considered the many heartless ways of ill fortune. Then Carrie spoke.

"I know from my own experience that a horse will understand one's troubles at least as well as any human," she said, as Bush nodded his assent vigorously.

"The emperor Caligula himself, for all his faults, knew this when he appointed his horse consul," he said.

"That is all very well," interjected Dan, "but we better let Mr. Bush go, else he will be caught out by Mrs. Bush, and a promising day will turn to cinders."

"You have hit the nail directly on the head there, my boy," Bush said, and with a slight bow and another tip of his hat he was off. They watched him for a moment.

"Did he not think it at all unusual to see the two of us here at this hour?" Dan asked after a moment.

"I don't think it ever occurred to him," said Carrie with a small laugh. "He's quite caught up in his own tangled doings."

They walked into the stable and slowly down its center aisle. The racehorses on each side turned to watch curiously as they passed by. Otherwise, the building was empty. At the far end, sunlight, becoming full and powerful, flooded through a big half-door and two open windows. They could hear the low conversation of several grooms a couple of stables down and the crackling of their small outdoor fire. They came to a partial enclosure where straw had been piled into a corner. Dan turned Carrie toward it. For once, she would be steered. The tumbling mound of straw showed golden in the bright light. She could already feel its radiating warmth. Dan put his arms around her waist and looked into her eyes.

"Will you love me, Carrie?" he asked. She noticed a slight tremor in his voice. He was nervous, too. Still a boy, really.

"Are we safe here?" she said.

He nodded and kissed her. She let herself open up to him as they kissed, and then he took her down onto the sunlit straw. She felt his cheek upon hers and his warm breath as he fought with his buttons and lifted her skirts. Conversation, she saw, was at an end. Looking high up into the rafters she noticed where swallows had built a nest and where one now flew quickly out and then back in again. She marveled at the sunstruck motes swirling in the ray of light that bathed them. Then she closed her eyes, for now Dan had discovered her. It was just what she wanted. He was inside her quickly and easily, and she was shocked at the intimacy of it. Because he was right on top of her, urgent and alive, too close to see, she imagined him at his most desirable—as he stood in the summer twilight on Matilda Street, full of ambition and bravado and dark good looks. Her mind began to turn to his dashing rescue in Five Points, but now he was suddenly no longer with her. She opened her eyes to see him already rising away from her, pulling up his trousers and looking rather furtively out one of the windows.

Carrie had not known what to expect, and now her thoughts raced. She enjoyed being physically attached to someone she was so attracted to and to feel his vital form against hers. But she wished they could have lingered, even for just a minute or two, in their makeshift lair. She wanted to understand Dan a little more, to gain even temporary entry into what she supposed was his vast hidden being. Now that sort of interlude clearly was not going to be possible. As Dan made ready to leave the stable for the outside world again, Carrie gathered that she had merely been seduced.

"I hope you don't mind, but I've got to report to work," Dan said, not unkindly. "It's going to be a hellishly busy day."

Carrie shifted her garments and rose to her feet. Dan stepped forward and brushed bits of straw off her backside. Was it peevish for Carrie to think his movements seemed more brisk and businesslike than affectionate?

"Will you walk with me back into town?" he asked.

"I will walk part way, but I have to get back to Mrs. Jensen's," Carrie replied. She had daydreamed only yesterday that they might be laughing or even singing together at this juncture rather than making such mundane arrangements.

They walked back through the stable and across the track to Union Avenue. Dan nattered on about the day's expected crowds, his many duties and the special card games devised for the post-race hours. But Carrie wasn't so eager to move on to the rest of the day—not on this Saturday morning. Her thoughts remained fixed on what had just transpired in Mr. Bush's stable. Aside from a few hesitant, ill-informed conversations with Elsie, Carrie's ideas about sexuality and the act itself had come largely from paintings and drawings. She had marveled at the nubile Venus of Titian, the dallying gods of Cranach the Elder, two or three forbidden French lithographs, and, very recently, the shocking lack of inhibition of Manet and other Parisian artists, which she had only heard about through breathless approximations. She had secretly imagined herself taking a half-reckless place in the midst of all of it, as when she'd worn the white dress to the opening at the Studio Building. But now she wondered if all those women so depicted were not actually disappointed as well, and whether their smiles and sleepy, satisfied languors were not just something self-servingly painted on by men.

They arrived at the corner of Union and Nelson, where Dan would continue on into town while Carrie turned off toward Spring Street.

"Carrie, this is a morning I will never forget," said Dan with a smile that an impartial observer would have no trouble calling satisfied. "I hope we can soon have that dinner at the hotel."

He leaned in for a kiss, but Carrie, still a bit lost in thought, offered only her cheek, a denial that Dan barely seemed to notice as he hurried away. Carrie walked on alone. She could say that on the one hand she admired Dan for his colorful, remarkable journey out of the horrors of Five Points, and enjoyed his looks and his attention toward her, but it seemed that somewhere along the way she had mistaken base urgency for something purer and more soulful. In one sense, she had found what she was looking for on that pile of straw; now, perhaps, she would have to find love, if that's what it was, elsewhere. But as matter-of-fact as she tried to be about it all, and as much as she now lifted her face toward the sun, she could not prevent herself from crying. And then, because of those damnable tears in her eyes, she nearly walked right past an animated cluster of women walking down Nelson Street in the opposite direction, armed with large anti-horseracing, anti-animal cruelty placards and headed toward the track. But in the event, she didn't walk past them, she bumped right into one, and in so doing, and in the brief conversation that followed, got her first glimpse at the bright road that would at last lead her away from her uncertain, meandering, altogether aimless ways.

# Chapter 12

The two women stood at the rail as the last light of day illumined the foaming waters of Long Island Sound and Calf Island in the middle distance to the north. They were aboard the Boston, Newport & New York Steamship Co.'s luxurious *Newport*, making its way east up the length of the Sound like a doge's floating palace. The women had already mingled agreeably with others in the main saloon, dined nicely on broiled snapper while luxuriating in the dining room's shining sea of cut glass and silver, and listened briefly to the strains of the estimable Farnsworth's Band. Now the older woman, who was in the vicinity of 50, was ready to retire to her stateroom, but first there were several more things she wished to go over with Carrie before their pre-dawn arrival and the rush of events that would follow.

"You will find the two cities as unalike as soap and cinnamon," Emily Warren Appleton was saying in her kind, patient, sensible voice—a voice that reminded Carrie very much of Alathea Kingsbury. "First of all, Boston is a fifth the size of New York, and as a rule much more civilized and comfortable. Its pace is slower and more measured, and its streets certainly less frantic. Second, the city's society is nearly perfectly well-ordered—cordial and predictable, with very little temperament for disruption. And third, it is in certain ways a wonderfully enlightened place, very well suited to the task we have set before us. Almost ideally suited."

Her voice trailed off, lost in the sound of the steamer's steady churning. Carrie welcomed Mrs. Appleton's tutorial. She had never been to Boston, had never given it much thought at all, save as the place that had produced Elsie Bentley. Now she was going to live there, leaving New York on what many might have considered little more than a whim.

Carrie had met her companion only two weeks earlier. She'd been busy at work in the New York office of the Society for the Prevention of Cruelty to Animals, going over strategies for fall with a small group of like-minded women as well as the organization's charismatic founder, Henry Bergh. Mrs. Appleton had been there as well, visiting from Boston on her own business; the two had met, discovered a shared passion, and now abruptly were on their way to Massachusetts to begin work with Bergh's first masculine disciple.

"What can you tell me of Mr. Angell?" Carrie asked of her boss-to-be. "I know his name but little else."

"He is very well cut out for the task," said Mrs. Appleton. "He brings a fervor quite similar to Mr. Bergh's. Two years ago, he witnessed the end of a race from Worcester to Brighton, a distance of more than 30 miles, two men up on each horse, running at a full gallop. I think both horses died from the effort, or perhaps one survived. In any event, Mr. Angell, once his anger subsided, began looking at ways to take up the animal cause, not just for horses but all animals."

"Which led him to you, I take it?"

"Not directly. I followed my own course to Mr. Bergh in New York. I visited him, asking for his help in Boston. He said I should use my connections to collect names on a petition that I could present to the governor, but that in order to be taken seriously I would need to find a man to lead the charge. A few weeks after that, I happened to read a passionate letter on the subject in the *Daily Advertiser* and knew that its author, George Thorndike Angell, had been ordained to me. He may as well have been wearing wings and a halo. I met with him, offered him solid financial backing and organizational support, and he agreed to open the Massachusetts branch of Bergh's Society, which he has just done."

Emily Appleton caught herself up. Moonlight now fell upon the *Newport*'s deck and a lone guiding light could clearly be seen on the Connecticut shore.

"You will never again hear me say so many words at once," she said, "but I am convinced of our cause, and grateful for your support."

"I don't know what took me so long," said Carrie. "I've always felt it in my heart. I've seen the terrible lives of horses in Manhattan and witnessed jockeys whip and spur their mounts, but I was too willing to accept it as being just in the normal course of things. If I hadn't stumbled into that group of Berghians on the sidewalk in Saratoga Springs two summers ago, I might still be doing little or nothing."

"Well, we are on the right road now," said Mrs. Appleton. "But I must ask you whether you have any remaining misgivings as we truly get under way."

Carrie paused just a moment.

"I am convinced of the cause and my work in Boston, but a little worried socially," she said. "I am an old unmarried woman now, quite nearly a spinster, and growing somewhat set and stubborn in my ways."

Mrs. Appleton laughed at Carrie's exaggeration.

"Don't be silly, dear," she said. "Boston may not be the hub of all things, as Mr. Holmes has declared, but certainly it is the place in America where a single, mature woman can feel most at home. You have nothing to fear on that count."

With that, the older woman said goodnight and stepped from the deck into her stateroom. Carrie lingered, watching the moon's reflection dance along the swell. Her room was far less commodious than Mrs. Appleton's. It was on another deck of the *Newport*, and she was in no hurry to get there. In fact, she was happy not to be hurrying anywhere. In all the packing and arranging and at long last leaving New York, she hadn't had much time for reflection on where she had been and where she was now going. Mrs. Appleton's recruitment of her to Boston had been so thorough and swift that she was barely able to make a proper goodbye to Henry Bergh, the man who had taken her in and found her a place to live and a job—indeed a whole series of jobs—to do.

After being told about Bergh and his mission by the band of protesters on Nelson Street in Saratoga, Carrie had made feverish haste to his headquarters in Manhattan. Her farewells in the Spa were brief and appropriate—with love and appreciation to Julie Beers and her daughters, good cheer to Mrs. Jensen and Genevieve, and nothing much to Dan Lyons save a note that was neither tear-stained nor sorrowful, nor angry, nor lovelorn. Her leaving was made easier by her certainty that although she might be remembered, no one would miss her too much, nor for too long.

As for Bergh, he made a strange first impression seated across from Carrie in what was no more than a small, rather disorganized room on Broadway at the corner of 4<sup>th</sup> Street. He was tall and gaunt, with straight black hair framing a long face, a drooping moustache, and piercing eyes. He made a formidable presence. His passion for reform flew off him like steam.

"Where are you from, girl?" were his first words to her. "Tell me, who is your family?" She was immediately aware that there may have been a touch of madness in his voice, but still she was drawn in. She soon established to Bergh's satisfaction that in her person and her pocketbook she would make a useful soldier in his new army. He became less imperious and more conversational.

"I spent many years in Europe," he said, after Carrie had asked about the origin of his campaign. "I can say with some pride that Prince Albert once bowed to me." He savored the memory briefly, like a minty little lozenge on his tongue. "But I was just drifting along, writing poetry and so forth. It wasn't until I was in St. Petersburg some years later that I was struck—it truly came upon me like a thunder clap—by the criminally overworked and harshly beaten horses on every street, down every lane and laboring in every field. Without a word of the language, I became a pest, but more than a pest—a meddler and a scourge. I didn't care. If I saw a mujik lashing his steed, I would order him to stop—and he would stop! Then I went searching out cruelties, which is what I've continued to do since returning home."

"I don't see how you can build much on that, sir," said Carrie respectfully. "You are starting from nothing and the challenge is so great."

"Oh, Carrie, it is such an age for reform—feminine rights, temperance, the Red Cross, penal improvement—we fit in perfectly! In addition, there's the model of London's Royal Society for the Prevention of Cruelty to Animals. I have in mind something similar for New York, and then for the nation. There are so many who feel as we do but fail to act, who only need a ready path to do so. I will need the help of people like you to bring them into the fold."

So Carrie, her zeal so recently uncorked and her indignation at a peak, signed right up. She became Bergh's third staff member. It meant staying in New York, which she hadn't planned on doing, but Bergh used his connections to find her a snug room in the eaves of The Church of the Ascension's rectory on West 10th Street, where the congregation held an especially kind and generous attitude toward the afflicted, even if they had four legs. Her new home was just down the block from the artists' Studio Building and all its many fond associations, but Carrie suddenly felt miles away from all that. She had a fire in her heart and a great deal to do, vastly more urgent and important, she thought, than putting paint to canvas.

The *Newport* was now steaming into the broader Sound, and the shores, both north and south, had become invisible in the dark. Carrie withdrew from the rail and found her way back to her room. She felt ready for sleep, but it did not come. She was excited to be on the move once again. As she lay on her bed, trying to find a narcotic rhythm in the vessel's inner workings, Bergh's face loomed before her once again.

She pictured him as he'd stood before a full house at Clinton Hall on a frigid evening in February, 1866. For months, Carrie and the others had helped him prepare for his lecture, which he had rather dryly entitled "Statistics Relating to the Cruelties Practiced Upon Animals." But the content was anything but dry, and he held the crowd, hand-picked though it may have been, in his grip. In striking detail he recounted many of the horrors commonly and endlessly inflicted upon what he called "the mute servants of mankind." It had been to a great degree left up to Carrie and her colleagues to collect many of the accounts Bergh used that night. She'd gone out to observe and interview in the streets of the city, but she'd also supplied the anecdotes of the jockeys' whips and spurs driving the racehorses at Saratoga, the tragic and thoughtless shipment of animals to Frederick Olmsted at Central Park, and the madness of caged live beasts burned to death during the Barnum's Museum fire, as well as other horrors she'd witnessed first hand. Carrie worked through the days with a fervor, and collapsed exhausted onto her bed each night. In so doing, she and the others built an undeniable case for Bergh to put forth, and when the time came he did so with the greatest burning conviction.

Within two months of his address, a charter incorporating the American Society for the Prevention of Cruelty to Animals had been signed by the governor of New York. Soon after that, an anti-cruelty law was passed granting the ASPCA the power to enforce it. Bergh now had his own army, with uniforms, badges and truncheons, and he would prove to be a most eager, aggressive and efficient general. Because of her sex, Carrie could not be a member of this enforcing militia, nor could she be an ASPCA officer or a member of its board, but she could get her ideas heard and sometimes acted upon, although often without credit. It was she, for example, who first brought up the need for an ambulance for animals one morning shortly after the organization was formed. She was also the one who recognized the desirability of providing drinking fountains for animals in public places and helped see the idea become reality. For her work, Bergh told her he thought of her as an "honorary" vice president, saying it was the best he could do, at least for the time being.

Finally, this long wave of tumbling recollections put Carrie to sleep. She would face her new circumstances when daylight came.

When Emily Appleton told her that an unattached woman would have nothing to fear from Boston society, Carrie did not quite believe her. A single female, 27 years old, would always approach a new social situation with trepidation, and sometimes even with the feeling that her every utterance was being watched and weighed against her age, appearance and availability. But in truth, Mrs. Appleton had not gone far enough. Within a matter of weeks, Carrie not only felt fully embraced by Boston society, she began to wonder if single women, in league with a small number of married female counterparts, didn't actually run the city.

This feeling took root in Carrie as she attended a series of receptions, luncheons and teas arranged by Emily Appleton to raise awareness, and funds, for George Angell's new organization from her friends and extended social circle. Carrie's job was to circulate through the ranks, speak persuasively about animal rights when called upon, recruit new members to the cause, and follow up with politely worded requests for money. Those in attendance were mostly female, accomplished and outspoken, and independent in ways she had never witnessed in Waterbury or even New York. Many had proudly slipped the mooring that traditionally attached them to men. Among the most prominent were woman's rights activists Julia Ward Howe and Caroline Severance, education reformer Elizabeth Peabody, performer and patron of the arts Charlotte Cushman, and the young writer Sarah Jewett, whose first story had just been published in *The Atlantic Monthly* and who had more or less been adopted by the older women.

But these were only the better-known few at the top. In each salon, Carrie felt the strength and self-assuredness of virtually all the women in attendance. There was a fierce camaraderie and a joy she hadn't experienced before, and more specifically a rallying around a cause that all felt was right and just. As for the men, they popped up here and there, balancing a teacup on a knee and nodding agreeably. For the most part they seemed to be college professors and physicians, with an occasional gentleman farmer (John Quincy Adams II) or philosopher (Ralph Waldo Emerson) tossed in for good measure. There were men in business as well, but, because it wasn't deemed polite by the ladies, they almost never spoke of it—a consideration that certainly never stopped the men in New York, or especially in Waterbury, where they billowed as endlessly as the smokestacks they owned.

Carrie was rather deep into these thoughts—and not strictly attending to her duties—when she became aware that the person before her, a rough-hewn, mannish yet handsome woman of about 40, was speaking about mountain climbing, and even more specifically about traipsing through New Hampshire's Presidential Range. The two of them were standing in the glorious front parlor of the Agassiz house on Quincy Street in Cambridge. The woman, Carrie now realized, had stopped speaking and was now looking at her expectantly.

"Excuse me," Carrie said, "but I don't think I quite caught your name."

"It is Augusta Warren," the woman said forthrightly.

"Are you something to Emily Appleton?"

"She is Emily Warren Appleton, as I'm sure you know, and, yes, I am her cousin."

Carrie nodded and smiled in what she feared was a slightly dotty manner.

"You are fond of rucksacking and scrambling and the mountains and so forth?" she managed to ask.

"As if I have been saying anything else for these past five minutes!" Augusta exclaimed with mock effrontery. Then she laughed warmly. "I see I will have to go back and begin again, as with a climb that sets off up the wrong trail."

"I wasn't attending and I apologize," Carrie said. "I am still taking in my new surroundings. But I'm very interested in the North Country. I've been wanting to go for ages!"

"These 'surroundings,' as you call them, as civilized as they are, crowd me out from time to time, as they do others. Some go to the ocean—your Mrs. Appleton has a place in Nahant—but I prefer the mountains, and I have found others who do as well."

"Is it to New Hampshire that you travel?"

"New Hampshire, Maine, Vermont, New York—although the East has been thoroughly discovered and trampled upon. But there is nothing like the Rockies. I have been once to Colorado, and am always daydreaming ways by which I may return."

They each paused to take a sip of tea.

"I hope you don't think it too bold of me to ask to go along with you on your next trip north," Carrie said. "I don't have experience, but I am fit and I don't believe I would hold you back."

"No, I daresay you wouldn't, not at your age," said Augusta, taking the opportunity to size Carrie up and down. "I'm certain we will go next month when the colors are at their peak—a small group, likely all female, roughing it in a cabin. We don't do great feats of climbing anymore, but it will be strenuous. Are you game?"

"Without a doubt," said Carrie.

With such a pleasant prospect leading the way forward, the late summer and fall in Boston progressed peaceably. Carrie had planned to live only temporarily with the Appletons in their house on Beacon Street, but the place was quite large, so she stayed on and on until her presence seemed normal to all, including the servants, who for a while were a bit flustered regarding her status. William Appleton was a scion of his family's international trading business, but chronic ill health limited the amount of work he could do. Indeed, both he and his wife were so quiet and self-effacing that Carrie thought she must have seemed a hellion by comparison. But she also knew that her work for George Angell and the MSPCA kept her well out of trouble. To her surprise, her belief in the cause was such that she actually looked forward to venturing out and asking people for money face-to-face, especially if she knew they had money to give. No one who had ever been out in the world at all could deny the validity of the animal-rights argument—there were examples everywhere, even in genteel Boston. By the end of one of her soliciting visits, as the last ladyfinger lay languishing on its serving dish, it was only up to Carrie to ask for an amount. By then, she had typically sized up the parlor, the house at large, the number of servants, the presence of pets, the rigging of the woman's outfit (for it was always a woman), and her general temperature regarding the cause.

"'A voice for the voiceless' is how Mr. Angell puts it," she usually said in bringing a visit to a close. "I think we all feel the rightness of that."

"Oh, yes," the hostess would say, for by now she had heard story after story of animal mistreatment, and had likely contributed one or two of her own.

"And now you have an opportunity to be one of Boston's leaders in fighting these grave injustices, of being in the forefront among your peers. It will only take $300."

"Well, my husband—"

"Surely you have views and can make decisions on your own, Mrs. _____? Your husband, as others do, will respect that you have given this matter intelligent thought and arrived at a prudent, wholly affordable amount."

This approach would not work everywhere, but in Boston, where no woman of a certain class wished to be seen as subservient, it seemed to do remarkably well. Of course, for the really big fish in the thousand-dollar class, George Angell himself would come in to take tea, but it was largely through the efforts of Carrie and her few colleagues that membership in the MSPCA quickly grew to more than 1,200, and the battle against animal abuse took its recognized place among the many other local causes.

As September wore on, Carrie more and more looked forward to her planned foray into the White Mountains. She had arranged with Augusta Warren to head north with her on the last day of the month, taking the train from Boston to Concord, and then a coach further north to Conway in New Hampshire, where a private wagon would take them up to the tiny mountain outpost of Jackson. There they would lodge one night at the Jackson Falls House before buying provisions and being guided on horseback to their cabin on Wildcat Ridge.

Augusta had earlier explained that they would at some point be joined by a couple of painters, Susie Barstow and Edith Cook, who were avid hikers and climbers and devoted companions, who had already scaled all the principal peaks of the Catskills, Adirondacks and White Mountains, as well as notable mountains in the Alps, Tyrol and Black Forest. She said they would be coming to hike on Wildcat Mountain and sketch Mount Washington and Carter Dome from various perspectives, but that for a night and day she and Carrie would be on their own.

"I am watching how you build and tend a fire," Carrie said, as she and Augusta settled in for their first night. "It's one of those skills, like carving a roast or mixing a punch, that falls almost entirely to men but is useful for anyone to know, regardless of sex."

"As with cooking, or the punch for that matter, the ingredients count for almost everything," responded Augusta as she crouched by the stone hearth. "If you've got good, dry hardwood and kindling, you can pile them in almost any way and they will ignite, although I prefer a crosswise approach. And some balled up newspaper is good for starters. I prefer the *Evening Transcript*, but it appears that this old copy of the *Manchester Local Union* burns perfectly well."

They watched the flames climb high, then settle back again. The interior of the cabin took on a warm, flickering aspect. To Carrie's secret relief, it wasn't the tiny, dank, spidery hovel her imagination had conjured up during their long haul north. Instead, it was more nearly a simple house, made of logs, yes, but with several large windows, a wide porch, a single living room dominated by a massive stone hearth used for both heat and cooking, and two lofts for sleeping, each accessible by its own ladder. There was an outhouse twenty or so paces up into the woods, a nearby stream for bathing, and all manner of kerosene lamps and lanterns for illumination, when needed.

But now she was content to sit in the near darkness, curled up into one corner of a slightly mildewed horsehair sofa while Augusta sat Indian-style on the floor, occasionally stirring the logs with a poker. They had spent so much time conversing on the train, stagecoach and wagon, and again as they set up the cabin to their liking and dined on pork chops and fresh corn, that they were now quite content to stare into the fire without a word. Each had told much to the other, more than enough to establish an agreeable closeness. In recounting her life in Waterbury and New York, and even Saratoga Springs, Carrie had tried to make herself seem interesting without revealing every detail. Augusta had said less, never straying far from the theme of being an outsider in what she felt to be an inbred Boston society. She longed constantly for big open spaces—something that was probably again on her mind as she broke the silence.

"You can see why your painterly types would enjoy coming up here from their crowded cities to do their sketching and think big thoughts," she said. "But I wonder what will be next for them, now that their cows and meadows and sunsets behind distant peaks have been played out, and even tiny Jackson has hotels and a hattery and railroad tracks being furiously laid in from Conway."

"They do move something like a herd," Carrie admitted.

"Or a flock," said Augusta. "Now with the first real chill in the night air they are surely flying back to Boston or New York, or wherever it is they winter."

They both laughed softly at the image. The artists' paint-smeared smocks, jewel-colored lounge jackets and tasseled smoking caps did not seem so far removed from avian plumage.

"I think they will continue to seek places further afield as the public begins to tire of the usual scenes," Augusta continued. "There are many painters in the West now, and along the Pacific, and others are setting up quite profitably in Florida."

"Don't leave out the lady sculptors in Rome," said Carrie, referring to the notorious band of female artists and camp followers, many from Boston, who had set the Eternal City aflame with their theatricality and open affection for each other.

"They are a somewhat different case," said Augusta, shoving a straying log back into formation. *Très outrées.* Unlike the rest of us, they could only find their desired stage and audience on the streets of an accommodating foreign capital. But some of their work is quite good."

"When you say 'unlike the rest of us,' I'm not sure who you mean," said Carrie.

"Why, the dreaded wearers of masculine clothing," Augusta answered with a smile. "The mannish spinsters, or the couples—and I'm sure you've met some of them—who are devotedly committed to so-called Boston marriages. Us." She looked plainly at Carrie. "Or at least me."

Some species of nocturnal creature cried out from deep within the surrounding woods, startling them both. As far as Carrie knew, it could have been a raccoon, or an owl, or even the wildcat that had given the mountain its name. She wondered if what they heard had been a cry of pain or triumph. She would have liked to change the conversation to cover these questions, but she felt the need to make an answer to the line Augusta had left hanging. She curled more tightly into the corner of the sofa.

"I am not certain where I fall in the nature of such things," she said, giving voice to thoughts she had often considered privately. "I am comfortable in the company of men but not in their arms. I enjoy a woman's attention and affection, but only up to a certain point. I do not think it's in me to want to *belong* to anyone—man or woman—nor to have anyone belong to me. I feel it very intensely. In truth, I have never been happier than during these last few months in Boston—working every day, enjoying the company I've found, living with your dear cousins, learning the ways of a new city—with none of these other complications. It seems to suit me perfectly."

After a long moment during which she seemed to be considering a great many things, Augusta reached up and took Carrie's hand. There was no aggression in the gesture.

"Well, tomorrow we will tramp and climb and picnic by a waterfall and gaze out at the snowy crest of Mount Washington," she said. "We will enjoy each other's company, and then the others will join us and we will turn into another sort of gathering."

"A party," said Carrie.

"Yes, a party—or our own little flock of birds," said Augusta. "And I hope you don't take it the wrong way if I suggest we sleep tonight in the same bed"—she glanced at her—"for warmth, simply, and protection against the great unknown that surrounds us. And the bed is extra large."

No arrangement could have seemed more suitable and natural to Carrie, nor to any other two people in the same circumstances, she thought.

The next day was precisely as Augusta had described it, intensified by deep blue skies and a gradually warming sun. After porridge and tea, the two women dressed for the scrambling and hiking that lay ahead. Only ten years earlier they would have been consigned to ankle-length woolen skirts, petticoats, stockings and heels; but now, thanks largely to the lead of no less than Queen Victoria and her well-chronicled outings in Scotland, they could attire themselves more comfortably in shorter skirts, chemises and boots. With rucksacks on their backs, they stepped away from the cabin and onto a path that took them directly along the ridge and up to one of Wildcat Mountain's five peaks. Below and among them, the beeches, maples, white birches and sumac were already approaching their brightest coloration, steadied by the deep abiding greens of spruce and balsam fir. As they progressed up and up along the mountain trail, they were startled as a shockingly enormous moose crashed across their path and into the underbrush. They navigated by a hermit's hut (Augusta claimed to see the tip of his hat peeking out from behind a nearby boulder) and at last stood at a precipitous lookout. Below them, raptors soared effortlessly up and down on unseen currents of air. Carrie reveled in a feeling of dominion over all things. With hands on hips, she looked out to the southeast through perfect clarity at what seemed like nothing less than the rim of the world. There was a cleansing, redemptive power in the view, as if she'd at last managed to climb up and away from all the error and evil she felt had marked so much of her life. And yet, one or two more short steps toward the edge would bring about her unequivocal self-destruction. She marveled at how close those two extremes—conquest and death—could become at such a height. Then she stepped back toward her friend.

"It is just as I had hoped," she said. "The air is of such a superior tonic quality; it gets down to one's very toes!"

"Then you must imagine the Colorado Rockies," said Augusta. "Two or three times our present height, the air thin but so very pure, and the vistas endlessly grand and theatrical. You really must find a way of getting there."

"Well, I shall grant you your Rockies and all that unseen splendor, but this will have to do for today, and I will do my best to enjoy it," said Carrie.

"Yes, of course you are right, Carrie," said Augusta, feeling the mild rebuke. "I have perhaps been here too many times now to see it with the eyes of a first-timer and appreciate it as fully as I should."

"I think it is you and not I who must find a way of getting to Colorado," said Carrie. "I don't think you will be happy until you do."

Carrie was returning to a subject the two had spoken of as they had lain together in their camp bed the night before. They had gone over their lives in Boston and the many people they knew in common there. Augusta said that despite the city's liberal attitudes, she felt closed in by its many conventions.

"They know you too well; they are the ones who know who you really are, or believe they do," Carrie had said, thinking of Waterbury and what it was like to go back there. "Your schoolmates, your teachers and neighbors—"

"They remember you at your worst," interrupted Augusta.

"I think maybe at your best, too," said Carrie, "but I was never able to show my best side—far from it—and then I went away, while you have stayed. I'm not sure I could ever go back."

"I feel like I am warmly accepted in Boston, but it's a calculating embrace," said Augusta. "It says, 'I love you' and then in a smaller voice, 'even though you are who you are.' It's such a superior attitude. There is no doubt that it will be better for me to be in a place where everyone has just recently come from somewhere else and where the rules have not yet been hammered into place."

Carrie wondered if the Bostonians she had met were really so calculating. Augusta offered one example that she claimed proved her point. Carrie replied that one swallow did not make a spring. After a few more similar exchanges, there followed a long silence into which they'd both drifted off to sleep. Later, in the middle of the night, Carrie awoke to find that Augusta's hand had crept onto her hip, whether by accident or with purpose, but instead of getting up and climbing into the other bed in the loft and pulling the blankets up around her, she let the hand stay. The woods had by then grown completely, even oppressively, silent. Not so much as an insect could be heard, nor a breeze riffling through the branches. Never in her experience had Carrie experienced such a sepulchral lack of sound, and as it pressed in against her she suddenly felt a terrible sense of uneasiness, even doom. Was this a foreshadowing of the "void" she'd heard so often mentioned in sermons and literature? Was it therefore an intimation of what comes inevitably to all creatures? She perversely imagined herself underground in an enclosed space among worms and burrowing beetles, and then she could not shake the thought. The silence weighed even more heavily and she began to feel a surge of panic. It was only when she cleared her throat loudly that she managed to break the mood—Augusta stirred with a harmonium wheeze, a few familiar sounds of the night came back to the outdoors, and Carrie once again found sleep.

All seemed so different now as the two women sat in the bright sunshine at the top of Wildcat Mountain and unpacked their sturdy lunch of boiled eggs, hard local cheese, bread and apples. Sitting there on a piece of rock ledge, she felt she understood Augusta's wild desire to leave the turmoil of civilization behind and set off on new adventures, seeking ever-higher peaks and purer forms of being—but she did not, at least for the moment, share it. Maybe her blood had settled. She had friends, a comfortable position, a place to live and work that mattered to her. She was from Boston now, proudly so; and a Bostonian may roam, but she always returns home.

When they got back to the cabin that afternoon they found that the painters, Susie Barstow and Edith Cook, had arrived and already taken a quick hike through the immediate environs. Carrie could see immediately that they made a redoubtable pair. In their similar clothing, language, humor, and the comfortable, fond glances between them as they spoke, they had shaped themselves into a rock-solid alliance. One could notice that Barstow might more often take the lead, but Cook stayed with her every step of the way, and sometimes forged ahead, whether deciding which route to take in the morning, cutting up carrots for a cabin stew, or venturing out at night for a pail of water. Both were delightfully gossipy and entertaining as well, with their many stories of derring-do abroad or memorable encounters with others in the painting crowd, all told with the practiced patter of an old married couple.

The week flew by. The weather held, the days were warm and the nights chilly, and the colors in the mountains seemed to grow more vibrant by the hour. Barstow and Cook could tramp 20 miles in a day, so they usually went their own way while Carrie and Augusta stayed closer to home. Carrie collected wildflowers and plants and pressed them into an album. She sat stock still by the mossy edge of a pond one morning until the moose—she was certain it was the same one they'd seen—approached shyly on the opposite shore and took a long drink. She attempted to make a late-season highbush blueberry pie, with disastrous prospects until Edith taught her how to reconfigure it into a passable cobbler. For Carrie, it was a week that would at length turn into a sweet, unassailable memory—an extended bubble of time she would carry with her always. There were no unpleasant returns of the vision that had haunted her first night in the cabin, nothing like it at all; in fact she was often lulled pleasantly to sleep by the voices of the other three women talking and laughing softly in front of the fire.

More trips up into the mountains followed in the years ahead—in every season and with variations in the cast of characters (although never a man)—and the physicality of them helped give Carrie a sense of completeness in her life. Her work for the MSPCA continued to be fulfilling, and she began to involve herself to a lesser degree as a volunteer in another of Emily Appleton's projects, a kindergarten for the blind, where she surprised herself with her feelings of tenderness and protectiveness for the children. Her circle in Boston continued to expand, especially with her membership in the New England Women's Club, where social do-gooders, artists, outdoorswomen and what amounted to all the bright lights of Boston gathered to listen to the likes of Emerson and Bronson Alcott, and discuss women's suffrage and other issues of the day. As to her older connections, she'd let them go almost entirely, perhaps feeling unhappy or uncertain about the person she had been then. She ran into Earl Covington once at an art opening where they spoke most cordially of the days in New York and his current situation, which included growing acclaim in his career and a happy young family at home—Elsie preferring to stay there at present rather than consort with creative types, which she felt she'd done enough of. Carrie also kept sporadic correspondence with Aaron Polk, whose humorous, news-filled dispatches kept her abreast of the New York scene; her mother, who wrote short letters full of wild dashes and half-completed thoughts; and Henry Bergh, whom she knew would never stay out of touch for long from any source of a potential windfall for his cause. As for her personal needs and desires, she buried them. She took the greatest pleasure in her friendships and in whatever warmth others might bestow upon her. On rare occasions when she felt especially lonely, she wondered if she could ever possess the faith that allowed others so much comfort in God and church. But in general she held firm. Her thirtieth birthday came and went with little fanfare (the Appletons produced a cake). She seemed set, as a Harvard man might put it, for the long term. And then one blustery March day in 1874, a telegram arrived at the Appletons' front door, addressed to Miss Caroline J. Welton.

"Mother ill," it read. "Calling for you."

And although her father's terse message didn't go so far as to demand she come home, Carrie knew that she had to. There was no way for her to know that she would never return.

# Part 3

## Chapter 13

My storytelling sense informs me that I should resume my account of Carrie Welton's life by relating the story of her father's sudden and calamitous death. In late March of 1874, Carrie had come back to Rose Hill at Joseph Welton's urging after his wife Jane had fallen into what seemed to be a terminally feverish state. I first learned she had returned one unseasonably cold, gray, flurrying noontime when I drove my rig home for lunch, as was my custom, and found Alathea waiting for me at the kitchen door, her eyes bright with news. I had seen the look many times before, of course, usually in relation to a ripe piece of family or neighborhood gossip. Although I liked to pretend otherwise, I was a bit of a gossip myself, so I was apt to receive these reports with my full attention and an occasional raised eyebrow.

"Well, what is it now?" I asked as I hung my overcoat and hat on hooks by the kitchen table, where I liked to take an unceremonious midday sandwich and glass of buttermilk.

"It's Carrie," said Alathea. "She has returned to be with Jane during her illness. According to Abel, she may be here from some period of time."

"I don't see why that should concern us," I said nonchalantly.

Alathea gave me a look.

"Don't be pompous, Frederick," she said. "It doesn't suit you."

And yet I felt entitled to my reaction. For all our closeness to Carrie, and fondness for her, she had not been a very energetic correspondent during her long absence from Waterbury. It had been 15 years since she rode off that spring morning for New York City, and although she'd written devotedly during the first year or two, she'd left far too many lengthy gaps in the time since. Yes, she'd dropped over to see us for a cup of tea during her infrequent and very brief trips home, and, yes, Alathea had gone to see her once or twice in New York—but in all, that was not nearly enough by my standards. Admittedly, I was, and still am, the most ardent, industrious, perhaps even compulsive correspondent, responding immediately and often at length to whatever letter lay upon my desk. Be that as it may, we knew not much more than that Carrie had been in New York and for the past several years in Boston, something general of her friends and surroundings, and that in recent years she'd begun working on behalf of animals. We'd also received letters postmarked from places like Cape Cod, Saratoga Springs and the White Mountains as she traveled. Her tone was unfailingly cordial and proper, but the letters lacked human details. Although she would rarely admit fault in Carrie, I knew this sparsity was especially frustrating to Alathea, who above all things wanted to know how Carrie was and who she now was, not whether she was sunbathing by the Nauset Light.

"If she is to be here for several days, she will want relief from the sickroom," said Alathea, returning me to my kitchen table. "Do you think she'd enjoy a Kingsbury family dinner?"

My peevish mood, really not very profound in the first place, quickly vanished at the prospect of showing off our brood to Carrie. Our girls were now more like young women, or nearly so—Mary was 17, Alice 15 and Edith 14, while Fred was 10. The girls could be quite ladylike upon occasion, but not when they were all together at home, where they tended to become coltish and quite boldly opinionated. Carrie knew virtually nothing about them, at least not in person, and it would be a delight to see her contending with the Waterbury stories and banter that would surely bounce back and forth across our table.

Carrie came to dine with us on what turned out to be the fateful day, March 26. In recognition of spring's recent arrival, by its calendar date at least, we set before her a vernal roast of lamb, but not before subjecting her to a program of music and verse. Mary performed a piece by Haydn at the piano, Alice and Edith for the two-hundredth time raced through two Mozart duets for violin and flute, and Fred, in long pants at last, delivered a thumping if high-pitched recitation of the opening 30 lines of "The Song of Hiawatha." Alathea looked on with what I thought to be the relief of a lion tamer who no longer requires a chair and pistol. As for myself, I strove for a look of equanimity while at the same time stealing sidelong glances at our guest, who I had not had the chance to observe so closely in many years.

Not surprisingly, she had turned into a handsome woman, not so very far removed in looks and manner from the girl I remembered. At the appointed hour she'd appeared at our front door, hatless and with a cape thrown over her shoulders for the short walk across the street. The children were polite and rather shy to begin with as they gathered round to say their hellos, but then while still in the vestibule Carrie produced several small paper bags from within her larger purse.

"I recall that sweet things go down very well in the Kingsbury household," she said, "so here are some treats for you to share—one bag of licorice, one molasses, one honey and one spearmint. How you manage them I leave up to you."

As the children, even Mary, scrambled for the sweets, with importuning looks to their mother, I couldn't help observing that Carrie may not have changed much in her appearance, but her voice had gotten older. Gone were the lively trills, the girlish ups and downs, the wild promise of earlier days, replaced by a flatter, more worldly intonation— maturity, one might call it, but I missed the fire of youth.

Carrie greeted Abel by name and allowed him to take her cloak as we all stepped into the parlor. The children were allowed one sweet each, which they sucked with gravid pleasure.

"Please forgive me for bringing up the delicate subject," said Alathea, "but how is your dear mother doing?"

"We had unexpected good news yesterday," she replied. "Mother's fever broke around noon. She sat up in bed and demanded a plate of toasted cheese. She was ready to get out of bed this morning, but the doctor told her one more day."

"Oh, that's such good news," said Alathea. "Had they ever decided upon a cause?"

"No one was quite sure, and now I suppose they will never know. She suffered no pain, nor did she exhibit any outward signs other than a slight flush in the cheeks and neck."

"Well, let us toast her full recovery," I said, producing a tray with glasses and a decanter of Madeira. "I imagine you have obligations in Boston that cannot be neglected for much longer."

We each took a glass and raised it to the health and long life of Jane Welton, our faces turned toward the parlor window that looked out upon Rose Hill.

"I am eager to get back," said Carrie. "I have become a perfectionist in my old age and I don't think anyone but I can do my job."

"I feel the same way, although I don't mind letting them try," I said with a laugh. "What is the exact nature of your work these days?"

With that uninspired opening, our talk for the remaining half-hour before dinner skipped lightly across several topics, including Carrie's recruitment and fundraising activities at the MSPCA, the ins and outs of Brahmin Boston, the glories of tramping and hill climbing, her delight in reuniting with her stallion Knight, who had been returned to Waterbury some months earlier for an undisclosed medical problem, and of course something of the changes in the neighborhood —more physicians arriving every day from Yale—and the city at large, where a bicentennial celebration was currently being contemplated. At dinner, Carrie dug into her minted lamb, spring potatoes and peas with a pleasing vigor. The conversation was dominated by the children, especially our daughters' colorful descriptions of life at their school— Collegiate Institute, on Grove Street—with Carrie wishing such a school had existed in Waterbury when she was their age. After Carrie had left for home, following a dessert of expert plum duff (our new cook's odd specialty), I congratulated Alathea for having put together such a delightful evening. We hadn't gotten any deeper into Carrie's situation and state of mind, I allowed, but we had reaffirmed our friendship with her, and perhaps even extended it into the next generation of Kingsburys.

It was only an hour or so later—I was seated in my study, looking rather absently through some Scovill's papers—when Abel appeared at the doorway. I was expecting him to say his usual goodnight and wonder if there was anything else he could do, but instead he had a look of genuine alarm on his face.

"A boy has just come over from Rose Hill," he said. "There apparently has been an accident in the stable."

Here Abel hesitated, then resumed.

"He said his master is dead from a horse's kick."

I stood automatically, astonished at the suddenness, brevity and finality of the report.

"Joseph Welton is dead?"

"Yes, sir, according to the boy."

"Just in this past ninety minutes since his daughter left us?"

"It seems so, sir."

I wasn't sure where my duty lay. Should I cross the street as a responsible neighbor and confirm the news, or should I rush upstairs to tell Alla?

"Fetch my overcoat, please," I said. No reason to wake her for what might turn out to be no more than a rumor.

The night was cool and overcast as I walked down our drive toward Prospect Street. I could see immediately that there was indeed unusual activity across the way. It was getting late—around 10:30 p.m.—yet many of Rose Hill's rooms were blazing with light and there was a secondary glow emanating from the vicinity of the stable down below. I entered Welton's drive with the disconcerting thought that it was his drive no more. I could make out the outline of a heavy closed wagon, dark and grim against all the illumination; Root & Son had wasted no time in getting its conveyance onto the scene for removal of the body to its new embalming cellar. Police Chief Laird and a detective named Egan were standing by the house's rear entrance. We exchanged the briefest of pleasantries, and then:

"He is gone?" I asked.

Both men nodded.

"A tremendous blow to the side of the head, just above the left ear," said Laird. "He must have dropped instantly. Doctor Castle has already pronounced it."

"His wife and daughter?"

"They are inside. Mrs. Welton is apparently not well and was in a terrible state when we arrived. She and Miss Welton were within one of the stalls, kneeling beside the body. The horse in question was fractious in the extreme. Miss Welton spent some time calming the animal—it was her stallion— and then they went up to the house when Root's wagon arrived."

"What will become of him now?" I asked.

"They will convey the corpse—forgive me for using the word—to their funeral parlor and embalm him and make him presentable, then return him in their hearse for a viewing at some point."

"Will you investigate?"

"We have preliminary statements from both Mrs. and Miss Welton, the stableman and the senior staff," said Egan. "All they know is that he went down to the stable for an unknown reason, perhaps to smoke a cigar. Miss Welton wondered why he hadn't returned and went down and found him there beyond reviving. There seems to be agreement among all parties, so we were just coming to the conclusion that further investigation was unwarranted at this time."

Men from Root's crew now carried the covered body on a stretcher up the hill to their wagon. I removed my hat, as did the officers, as Joseph Welton's lifeless form passed by. I imagined his eternally glowering visage beneath the blanket, then wondered if his final expression might instead be one of flat-out shock and surprise. People were kicked by horses all the time, of course, but to die from a kick, although not unheard of, was unlucky in the extreme. We watched as they loaded the wagon and then moved off down the hill.

"Would it be permissible at all for me to leave a message at the back door?" I asked Laird.

"Of course, sir," he answered. "You are known to be a friend of the family."

It was Steeves, ancient and bedraggled, who answered my knock. Her gray hair was down in a wavy, recently unbraided state and she was only partially dressed into her livery. She seemed to be in some form of shock. I began to speak but she seized me by both forearms and pulled me inside.

"I don't want to disturb anyone," I said. "I just want to offer any assistance—"

"Oh, no, sir, she will want to see you," Steeves interrupted. "I will go find her."

I stood only for a moment before Carrie came in from another room. She was attired the way she had been at dinner, and she'd been crying. Her face was streaked and blotchy. She stopped short upon seeing me and then rushed forward into an embrace, and her tears came again.

"It's a terrible thing," I said softly. "Unimaginable."

She said nothing, only resting her head against my chest. We were silent for a long moment. It was not at all a time to speak in any way, even veiled, of her troubled past and her father's role in it.

"Please tell your mother that Alathea and I, and our servants for that matter, are at her disposal, and yours, too," I managed to say. "We will speak again soon, but for this long night you must know that you have our love and support."

"Thank you," she said, and then I turned away, left the house and went back across the street to awaken my wife.

The news that one of Waterbury's most prominent citizens had been kicked to death by his daughter's horse spread through town in no time. By morning it was on everyone's lips, and by noon it had already been pretty much chewed over and talked out. Welton had been a distant, unapproachable figure except to those directly under his employ, so there were no great feelings of admiration or loss, nor too much to say, save to comment on the strange, unfortunate and certainly unwished-for nature of his passing. He did, however, represent what was still the most prominent private dwelling in the city, so an almost inborn respect for wealth and grandeur brought many sightseers to the street and sidewalk in front of Rose Hill (and our house as well), where they dawdled and gaped and dropped litter into the gutters. And Jane Welton soon gave them something to gape at—for no matter how bedridden she might just have been, if mourning was to be the thing called for, no one would top her for it. Within two days she transformed her house with an effort that reminded many of us of the Belgian pavilion she'd put up in her side yard so many years earlier. All of Rose Hill's windows were draped in black, while equally black wreaths appeared upon every door. The staff and even the yardsmen were clad in black from head to foot, and the Welton coach horses were fitted out with black leather harnesses and black drapes and plumes. It was our own Mary who suggested Jane might paint the entire exterior of the house black and then back again to its original rosy hue once an appropriate period had passed—a bet I wouldn't have taken.

We were of course obliged to go over to the house during calling hours, before the body was removed and transported to Riverside Cemetery for burial.

"He wasn't all bad, was he?" I said to Alathea as we made our last adjustments before going across the street. "It took a long while, but I had some quite decent talks with him about local affairs and his former life traveling through the South. He seemed to ease up a bit once his daughter was gone."

"You mean once he banished his only child from his life," said Alathea with indignation. "I honestly don't see how you can just put that to the side."

"Of course I don't," I said. "I just hate to send someone into the ground without any feelings of loss at all, or even the slightest sense that he has earned his eternal reward."

Alathea uttered something under her breath and I asked her to repeat it. She turned to me with something approaching fury in her eyes.

"God forgive me, Frederick, but in my view that man makes a very good case for Hell. As Carrie sat at our dinner table the other night, I saw once again the girl who used to come to our back door all teary and disarranged, so grievously unhappy, and I also saw the woman so deeply hurt and distrustful of others despite her great, good natured efforts to be otherwise. And you want me to mourn the person most responsible, almost singularly responsible, for it all? Thank you, but I don't think I shall."

"I didn't ask you to mourn for anyone," I said rather helplessly. "And I don't disagree with a single word you've just said about Welton."

I consulted my pocket watch.

"Anyway, you are free not to accompany me to the viewing," I said.

"Of course I am going to the viewing," Alathea said, "Why would I ever not go to the viewing? Sometimes I just don't understand you at all."

As we approached Rose Hill, hand in hand, I thought of how we had outlived two masters of the mansion, Alla's father and now Joseph Welton, and wondered what its fate would be. The place, as I have mentioned, had been magnificently rigged for mourning but there was no line of visitors passing from the front door down to the street, as there might have been for others among the city's leading industrialists. We were let though the big door and brought into the parlor, where family members and friends, mostly from the neighborhood, stood or sat in small groups. The deceased was laid out in an open casket raised up in front of the fireplace. In a single chair beside the casket, and beneath a portrait of her late husband, sat Jane Welton. As custom had it, she wore all black but for the widow's white collar that would distinguish her from the other mourners. From a side room came the drear notes of a portable organ. We approached and expressed our gravest condolences and asked after her own health. She offered a wan smile.

"My own health is nothing," she said softly. "It is only that the suddenness of the incident gave him no chance to be spiritually ready for the next life."

Alathea checked her own thoughts on the matter and, because no one was behind us, she continued the small conversation. I took the opportunity to study Welton in his final repose. The experts at Root's had been unable to soften the natural cruel slash of his mouth, but otherwise he had been made quite presentable. The area of the fatal blow was hidden from my view. I could not help but reflect upon the fact that, as he lay there in his best suit of clothes, the vital spark had left him: his heart no longer pumped, his brain had ceased its calculations. Was he nothing now, I wondered, or was he still something? After his burial, he would exist only in our memories, forever unable to change or make amends—or to hurt. For some, of course, his memory would always hurt, although perhaps less so with time.

These were not thoughts for standing up in front of one so newly widowed, and I was relieved when my wife finally grabbed my cuff and led me away. We went into the dining room, where food and drink had been laid out on the table and sideboard, and where Carrie sat in a sort of secondary mourning position in a corner by a window. A couple of straight-back chairs were set up alongside hers, but she was sitting by herself, a vision in long black, cradling a cup of eggnog in her hands. She stared straight ahead and did not notice us, so we went over to sit with her. After we expressed our sorrow—Alathea quite touchingly, and directed mostly at Carrie's state of mind—Carrie apologized for not being seated in the parlor.

"As you will understand more than most, I just couldn't sit beside him and accept a flow of compliments about his life," she said in a low voice. "My mother didn't argue, but suggested I make myself available elsewhere in the house, which I have done. I find that most people quite spend themselves on my mother and by the time they get into this room they have little energy for more than a brief greeting and a sad shake of the head, and then refreshments."

"Which suits you, I gather," I said.

"It suits me very well," she replied.

After a pause she spoke again.

"I don't know how to feel," she said. "I have outlived him."

Another pause.

"For a long time, I feared I'd never know a life without him in it."

We let her consider her own words. It seemed to us that a great weight had been lifted, however tragically, and that she could now be judged for who she was, not criticized for what she wasn't and could never be, and that she was, at long last, free. That feeling of freedom might take a while to manifest itself, I thought; perhaps not until after the shock had worn off. For now, as we left her, she had resumed staring out into the room in an unseeing way, neither truly grieving nor putting on a show of false high spirits, as so many are known to do at last viewings.

"'Numb,' that's the word I'd use," said Alathea as we walked home. "Jane, on the other hand, was the perfect picture in her widow's weeds. I suspect she is feeling a tremendous sense of loss right now, but that she will recover, probably quite handsomely."

"Carrie is another case?" I asked.

"More complicated, I dare say. The great fact of her life has been taken away. Will she need us and other friends less now, or more? I cannot tell. Will she return to Boston feeling unencumbered and at peace with herself and the world? I don't know. And," she looked up at me sweetly as we crossed onto our property, "I don't think I'd put out anything as frivolous as a rainbow trifle for your visiting hours."

"Well, thank you—but I'd rather you not start planning the menu quite yet," I said as we walked up the front steps and entered our house.

It took us a long time, nearly as long as it took for spring to finally arrive that year, for us to realize that Carrie wasn't going back to Boston. She was of course required to stay in Waterbury for her father's burial, which proceeded without incident, and the initial determination of his assets. Welton had died without leaving a will behind, so it was up to the local probate judge to count up his holdings in property, stocks and cash—around $250,000—and eventually divvy it up between his wife and daughter. In the meantime, and without any other claimants to the fortune, they would have access to the funds for their household needs, as well as to whatever individual resources they possessed.

In the first days and weeks following the flurry of post-mortem events, we were not surprised to see Carrie remain at home. As May approached and the days grew warmer, we (by which I mean Alathea and, increasingly, our daughters) saw her walking together with her mother through Rose Hill's network of paths and gardens. With Jane remaining in her mourning garb and Carrie not, they moved slowly and deliberately, their heads bowed toward each other in nearly constant conversation. As far as we could tell, they made no effort to leave the property, not even for church on Sunday or Carrie's forays on horseback.

"I wonder if they will put Knight down," our Alice asked one evening at the dinner table. It was a thought each of us had no doubt considered but not put before the others.

"If they didn't do it right away, I don't see how they can do it now," I said. "It would seem too cold-blooded. Anyway, can one really blame the horse for an accident like that?"

"I agree," said Mary. "Carrie would never do anything to harm Knight. And, anyway, what was Mr. Welton doing in the stall in the first place?"

"Maybe he did something to startle Knight," suggested Alice.

"Like what?" asked Fred, now quite interested in the turn the conversation was taking.

"It could have been as innocent as a cough," said Mary.

"Or a sudden move from behind," said Alathea.

"Or maybe he stubbed his cigar out on the horse's flank," said Alice, who was more sensitive than the others and seemed able to extract out of thin air her parents' feelings toward Welton. Perhaps she had inferred them from our gestures and intonations, as we had never spoken openly or plainly against the man in front of them. I managed to change the subject to something slightly less morbid, but the conversation did show how avidly we followed the continuing drama across the street.

However, as the weeks turned into months, we saw that the story was not going to play out as we thought it would. Carrie remained ensconced and unavailable. Alathea sent her a kind note, wondering about her situation and asking her, with her mother or not, over for tea. But Carrie's reply said she could not do so, and it left no opening for another try. Although it didn't conform with anything we knew about the Welton women and their feelings about the late patriarch, it seemed that Rose Hill had turned into an island of grief and mourning. Servants and tradesmen were allowed passage on and off the island, but no one else, not even family members, could visit.

The total embargo remained until early summer, when we noticed that someone we had never seen before began to appear with some regularity, strolling with both Jane and Carrie and sitting out with them in the evening on one of the house's porches. The women and girls in our house came up with any number of hasty descriptions of the man, some in direct conflict with others, but it was not until he passed by me one mid-afternoon in an open carriage that I caught him cold. He was a tall, thin man with an imperious expression and a narrow face elongated even further by a drooping moustache and top hat. He was dressed rather sharpish by Waterbury standards, and on the seat beside him was an overnight bag of rich tan leather. I raised my walking stick in a gesture of friendly greeting as he passed by, and for the first time in my life had the experience of being "looked through" by another man. My dislike for him was immediate and intense.

When I got back inside I decided that, snooping or not snooping, we could stand the mystery no longer. I called for Abel, described for him the stranger and commanded him to find out who it was. Abel waited until I was done, paused for one delicious moment and then spoke.

"We have already determined his identity, sir," he said. "In fact, I have gotten it several different ways—from Sanderson the grocer, our own groom Mr. Joines, and most recently from Jerusha Steeves herself, over the backyard fence, so to speak."

For Abel, this amounted to a flamboyant oration, but I would not give him the satisfaction of a reply or even of any change in expression. I drummed my fingers on my desk blotter. At last he spoke again.

"He is Mr. Henry Bergh, the friend of animals from New York," Abel said. "It is generally believed at Rose Hill that he has come seeking donations from Miss Welton and also from her mother."

"He is a particular friend of Caroline Welton, I believe," I said.

"They don't like him over there," Abel replied.

"Why not?"

"They see him as taking advantage during a difficult time."

"But he's there by invitation, certainly."

"Only after his initial contact," said Abel.

I thanked my remarkable manservant and went back to drumming my fingers. Both women would be susceptible to a clever sales pitch, I thought, especially for an admittedly worthy cause so close to Carrie's heart, and at a time of such emotional disruption. It could therefore never be a surprise to me that Bergh and his organization would end up with almost all of Carrie's money, and indeed that the man would end up being the executor of Carrie's estate.

# Chapter 14

.*It* was with a feeling of helplessness that we witnessed Carrie's long retreat into the mysterious surrounds of Rose Hill. What she had once so openly hated and wished to escape now became the place she evidently most wanted to be, perhaps the only place. Her seclusion lasted something like 14 months, during which time she became a truly remote figure to us, occasionally seen strolling alone or with her mother or the ubiquitous Bergh, gathering flowers to take inside, reading on a shady porch, or, in the winter gloom, only as a shadow passing occasionally in a lighted window. It's not that we were spying on her. After our initial intense curiosity we stopped making a point of looking. Even the girls to some degree eventually lowered their eager level of interest. It was clear that Carrie preferred to live without us, however greatly she had once depended upon our council and reliably warm welcome. For me, it was almost as if one of our own daughters had decided to disavow us. Alathea, for her part, was at first devastated and occasionally reduced to tears by the whole thing. It was an enigma to her, but at length even Alathea took on at least an air of detachment. We pretty much stopped speaking of Carrie. But inwardly, quietly, we remained attuned to any shift in the weather across the street.

The first glimmer of a change came when Carrie's beloved Knight grew gravely ill and had to be put to death in the spring of 1875 at the age of 20. We had long since noticed that Carrie had stopped riding, but we supposed it was due to her reluctance to leave her home rather than the horse's failing health. Probably it was both. Knight, the faithful, strong, unquestioning companion who had taken the rebellious young girl racing through the streets of Waterbury all those years ago, and then on her precocious journey down to New York, back and forth across Central Park and through the rest of the great city, and even on jaunts in the famous Common of Boston until he was no longer fit to do so, was gone. For us, he was a neighbor almost as surely as any human was or could be. We heard through channels that he was buried with significant pomp in a grove beneath a spreading walnut tree on another Welton property, with only a couple of cousins, a Porter uncle and his old groom Michael Walsh in attendance with Carrie and Jane. Some thought the pomp quite inappropriate, given the stallion's signal role in Joseph Welton's death. Further, gossip among the gravediggers had it that Carrie had scandalously placed hundreds of dollars worth of blankets around Knight to go into his grave with him, and that she'd taken his shoes and bits to have them plated with gold. By all accounts she had maintained a steady, sensible composure at the graveside but was clearly heartbroken.

The first real thaw in the Weltons' icy distancing came not too long after. It arrived with a wholly unanticipated bang. Several weeks after Knight's burial, an invitation was delivered to our door—asking us to attend a big afternoon party at Rose Hill. Even though Jane Welton had thrown occasional galas, some of them quite grand, in the years before her husband died, this summons seemed to us like a relic from a lost time. The beneficiary would, not surprisingly, be the Society for the Prevention of Cruelty to Animals, and we would be expected at some point to make a donation or even join up. But if you think Alathea was inclined to turn her back on the invitation as those across the street had turned their backs on her, you don't have her figured.

"Do you somehow feel obliged to attend?" I asked her as we read together in our parlor armchairs late in the day on which the invitation had arrived. "I mean as a neighbor and old friend."

"If anything, I should feel obliged *not* to attend," she replied. "But I am very curious to see how things are over there after all these months. Or maybe *concerned* is a better word. But I am not angry or bitter. After a great deal of thought, I find that I don't hold them fully accountable for their actions. Anyone is entitled to pull back if they want. They haven't hurt anyone. Distress can sometimes turn into prolonged sadness."

"I think they've hurt you," I said.

"It's just the way they are now. I have to accept it. It's like being a teacher who molds and influences a child, who makes a child better, and then never sees her again."

"They live right across the street," I said after a pause. "You have seen her and she's seen you."

"I'm aware of that, Frederick," she said a bit impatiently. "And all right, we know that it's become a terrific mystery— why she stayed, what's driven them into such otherworldly seclusion, why they're suddenly throwing a big party instead of gradually tiptoeing back into society."

"I can answer the last part, I think," I said.

Alathea looked up from her book.

"Carrie and her mother are not just steady friends with this man Bergh, but are now, to an unhealthy degree, under his sway," I began. "I have no doubt of it. I believe he's staked a claim on their fortune in the long term but that he senses another opportunity right now, following Knight's death, to raise money from the Weltons' network of well-to-do Waterbury friends. He sees it as a moment that must be capitalized on without delay."

"And they will do as he wishes?" Alathea asked.

"Could you want better proof?" I replied. "He is known to be absolutely single-minded in his crusade, and most persuasive in the rightness of his cause. He appealed to their love of animals and especially to the memory of Carrie's stallion, and now here we all are, lining up to contribute to his coffers."

I finished my argument with what I'm sure was a look of satisfaction.

"You should have remained a lawyer," Alathea said with a sniff, returning to her reading. But it was a very long time before she turned a page.


I have several times in this account mentioned Waterbury's status as a growing city, and in fact its emergence as one of the leading cities in America, but I think it is necessary for me to do so once again. Since I last spoke of it, the city's resident well-to-do population had quadrupled or possibly quintupled in number. Picking up a trend that had faltered during the post-war period, they were once again building grand houses and putting down stakes, not only on our old hill but all around the town's central valley. Some of the stubborn old families remained, and some, like me, were still in titular charge of the larger industrial operations. But the factories, so many of them producing brass goods, had expanded to such a degree that now a whole new, thoroughly modernized level of managerial men was needed, as well as key salesmen, and inventive and technical types, and even foremen on the various shop floors. All were well paid for their efforts. In addition, many of the most ambitious, having learned all the ways of their trade, had gone off to start their own businesses, either in service to the larger companies or as independents. By 1875, there were dozens if not scores of manufacturing shops crisscrossing the valley, producing everything from brass tubing to coin blanks to cameras, and of course pouring out rivers of buttons, pins, eyelets and other fasteners. It did not take a genius to make a very good living, or even a fortune.

I mention this because as I made my way through the crowd at the Weltons' fundraising party I found myself nodding genially but blankly to many faces I didn't recognize, or had only seen in passing at church or in a club room. They were by and large a handsome, fit-looking cohort of young men and women, a new generation, demonstrably more robust in bearing than my own drooping contemporaries had become, speaking with vigor, confident in what could be an intimidating social milieu, and in all making me feel just a wee bit invisible.

I naturally gravitated to my own circle, where the conversation would be easy and familiar, but I kept an eye peeled for our hostesses as well. Jane had taken on the role of standing by Bergh's side and introducing him to her guests as they came through. She had pulled out one of her best red wigs for the occasion, affixed an unnecessary tiara to it, and pinched and brushed a good deal of color into her cheeks. My old friend Kellogg and I were giving her credit for the effort when he interrupted me with a sudden hand on my forearm.

"Don't look now," he said, "but behind you, Fred, isn't that Carrie on the landing?"

I did of course immediately turn and look up, and saw her familiar form framed by the commodious bay and its windows. She stood a step or two back from the rail, almost entirely in shadow, surveying the crowd below as if deciding when, or whether, she should make her appearance.

"I'd say that she has a look of great uncertainty," Kellogg continued.

"I don't blame her," I said. "She probably knows fewer people here than we do, although she told us once that she had organized and attended many such gatherings in Boston."

"Maybe not as expertly put together as this one," Kellogg said.

"Oh, I don't know about that. I think some of them know how to put on a do up there," I said, and then, more nearly to myself, as Kellogg was pulled away by another friend, "I find it impossible to credit, but I haven't spoken with her in over a year."

Carrie wore a worried, distracted expression, I thought, but her gaze was quite determined, and fixed upon another quarter of the room below. Her intense focus allowed me some freedom in observing of her, although I remained secretive enough so others would not follow my lead. She was wearing something very light green and summerlike, perhaps brocade and silk. I couldn't see any more detail of her clothing than that. I thought I noticed her shift her weight warily as she stood there, as if the slightest alarm would send her scurrying. But the question in my mind was: Who among the invited guests was she looking at so intently?

I carefully followed her line into the by now animated crowd and was surprised to find my gaze at last resting upon my own wife, deep in conversation with two neighborhood friends, and unaware that she was being watched from above. Then I followed the line back up to Carrie and, to my further shock, straight into her eyes, as she was now looking directly at me.

Alas, my pen is not up to the task of describing the look upon her face. It spoke volumes, yet said nothing. It was somehow intimate yet strangely remote. As I say, impossible. In any event, my modesty made me turn away, and then when I dared to look back a moment later she was gone. All my buried feelings for her came rushing to the surface. It was painfully clear to me that she had once again fallen into a sort of nervous despair, a wish not to engage with the world, even the one gathered in her own living room. I wanted to chase up the stairs after her and take her across the street to our own kitchen table as we might have done in the old days, but of course I couldn't possibly. In any event, her mother was just then calling the gathering to order.

As Jane Welton delivered her brief encomium on Bergh's behalf ("an American saint," "the conscience of us all"), and then as the great man began his account of deeply wronged cattle and languishing dray horses, I tried to catch Alathea's eye. I could tell that as Bergh spoke she was searching the faces for Carrie's. At last, as Bergh continued on, I wound my way through the gathering to Alathea's side and suggested with a quick nod of the head that we go into an adjoining room.

"Did you see Carrie?" I whispered as we tucked ourselves head-to-head a corner away from the doorway. "She was up on the landing. You really had to know she was there in order to see her."

Alathea shook her head.

"I think she was looking directly at you," I continued, "as if she was waiting for you to look up."

"I had an eye out for her but got caught up with the Whitechurch sisters," she said.

"Well, she was very furtive," I said. "She retreated when she knew I'd seen her. I don't think she'll be coming down."

We had both seen this behavior enough in Carrie over the years, and it didn't require further description.

"I thought this was to be her coming out. And I thought the death of her father and then a long period of recovery might have created an improvement, a steadying in her moods," Alathea said after a moment. "How wrong we can be about people!"

"Maybe the opposite occurred after he died," I offered. "Maybe it threw things between them into an unresolved state—a sort of permanent discomfort."

"More than discomfort, surely."

"Confusion? Unease? Imbalance?"

"At least that, or all of them, I would judge. Anyway, enough to keep her from going back to Boston."

"Even though we believed her when she told us she'd found her lasting happiness there."

"It's a tragedy, Frederick, nothing less, virtually on our own doorstep, and we are helpless to do anything about it."

Bergh was now dragging a bit. Scattered throat clearings and coughs should have told him he ought to draw things to a close, but he had likely picked out the true believers in the room and was at this point in essence speaking only to them.

"I was thinking wildly of how we could rescue her again," I said finally, "but she's not asking to be rescued this time. Her exile is self-imposed."

Both of us had thought this party might serve to bring us back into contact with Carrie. We'd supposed that afterward we'd be able to resume the friendly, open, understanding relationship we'd once known. It was hard for us to realize we weren't going to get our way in this matter. We were used to winning people over, and secretly prided ourselves in our ability to do so. But in Carrie's case it was perhaps time at last to throw in the cards and admit defeat.

Without a further word between us, we rejoined the others in the parlor as Bergh wound into his concluding plea. Despite myself, I looked back up to the landing, but Carrie was not there and did not reappear. Bergh's final line—something about giving a voice to the voiceless—drew handsome applause, and then the room came back to chattering life. Bergh was quickly surrounded by those five or six he'd attached himself to during his speech and who now felt the pull of his special attention. A big cake in the shape of a horseshoe was wheeled out, cut into slices and served with coffee. We caught up with several more of our friends, left a meaningful check on the mail table in the entrance hall, and made our way out the front door, where we found Jane Welton just entering after seeing off a carriage conveying some long-distance visitors. She gave us a smile that was just a bit weary at the edges. In the light of day, her red wig and its slightly askew tiara suddenly looked preposterous.

"Henry is doing great things," she said of Bergh.

"And you are so good to open your house to his cause," said Alathea. "Carrie, too, although I don't believe we saw her."

Jane gave us a confiding tilt of the head.

"I haven't spoken with her, but I gather that at the last minute she didn't feel up to joining us," she said. "We—the two of us—have had the most difficult time since her father's terrible death. We've gotten all bottled up in our woes, especially Carrie. We agreed at long last, with Henry's urging, that a party might help, but obviously it hasn't."

"What is the nature of her discomfort?" I asked, groping for even the slightest clue to Carrie's prolonged unhappiness. "Is there anything a doctor might do to help—or that we as old friends can do?"

Jane smiled again but said nothing. She now clearly wished to move past us and back into the house.

"Have you given any thought to getting away?" Alathea asked quickly. "Sometimes it can answer perfectly."

"We soon will be going to Watch Hill, of course, and then —you are right, Alathea—we have made plans for California in the fall. It will be in the nature of an excursion or a grand tour, taking in many of the western highlights. There's nothing like a long trip, staying on the move, for holding the demons at bay. And now if you will excuse me, I must rejoin my guests."

And with one last smile and a quick step or two inside, Jane made sure the teasing "demons" would exist in name only for us and for the outside world in general, unknown and unexamined for a very long time to come.


Looking back at the way Carrie's behavior deteriorated over the ensuing years, I'm not sure there was anything that I, or my wife, or anyone, could have done to help her. Following her trip to California with her mother and their return east in July 1876 for the Centennial celebration in Philadelphia, she once again removed herself to Rose Hill and her former shuttered ways—only once in a while venturing out, never for church, and exhibiting an icy aloofness if she did happen to pass by. She may as well have thrown herself off a building or in front of a train, so determined was she to bury herself—to shrug off whatever progress she'd made in recent years and give in to her own increasingly eccentric ways and not interact with others, especially those who could love and help her. It's not quite true that I never saw or spoke with her, however—our proximity worked against that. Until she departed one last time for the western states in 1883, our paths crossed several times, encounters that were always accidental, as the day I chanced to see her leaving to have her portrait painted, unfailingly strained and, on her part, hurriedly concluded. Never did we resume the cordial tone we once enjoyed. Indeed, it seemed to me that Carrie's former kind feelings toward me had been replaced by nothing less than open unease and an urge to flee, as if she were afraid where a real conversation with me might lead. Alathea felt much the same way as I did.

"It breaks my heart—it still has that power—but she seems to be in permanent retreat," Alla said to me one autumn day after she'd looked up from supervising the planting of tulip beds in our front yard to see Carrie across the way, standing by the same chestnut tree where we'd encountered her so many years before. She told me she had waved across to Carrie and that Carrie had called out in a tremulous voice something about having seen our Freddie walking by and how he was turning into a fine young man. It had been a shockingly extroverted thing for Carrie to do at that point, to call out that way, but by the time her words were out she'd already turned and nearly run back into the house, leaving Alla no chance of further conversation. "If there is no interaction with others, even if it's just the daily inanities we all suffer, it will be impossible for her to improve," she said. And she was right.

During these years, we remained well occupied with our family matters and our hectic checkerboard of business, civic and social interests, but Alathea and I, and to a lesser extent our children, did continue to keep a casual, neighborly eye on Rose Hill. We were no longer high up in the rigging shouting down news of every visitor and movement, as we once had done, but we did possess a reasonable human curiosity—most of which was satisfied by the reporting of our servants. This is not to say we relished every new piece of intelligence. To the contrary, as time went by we frankly came to dread them.

First came the stories of Carrie's increasing obsession with the welfare of animals. We'd long known that this was a special interest of hers, of course, but it wasn't until one rainy day in the spring of 1878 that I realized how far it had gone. I'd been walking along West Main Street on my way from my bank to my club for a late afternoon social hour when a sudden downpour sent me scurrying into a convenient doorway. I saw the jacket and cap of another figure, a diminutive, white-haired one, huddled there as I entered, and when he looked up I recognized the pale face of Michael Walsh, the Welton's longtime groom, and a particularly devoted servant to Carrie. We had spoken many, many times over the years, always out of doors, usually touching in some way upon horseflesh, and we'd established something that approached friendship. Now we exchanged a few words about the weather and the winter just past, and then we calculated how long it had been since last we'd seen each other to speak to, as it had been many months.

"And what have I been missing during all that time?" I asked with a meaningful look. He knew my intention. Either he would engage or not, unburden himself even—it would be entirely up to him.

"Oh, just a small thing or two," he said with just enough of a conspiratorial smile to invite a certain line of questioning.

"To begin with, how does your mistress do?" I asked. "I understand she has a new horse."

"She has. A strong, unfriendly gelding called Bunch."

"Nothing like Knight, I gather."

"Could never be another like him, sir."

"And does she go out on Bunch?"

"She does. Out the back way, but not often, not over twice a week."

A silence grew as we watched the rain pound the pavement and run down the gutter.

"She's gone daft on animals," Walsh said finally and a little softly, as if reluctantly saying something that had to be said.

"How do you mean, Michael?"

"Well, you know how partial I am to my horses and the other creatures you'd find in a barnyard or out in a domesticated field—"

"Of course I do."

"And I would never see them come to harm."

"Never."

"Carrie goes beyond that, and then she goes beyond beyond."

I waited for an example.

"If she's out, which, as I say, isn't often, but *if* she's out on horseback or in a carriage, she can't pass by neither horse nor ox nor milk cow without studying all the angles for possible ill treatment. And woe to the owners if she finds anything. She'll get down and walk right up to them and demand they shift the load or ease the yoke or repair the shoe. Right or wrong, she won't take no for an answer. She will soon be known for it—already is—and not in a kindly way."

"Well, I think I know where that comes from," I said. "Have you met the man Henry Bergh?"

"Yes, he's visited the stable on a number of occasions," Walsh said. "He looks out for animals in the most minute way, yet he treats human creatures, at least those in service, with contempt."

"That's his way of operating," I said. "He confronts what he sees as injustices and he teaches others to do the same. Carrie is one of his most devoted followers."

"It's more than just that," said Walsh. "She has us box-trapping stray cats and finding new homes for them among relations and people we know, and she must have ten of her own, each with a name. She gets a special supply of milk delivered just for them, and she talks to them like I'm talking to you right now."

I shook my head.

"And then there are the pigeons," he continued. "They are filthy birds, as you surely know, sir, and no one wants them living in and around a barn or a house, but we are ordered to lavish them with kindness and even feed them, and then clean up after them—common pigeons, these are! She believes they suffer from general ill treatment and it is up to us not to do them any disrespect. We wonder if rats and miller moths might not be next."

The rain had by now let up and people were walking up and down the sidewalk once again, but Walsh was not quite ready to join them. He was confirming so much that Alathea and I had only heard in piecemeal fashion, and I wondered, if he saw me as an old and reliable acquaintance, whether he might be willing to go even further.

"And what of Carrie's general state of mind?" I asked.

"You know I am fond of Carrie above all things," Walsh said, looking hard at me, "but I am worried. We all are, what with her spells."

"Spells?"

"As when she's speaking to the cats or the birds, sir, and nods or laughs as if they're answering her back. I think of her when she was a girl and I first came to Rose Hill and grew to know her and learn how fragile she was and how miserable and lost in her own world she could get. There were times when I couldn't see how she would survive it. Then, as you know well, as you and Mrs. Kingsbury both know, she broke away, and we were all so proud of her and happy for her, following the story along year by year as well as we could. And then to top it all, himself gets taken out of the picture as clean and abrupt as anybody could wish for. Nothing but blue skies for our Carrie, it seemed." He spread his arms out in a helpless way. "But now she's right back where she was, worse even, older, without prospects, and with far too much time to ponder it all."

"Isn't there a doctor who could—"

But here Walsh at last cut me off; perhaps he had said too much.

"Not my department, sir. Not for me to say," he said. He looked out at the town green and sighed. "Now I really must be getting back up the hill."

At around that same time, Alathea returned from a visit with one of her neighborhood friends, Sarah Nash, with an anecdote that left us both in a terribly disturbed state. As a result of the ASPCA benefit at Rose Hill, Mrs. Nash had emerged as a most vocal and generous advocate on behalf of animals, enough so that she'd earned a return for tea with Carrie and her mother. As they sat down, and before the tea was poured, Carrie drew attention to a living three-inch-long bug, or beetle, that she wore on her shoulder, tethered there by a tiny chain attached to a collar. She said the bug was Brazilian and that Tiffany had procured it for her and had gilded its backmost legs. His name, she said, was Paris. She further explained that, when alone, he lived in a plush-lined house especially constructed for him with bedroom, bathroom and so forth. "I asked her what he lived on," said Mrs. Nash, "and she said she didn't have to feed him since he seemed happy living on just air. And then she said, 'Let me show you how he knows his voice and my name.' She put him down on the floor and he crept into his box and then she called, 'Paris, little Paris, come out!' And when she pulled hard enough on his chain he came out, as he was compelled to do. And then she said she would soon have his collar set with diamonds."

"I asked Sarah what Jane Welton's reaction had been," Alathea told me. "And she said she only sat by with a bemused look on her face, which I guess is the best anyone could manage under those circumstances."

If that, even that, turned out to be the worst of it—if she merely moved back and forth across the line that separates humans and the rest of our Creator's menagerie—maybe Carrie could have lived on fairly peaceably as a spinsterish, rather harmless eccentric. But that wasn't the worst of it, not even close. At some point late in that year of 1878, Carrie broke with her mother. To my mind, their companionship since Joseph Welton's death, their trips together, their long hours spent within the confines of Rose Hill, had never been very convincing. Jane Welton was a social creature by nature, one who judged her own worth by how well she could exist within a large, active circle of friends and relations. Her daughter, as we know, was not built the same way. Where Jane was outgoing, Carrie was tentative; where Jane possessed an extraordinary social compass, Carrie was often lost and without direction. Which is why the idea of the two of them simply living their days out together in splendid isolation did not make sense to me. I thought then and I think now that Jane was suppressing her proclivities in order to help Carrie along. It couldn't last forever.

No one seemed to know what caused the estrangement when it came, at least not for certain. Through my Waterbury contacts, I had heard (from what source I can never reveal) that it might have been a matter of Carrie's will. Under the original document, drawn up not long after her inheritance from her father was made final, she gave all to Jane, and Jane, in turn, had done the same for her, with each serving as executor for the other. But in late 1878, likely following a major disagreement, Carrie rewrote her will, cutting out her mother and turning over the great bulk of her estate instead to the American Society for the Prevention of Cruelty to Animals, with Bergh now entering the picture as a co-executor. Whether he had a direct hand in this, no one could know, but the love and trust between mother and daughter was shattered, and it would never be restored. In the months that followed, Carrie continued to spiral out into her own version of reality, while Jane, thoroughly devastated, could only wring her hands and watch. As for the rest of us in Waterbury, we were well aware of the drama, and many of its particulars, but as bystanders only. There was no other role for us to play.

At length, Carrie began to distrust her mother extremely. In the presence of two or three cousins with whom she'd remained close, she claimed, without evidence and only a few specific details, that Jane planned to have her committed to an asylum and was acting in concert with local authorities to do so. She cited a visit her mother had arranged from Alfred North, a local physician of the highest reputation, who asked questions about her health and well-being, but also about her behavior. Nothing came of it (and maybe her suspicions were justified), but at around this time she began referring to Rose Hill as "Echo Hill" for the voices she felt were arrayed against her there. She unfairly began accusing her mother behind her back of immodesty and immorality, and then she started providing herself with her own supply of drinking water after she found a white deposit on a glass that she suspected might be arsenic. And finally one day, in late 1880, she could stand no more and she left Rose Hill forever.

For three years, Carrie roamed restlessly. She took a room for a period in a New York City hotel, then, as if unsure about where else she could go, she came back to Waterbury and for eighteen months stayed with her cousin, Ellen Johnson. She continued to display antisocial behavior, ordering double locks for her door and purchasing a five-cylinder Smith & Wesson revolver. And although she was perfectly capable of acting normally, carrying herself with great propriety and style, and even conversing with wit and intelligence, she could also be deeply suspicious of some of those who spoke with her, be it and old friend or the man delivering ice. She repeatedly found special meaning in words spoken innocently by others. It was a decline that seemed to know no boundaries, but then in May 1882 there was a signal change. I believe that someone in her life, someone who could still reach her, advised her for her own good to leave not only Rose Hill, as she had already done, but Waterbury, too. She first found rooms in New Jersey, close to where two of her uncles, Jane's brothers, lived and practiced law. Somehow she'd managed to remain friendly with them even while estranging herself from their sister. But that was merely an *entr'acte*. As it later became vividly clear to all of us, her attention had by now had truly and finally turned to the West. During the summer of 1883, she made a trip out to Colorado Springs, where an old friend from Boston, Augusta Warren, ran a popular boarding house. While there, she climbed the 14,110-foot Pikes Peak, and the thrill of the achievement, or maybe it was the view from the top or just the marvelous sense of escape, must have stayed with her. She returned to New Jersey, but not for long. Mountains, big ones, whole ranges of them, now loomed in her future. As soon as the weather warmed, she packed what few belongings she required and headed back across the Mississippi, and the Missouri, too, out to the wild country.

# Chapter 15

$\mathcal{I}$t is impossible to know all the twists and turns that Carrie's journey West took in 1884. If she wrote to anyone back in Waterbury, I never learned of it, and she was no longer in any meaningful contact with family members. Her idea was to leave, after all, and she seemed intent on cutting all ties. My recounting here of her last days comes mostly from the Colorado newspapers that picked up Carrie's story at the end and reported it with a high level of energy (and a somewhat lower level of accuracy). Some of their work ended up in the Waterbury papers as well. We must accept the fact that there are many pieces that will always remain missing, and of course most of Carrie's own thoughts during this period will never be known.

She arrived in the West that spring and traveled first by Northern Pacific Railway to Yellowstone Park. Staying at the Old Faithful Hotel and the similar resorts at Mammoth Hot Springs and the Norris Geyser Basin, she spent several weeks hiking, horseback riding, climbing and exploring all the park's natural sensations—the rivers, waterfalls, hot springs and geysers. Having freed herself from the confines of her small apartment in New Jersey and, earlier, her room in

Waterbury—with its double-locked door!—she must have felt the greatest elation at being out in the big world once again.

In June, she traveled south from Yellowstone back to Colorado Springs, where she counted herself among the very first residents at the brand-new Antlers Hotel on Cascade Avenue. The seventy-five room hotel was perfectly suited to all Carrie's needs: it was comfortable, thoroughly up to date (including a music room and Turkish bath), very convenient to the mountains, and it provided her with the daily companionship of her old friend and climbing companion, Augusta Warren, who had moved up from her former boarding house proprietorship to become the new hotel's manager.

I did once hear from Warren, who replied to an inquiry I'd made some years ago regarding Carrie. She wrote me a brief note, explaining how they had met in Boston, tramped through the New England mountains together, and reunited in Colorado upon her invitation. But Carrie didn't spend all her time in the company of Warren. She also fell in with a group of female artists, probably through an earlier connection back East. A painter named Emaline Culver met Carrie in August of that year when they traveled up Gray's Peak together, albeit by carriage to a point four miles from the top, and then by horseback. Along the way, both women discovered a common love for cats, and Carrie expressed a horror regarding how livestock in the Great Plains must suffer during the long winters. She added that she had written Mr. Bergh in New York seeking a solution. Mrs. Culver described her companion as "reticent and dignified" but "driven by a great inner spring." Carrie told her she would next be going by horseback to the Chicago Lakes, up in the terra incognita by Mount Evans, but Mrs. Culver begged off, saying she did not think she could manage such a journey, especially with so much snow still covering the more remote trails.

Carrie seemed to take the snow as a challenge. She wanted to repeat her Pikes Peak climb of the summer before, and she became especially determined when she learned she might be the first of the season to do so. The previous winter had been especially snowy and cold, and even as the weather grew warm down below, the mountain's upper reaches remained nearly impassable. Indeed, when she stated her intention to some acquaintances she'd made in Manitou, they told her it would be a foolish thing to try. Still, she managed to buy the services of two guides and set off from Manitou at midnight. It was by the guides' account a difficult, at times harrowing, ascent, but they reached the summit. And as Carrie stood there, breathing hard in the thin air, perhaps she looked out to the north—undoubtedly she would have done so—and fell under the fatal spell of the Front Range's other great massif: Longs Peak.

Even from my civilized, altogether domesticated perch here in Waterbury, I have been able to learn a few things about Longs Peak. At 14,259 feet, it is one of the most prominent mountains in the entire Rocky Mountain chain. There are several ways for hikers to get to the top. The most common is to go by horseback along the trail, then dismount and proceed by foot along the so-called Keyhole Route. The hike from the trailhead to the summit is 8.4 miles, crossing an extensive boulder field, teetering along narrow ledges and finishing with a steep climb to the flat summit. It is a significantly more difficult climb than the one at Pikes Peak. The best time to attack Longs is from mid-July through early September, before the first snow and ice of the season begin to make the trip treacherous. Even in welcoming weather, most hikers set out before dawn in order to reach the top and return below the tree line before the frequent afternoon storms set in.

It was already mid-September and arguably too late in the season when Carrie took a train north from Colorado Spring to Denver and checked into a room at the Brown Palace Hotel. She spent several days visiting with friends there, then traveled further north to Estes Park, a small resort town located alongside the Big Thompson River and nearly surrounded by towering peaks. Arriving the week of September 14, she took up residence at the Estes Park Hotel and for a few more days went sightseeing on horseback all through the pristine valley. But the lure of the mountaintop was too strong. She told the hotel's manager that on Monday, September 22, she would leave to climb Longs Peak. She showed him her riding crop and said she would have a gold band put around the handle for each peak she climbed. Citing the lateness of the season and the possibility of real danger, the manager tried to dissuade her, but Carrie was adamant.

On Monday afternoon, she checked out of the hotel. She left behind a small package for safekeeping, but took her jewelry. She engaged an Estes Park livery operator to take her to Lamb's Ranch, where for years members of the Lamb family had provided rough cabins for hikers as well as guided climbs to the top of Longs Peak. Carrie made arrangements with Carlyle Lamb, age of 19, to guide her on the ascent the following day. The man from the livery stable departed, stating that one of his drivers would return to the ranch and take Carrie back to Estes Park early on Wednesday morning.

After spending Monday night at the ranch, Carrie shared a hasty breakfast with Lamb and they departed on horseback at 5 a.m. According to a later report in the *Denver Tribune*

*Republican,* "Over a pair of black broadcloth riding pants she wore a black alpaca dress and a heavy black sacque in addition to a black dolman coat trimmed with fur. In addition, she wore a heavy cashmere shawl around her neck and a pair of heavy kid gloves." By any standard of the day, she was dressed for cold and difficult conditions. She also carried a gossamer raincoat, which she would later put on against the weather, and covered her face with a pink silk domino mask as protection from the sun and wind.

The day began sunny and warm and seemingly ideal for riding, but the snows of the preceding winter were still deep along the trail, at times obscuring it completely. The horses' hoofs kept breaking through the thin icy crust. It took them five hours to make the first seven miles, and they had yet to reach the timberline and the most difficult stretch of the climb. The going on horseback was proving so difficult that Carlyle and Carrie decided between them to leave the horses well below the usual tethering place at the boulder field. They were lighter than the horses, they figured, and could stay on top of the crust. Some have blamed that decision, made in sunshine while the two climbers were still fresh and confident, for the loss of Carrie's life.

Still ascending, the two made their way on foot across the field of boulders, where it was sometimes necessary to jump from rock to rock in order to avoid falling into 100-foot crevices. Then the Key Hole beckoned, the jagged opening with its rocky overhang on the northeastern side of the peak through which they had to pass in order to reach the summit.

It was at the Key Hole that the weather reportedly began to turn against them. A cold wind sprang up and dark clouds moved in around and below them, a sign of very bad weather to come. At this point, Lamb, who had led climbing parties on Longs Peak for two years, advised retreat, telling Carrie that even if they did succeed in gaining the summit there would be no view. Many times before, under just such rapidly changing conditions, Lamb had turned around and brought climbers back down before it was too late. But Carrie would have none of it. She hadn't been put off by objections like this at Pikes Peak, and she wouldn't be now. Her response, Carlyle Lamb later told his father, was that "she had never undertaken anything and given it up." They proceeded with the climb.

By the time Carrie and her guide reached the summit it was very cold and quite late—3 or 4 p.m. by the elder Lamb's later reckoning. Carrie was by now weary, and their stay at the top was brief. As Lamb had feared, the dark clouds had intensified, and their roiling and tumbling signified that a storm had likely already set in below. As they left the summit, the clouds briefly parted, but then, as they descended through areas known as the Narrows and the Trough, they found themselves trapped inside a fearsome, blinding snowstorm—the worst, Lamb would later report, that he ever had seen in any part of the mountains. Their progress became painfully slow. Carrie soon began to complain of weariness, and by the time they reached the bottom of the Trough, she displayed all the signs of extreme exhaustion. And here I will say what no one mentions in any of the accounts that have found their way back East: Carrie was no longer 22 or even 27 years old and blessed with all the strength, endurance and brash confidence of youth; she was 42, less sure-footed and far more prone to fatigue. During the next two brutally torturous hours, groping their way in the dark, she and her guide covered no more than two-thirds of a mile, with Lamb alternately leading Carrie and carrying her. Fully dressed in all her gear, she must have weighed about 150 pounds, and Lamb, for all his youth, naturally began to tire as well. They struggled to the Key Hole, but by then Carrie, growing increasingly numb from the cold, had become, as Lamb recalled, "so utterly exhausted and chilled that she could not stand alone." The moment of crisis and decision had arrived. It was now 10 o'clock at night, it was still snowing, and there was a foot of fresh powder already on the ground.

After descending a short distance below the Key Hole, over terrain so rough and steep that it was almost impossible for one person to assist, let alone carry, another, Carlyle Lamb called a halt. Sitting down, he confided to Carrie that he, too, was exhausted and so cold that he could scarcely walk. The only chance that either of them had for survival, he told her, was for him to leave her and go ahead for help. At first, Carrie objected to being left. Finally, she agreed to remain where she was until he could return. Lamb removed his vest and tied it around her feet, arranged her waterproof and shawl as best he could against the cold and wind, and then set off, down into the darkness.

It isn't likely that Carrie lasted long on that ledge. Later examination showed that as her guide made his way back to the horses and from there to his father's ranch, she at some point had risen from where he'd left her and struggled about ten feet to where she fell over a rock, bruising her head and wrist. She was found lying in a snow bank, still wearing her pink silk mask. Beside her was the ivory-handled riding crop upon which she had hoped to record her mountaineering exploits. In her belt was her revolver loaded with two bullets in their chambers. A gold watch was fastened to her dress with a black silk cord, and on her breast she carried a small chamois bag containing three elegant rings, one of them inlaid with a large solitaire diamond.

There is a symmetry to Carrie's story that doesn't escape me. The first time I set eyes upon her, she was a girl riding bravely but also heedlessly through a snowstorm, and that, more or less, is the way she had ended things. About a week after Carrie died, a business associate of mine from the western copper fields sent me this from the *Denver Times*:

> Miss Welton seems to have been unusually romantic, or peculiarly persistent in her desire to behold the glories of the mountain world. Hers was in a woman something of the same spirit which in a man carries one off in search of the North Pole and the open sea of the Arctics; and, as so many of the men who have fallen under this influence have done, she surrendered her life in—shall we call it the satisfaction of her curiosity, the gratification of a whim?—or shall we say it was all an accident, and that it could not have been avoided? Call it what we may, there is something very sad in the thought of a young woman, who had evidently been reared in the lap of luxury, breathing her last in the dark hours of the night on the side of a barren mountain so far above the haunts of life that the wild animals would not even lend their presence to the scene; with no hand except that of the icy blast to soothe her last moments, and no voice to cheer her in the dread ordeal except that of the shrill blast of the mountain wind.

Had her death been due to curiosity or a mere whim, as the writer suggests, or had it sprung from a more decadent urge? Had she been teasing death in those last months, or had she truly been looking for something—some kind of inspiration or spiritual rebirth—in the mountains? Those are

273

not questions that I can answer, and there are no clues, or precious few of them, in the sad little pile of newspaper clippings here on my desk. At least she had found death in what could be termed a manner of her choosing, a condition that eludes most of us. But, as Alathea put it to me, it's impossible for us, who knew her so well and intimately, to read the description of how she was found in the snow, and how she was dressed, and what she carried with her, without forever being heartbroken.

# Chapter 16

Carrie's death, and especially the way she died, caused something of a sensation in her hometown. As the accounts flowed in from Colorado—some of them quite breathless concerning Lamb's behavior during the descent, and whether he had abandoned Carrie on the mountainside—townspeople gathered to discuss them and also to relate their own recollections of Carrie and the Weltons and the goings-on at Rose Hill in general. Needless to say, many of the memories lacked accuracy, and some bordered on pure fantasy, but it did soon become clear that the alchemy of a sudden, tragic, accidental, distant death had converted the former widespread disapproval of Carrie's reckless ways into fondness for her and even a kind of nostalgic admiration.

As her body made its way back by train from the foothills of the Rockies to the chapel at Riverside Cemetery, Jane Welton steamed home from an extended trip to Europe. It was later revealed that she'd been visiting the great museums and sketching the works of the likes of Rubens and Raphael, which she was later to reproduce in giant size in oils, install in frames, and hang on the walls of Rose Hill—an eccentric gesture to match anything her late daughter had ever devised. When Jane got back to Waterbury, she gathered in her many Porter relations and once again went into full mourning mode, and it was hard not to feel a good measure of sympathy for her. She may have erred grievously in her handling of Carrie's upbringing, but by all appearances she had tried her best to help and provide comfort to her daughter in the first years following Joseph Welton's death. She had kept her near, offered her companionship, even literally bought into the work of Henry Bergh in order to maintain that closeness with Carrie. But none of it was enough in the end.

The service was modest in nature and in size. Alathea and I attended with three of our children and Georgiana Lewis (Abel, God bless his soul, had been taken from us six months prior), while a good number of old neighbors were on hand as well. Our Freddie, now 21, helped Jerusha Steeves up the chapel steps and to her seat inside. Michael Walsh came in, stooped and grave. But the pews were only about half occupied. Presiding was the associate vicar from St. John's. He knew Jane Welton, but not her daughter, nor her full story; so even though he held his remarks to a minimum, he got quite a bit wrong, and every time he erred I got an elbow in the ribs from Alathea on one side or Alice on the other. The poor man referred to her at one point as "a loyal daughter," and as "humble" and "God-loving." But at least he didn't venture further onto those dangerous shoals, as so many in his profession are prone to do, and was soon back in his seat. There were several readings and hymns, but no one else spoke. I'm not sure who chose the music, but it was during "Rock of Ages" that I was overcome, unable to look up, my face buried in my hands—the wild girl on horseback, the brave one in our kitchen, the singular soul in our lives and in our hearts, and finally the one lost, helpless and all alone on the western mountainside:

While I draw this fleeting breath,
When mine eyes shall close in death,
When I soar to worlds unknown,
See Thee on Thy judgment throne,
Rock of Ages, cleft for me,
Let me hide myself in Thee.

Later, as we all walked back home, we tried to think of who might have profitably said a few words on Carrie's behalf. The girls thought Alathea would have done the best job, and I agreed, although we all knew her genius was for private conversation rather than public speaking. Anyway, there had been no opportunity given for those present to say a few words—a measure no doubt put in place by Jane, who understandably feared what episodes from Carrie's present or distant past might be brought up by people she didn't know.

And, indeed, there were several strangers present, each of whom I made a point of greeting following the service as we gathered outside the chapel and sipped apple cider.

There was a delegation of five from the New York office of the ASPCA, including Henry Bergh himself. They'd sat front and center in the chapel with what I took to be a sense of ownership over the proceedings, but they had lost a very good friend and their sorrow seemed genuine.

Carrie's great benefactor in Boston, Emily Appleton, was present with an attendant, having ridden by rail down from Massachusetts. She told us a little of Carrie's life in Boston, how she'd grown there and found what seemed to be happiness and a full life. She spoke further of her great puzzlement—everyone's puzzlement—when Carrie failed to return following her father's death.

277

"We kept her room in our house and Mr. Angell kept her job open awaiting her return, but we never saw Carrie again," Mrs. Appleton said.

"Did she ever write to you and give you a reason?" Alathea asked.

"She wrote that she could not do it, never any more than that. Mr. Angell received the same response. I even wrote to her mother, hoping for some kind of explanation, but only got a cordial, uninformative paragraph in return."

And there were the three who sat together near the rear of the chapel during the service: Mr. and Mrs. Covington and Mr. Polk. All, they said, had been best of friends with Carrie when she lived in New York. They'd all been part of the same artistic and social circles, Polk said, and they'd enjoyed many youthful adventures together.

"I dare say those were our best years," he went on, "or at least they were for me. The world was opening up before us— New York, no less!—and we stepped right through the door together. Carrie was so brave and unusual. I loved her, actually, but I never told her, not in so many words. That is something I will now always regret."

Covington remembered that Carrie once wore a flowing white dress—very bold and unusual—for an art opening, creating an impression so indelible that he claimed not a month had passed ever since without his thinking of it.

"And it wasn't just the gown, of course," he said. "It was the vital, unforgettable creature who wore it."

Following several more such memories, including Elsie Covington's tales of horseback riding with Carrie into every remote corner of the city, and many questions regarding Carrie's subsequent years, the gathering broke up at last and we all went our separate ways. Burial took place a day later in a plot about 100 yards west of the chapel and up a gentle slope, along one of the cemetery's prime avenues. I chose not to attend. I didn't want to see her put into the ground alongside her father.

And that should have been the end of it. With the exception of stories and recollections of Carrie whenever our Kingsbury family was together, or between Alathea and me alone, or with neighbors or an old servant or two, that should have been it for Carrie—a fond farewell and a Christian burial beneath a line of sturdy oaks.

So it was a surprise when I received a telephone call in late October from Greene Kendrick, a successful local attorney-at-law and a friend of the Weltons. He wondered if I might pay a visit to his office, where he had several items of interest having to do with the Caroline Welton estate.

"For the moment, I have care of the contents," Kendrick told me upon my arrival, "but I doubt I shall have it for long."

"There will be a challenge?" I ventured.

""Undoubtedly," he said. "Carrie has directed that the great bulk of her estate go to the animal society in New York, and fairly late in the game she made Henry Bergh the sole executor. I've already heard that some Welton and Porter connections are ready to make a fight of it."

"On what grounds, do you suppose?"

"I believe they will challenge her state of mind—her sanity—at the time she drew up the final will. There's a good deal of money involved, and we all know that her behavior became quite strange toward the end. I'm certain that at some point Bergh will bring in his own high-priced legal team, and I will be back to fence-line disputes and barking dogs."

Kendrick paused as he pulled a packet of material from a drawer and placed it between us on his desk.

"In the meantime, however, I have some items to call to your attention. First are these letters, a few from you, but most from Alathea, that Carrie bundled together and kept in a metal box beneath her bed."

There were several dozen bound up by a blue ribbon. I had no idea that my wife had written so many. I took them with the idea of showing them to Alathea so she could decide whether to keep or destroy them. I had no intention of reading them without her permission.

"The box was evidently where she put her special keepsakes," Kendrick went on, passing over to me a piece of white cloth. "This handkerchief was in with the other things. Its 'ASK' monogram made me think it may have belonged to Mrs. Kingsbury."

I took the item and spread it out on the table before me. For a long moment I couldn't place it, but then with a jolt I remembered.

"The first time they met, Alathea offered this to Carrie to dry her tears," I said. "We were standing on Rose Hill's front walk, beneath the big chestnut tree, just having paid a visit of welcome to Jane Welton." I paused, looking at my wife's initials and wondering how often Carrie might have done the same. "I am amazed that she kept it, and it stirs me most profoundly to see it here," I said at last. "Alathea and I wondered back then what the future might hold for this new family living in the house her father had built—but I'm afraid our imaginations weren't nearly up to the task."

I put the handkerchief in a pocket and prepared to leave, but now Kendrick held up an envelope before me.

"Just one more thing, Frederick," he said. "This is a letter, never opened, that was filed with Carrie's will and several other legal documents. It's addressed to you and Alathea, and I think you should take it now rather than risk having it get caught up in the legal machinations to come."

I took the envelope. Across its front was written "Mr. and Mrs. Frederick Kingsbury" in Carrie's recognizable scrawl. I stood, thanked Kendrick for his kind consideration, and left.

The letter weighed heavily in my coat pocket during the short walk back to my office. I went through all the possible reasons why Carrie might have written, but I came up blank. We weren't relatives or possible beneficiaries of her fortune; there were no legal matters that stood between us, or specific unfinished personal business that I knew of. I did determine during that walk, however, that I would read the letter first and then pass it along to Alathea later, when I got home. I'm sure you will understand that I felt a certain amount of dread concerning the letter's contents. What message from the grave might Carrie have devised? I couldn't say. But I thought my wife might benefit from some type of preparation or warning on my part before she read it herself.

I got back to the bank and hurried to my office. I asked my secretary that I not be disturbed and poured out a glass of water from a pitcher on a side table. I sat in the room's only armchair, cut into the envelope with my ivory opener, pulled out the sheets within, unfolded them and began to read.

Dear Alathea and Frederick,

If you are reading this, it means that either you have lived to be very old or I have died quite young.

I am writing this letter on the afternoon of the party for Henry Bergh and the ASPCA here at Rose Hill. Everyone has gathered in perfect finery except for me. I have just seen you minutes ago, Frederick, from the shadows of the landing. I tried to catch your eye, too, Alathea, but was unable to do so. I have wanted to speak to both of you for the longest time, but things have gotten too hopelessly complicated and difficult. These words, written at my little blue childhood desk, will have to do instead.

It is necessary for me to tell you all that happened on March 26th, 1873, the night my father died. You may recall that I dined that evening with your wonderful family. After our goodbyes on your front porch I returned home to find my father waiting for me. He was in a terrifying state. Upon seeing me, he entered into an attack so loud and incoherent and filled with threats that it took me some time to determine its cause. It seems that while I was dining at your house, he was opening a letter addressed to me that had arrived in the late post. It was from my dear friend Augusta Warren, filling me in on events that had occurred in Boston since I'd left to care for my mother in Waterbury. In closing, however, she happened to express in the most open terms her affection for me and fondly recall several nights in which we'd shared the same bed while off in the mountains together. However innocent all this was—and it was—it enraged my father. He said he considered that sort of friendship to be the ultimate sin, the final insult to him, and that he could no longer have me for a daughter. I raised my voice to him, saying he had no right to open my private mail. He then slapped me across the face. You can imagine the danger I felt I was in. I hurried out of the room but he followed, both arms raised against me. I ran out the back door and down to the stable. He ran after me. I went into

Knight's bay, grabbed the first thing I could find, an old mucking shovel, and as my father came in the door, before he could lay his hands on me, I struck a single blow to the side of his head and killed him.

Everything else has flowed from that moment. My mother's involvement was immediate, as she had followed us down to the stable. On the spot, we devised the story of the horse's kick. I had the presence of mind to lean the shovel back against the wall. I don't think anyone, not our own servants nor the city detectives, ever suspected any other cause of death. For many days, I was sick and distraught and couldn't face anyone, especially not the two of you. Had I seen you, I would have told you everything and either placed an unspeakable strain upon you or ended up at your insistence confessing the truth to the authorities (which is something I cannot do!). Nor could I resume my former life in Boston. I've played over the prospect of returning there many, many times, almost obsessively and even in my dreams, picturing myself at work or with friends, rejoining my former happy life, but I knew it could never happen. The incident had changed me too much. I feel very strongly that the act I committed, whatever the circumstances, was wrong, horribly wrong, and that I am no longer deserving of any kind of happiness. At the same time, the bleaker truth has become evident to me: in our lifelong drama, my father has won out in the end.

As for my mother, she and I have shared this secret for more than a year now, and I suspect we shall carry it between us forever, or at least until you or someone else reads these words. I don't know what our prospects together are at this point. She is already showing an impatience for this isolated life and I have the feeling that we must eventually go our separate ways. I beg that you treat her kindly and forgivingly if she is still living. She is far from perfect, but she has done nothing to deserve such a burden.

Now you know all and I am no longer! How very liberating it is to write those words! I realize that I have always been a hopeless case—now more hopeless than ever—but you have unfailingly shown the greatest interest in me, and afforded me the greatest patience and kindness, too. I only wish I could have done more in return.

Please keep me in your hearts as you always have been in mine.

Love,
Carrie

It has been nearly 20 years since I first read those words. I am now an old man, nearly 80 years of age, long retired from the bank and factory, and now working, if you can call it that, at home, seated at my desk with a blanket thrown across my knees. I can tell you that Jane Welton never knew of the letter. After Carrie's death and the successful defense of her will following a protracted court battle, her mother resumed her travels in Europe, returned for a brief period to Waterbury, then gave up Rose Hill and moved to Philadelphia, perhaps to escape the "demons" she had once spoken of. She died two years ago, in 1901, and is buried with her husband and daughter in a plot that seems much too small to contain the three of them and what promises to be their unending state of conflict.

Alathea and I decided not to share the letter with any of our children, either. As the years went by, she and I often privately agreed that this was the correct, prudent course to take. I must report, however, that when I speak of Carrie or anything else to my dear wife these days, it is to the photograph of her that stands on my night table. Alla, my soul, was taken from us very abruptly and unfairly four years ago while she was visiting her sister in New York. Since that day, I have had the joy of grandchildren and wonderful family holidays, and even great festive events in Waterbury and the nation, but I haven't had one happy day straight through. If you've read this account in its entirety, I think you know why.

So now it is just me, ancient and aching, poking the air with an index finger to conjure up a name or stray fact as I seek an end to this tale. I have told Carrie's story, as I set out to do, and perhaps some others along the way, but I don't know that I ever did penetrate her inner engine, or find exactly what it was that made her Carrie and not the next person, or the next one after that, on life's great stage. Perhaps setting that sort of goal will always end in frustration. Even I, outwardly such an uncomplicated man, might well turn out to be a mystery to someone trying to recount and understand my life. Maybe just telling the story, one thing after the other, is enough.

In the end, I am left where we began, with Carrie's searching gaze. What was it in those eyes and that look— from the first time they pinned me at Lamson Scovill's funeral, to the last time they connected from the landing at Rose Hill, to the yearning depths captured forever in Anderson's portrait—what was it exactly that I saw there, and see there still? Could it be something so encompassing as all the complicated richness and sadness of a human life? Is it the promise of this world, and then another yet to come? Or was it all—her eyes, her face and all the rest of it—just a nearly random pile of atoms and jots, by now long since disassembled and scattered away like dust to other uses? All good questions that deserve a proper going over, to be sure— but, alas, I am now very tired, and Alathea will be impatient to know the details of my day. Those questions won't mind if we wait until tomorrow.

*The End*

# Acknowledgements

*Carrie Welton* is fiction, but in order to get the settings, characters and events as true-to-life as possible, I depended upon many sources.

The book could not have been written at all had it not been for the comprehensive, highly readable, altogether magnificent *The Town and City of Waterbury, Connecticut, from the Aboriginal Period to the Year Eighteen Hundred and Ninety-Five*, a three-volume work edited by Joseph Anderson, D.D.

My depiction of the artists of the day and their milieu was aided greatly by what I found in *The Artist in American Society: The Formative Years* by Neil Harris and "Women Artists of the Hudson River School" by Jennifer C. Krieger, which appeared in the magazine *Antiques & Fine Art*.

I used accounts from *The New York Times* to help me describe the racing scene at Saratoga Springs in 1865 and also that same summer's catastrophic fire at Barnum's American Museum in New York. Look up the *Times'* account of that blaze and you will see all a newspaper could accomplish under deadline in those days.

I learned much about Henry Bergh and the animal rights movement from *Angel in Top Hat* by Zulma Steele and *For the Prevention of Cruelty: The History and Legacy of Animal Rights* by Diane L. Beers.

"Alone Amid the Wind's Mad Revelry: The Death of Carrie Welton," by James H. Pickering appeared in the Summer 1998 edition of *Colorado Heritage* magazine; it expertly summarizes the contemporary newspaper and journal accounts of Carrie's death and I made extensive use of it in describing her final ordeal.

Online, "The Vault at Pfaff's" website provided much good information about New York's Bohemian scene in the 1860s, while many, many Wikipedia entries were valuable, including those for the Tenth Street Studio Building, the Fifth Avenue Hotel, John Morrissey and Frederic Church's "The Heart of the Andes," to name just a few.

The staff at Waterbury's Mattatuck Museum was most obliging in showing me the original journals kept by Frederick Kingsbury, as well as his unpublished autobiography. Waterbury City Historian Philip Benevento was kind enough to share with me a trove of Carrie Welton clippings and other material gathered by Carrie enthusiast Pat Joy. Thanks to both of them. The Southbury (CT) Public Library provided an ideal atmosphere for my writing—in fact, I still occasionally find myself longing for that wonderful HVAC-system hum.

At Penmore Press, my thanks to Michael James for agreeing to publish *Carrie* and seeing it through the publishing process, to Chris Wozney for her steady editorial hand, and to Midori Snyder, *Carrie*'s crucial marketing link between my Word document and the world.

I am forever grateful for the close reading of the manuscript and many useful suggestions from my sister Laura Monagan. June Gaston and Nancy McNamara also helped out greatly with their early readings and comments. Michael Monagan and Susie Monagan offered enthusiasm and encouragement, as did Shelley Donahue. As always, my wife Marcia read along pretty much as I wrote, and doled out roughly equal measures of criticism and praise. Thanks, Honey.

# About The Author

## Charles Monagan

Charles Monagan has been a writer and editor since 1972, when he graduated from Dartmouth College. His work has appeared in many magazines and newspapers, and from 1989 to 2013 he was the editor of *Connecticut Magazine*. In 1997, he won the Gold Medal for Reporting from the national City and Regional Magazine Association. In 2012, he received the Connecticut Press Club's Mark Twain Award for Distinguished Journalism, a lifetime award.

Monagan is the author of 10 books, including *The Neurotic's Handbook*, *The Reluctant Naturalist*, and *How to Get a Monkey into Harvard*. Additionally, he wrote the book and lyrics for the musical *Mad Bomber*, which was produced in 2011 and won first place in the Academy for New Musical Theatre's 2012 international Search for New Musicals.

Like many who grew up in Waterbury, Connecticut, Monagan became familiar with Carrie Welton's name due to the presence of a striking drinking fountain for horses, topped by a life-size bronze stallion, known familiarly as the Carrie Welton Fountain. Much later, he became intrigued with the scant but colorful details of Carrie's youth and her terrible death, and he took up the challenge of giving her a full life in fiction. *Carrie Welton* is Monagan's first novel.

Monagan and his wife, Marcia, live in Connecticut. For more information about the author and his work, visit **Charles Monagan: Stray Voltage**.

# If You Enjoyed This Book
## Visit

## PENMORE PRESS
www.penmorepress.com

All Penmore Press books are available directly through our website, amazon.com, Barnes and Noble and Nook, Sony Reader, Apple iTunes, Kobo books and via leading bookshops across the United States, Canada, the UK, Australia and Europe.

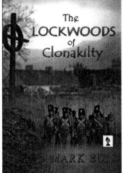

# The Lockwoods

## of Clonakilty

*by*

# Mark Bois

Lieutenant James Lockwood of the Inniskilling Regiment has returned to family, home and hearth after being wounded, almost fatally, at the Battle of Waterloo, where his regiment was decisive in securing Wellington's victory and bringing the Napoleonic Wars to an end. But home is not the refuge and haven he hoped to find. Irish uprisings polarize the citizens, and violence against English landholders – including James' father and brother – is bringing down wrath and retribution from England. More than one member of the household sympathizes with the desire for Irish independence, and Cassie, the Lockwood's spirited daughter, plays an active part in the rebellion.

Estranged from his English family for the "crime" of marrying a Irish Catholic woman, James Lockwood must take difficult and desperate steps to preserve his family. If his injuries don't kill him, or his addiction to laudanum, he just might live long enough to confront his nemesis. For Captain Charles Barr, maddened by syphilis and no longer restrained by the bounds of honor, sets out to utterly destroy the Lockwood family, from James' patriarchal father to the youngest child, and nothing but death with stop him – his own, or James Lockwood's.

PENMORE PRESS
www.penmorepress.com

# THE BOTTOM DWELLERS

BY

## LEAH DEVLIN

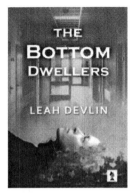

Bioengineer and Party Girl...

Lindsey Nolan has it all: inventions paying large dividends, a dream job in the scientific village of Woods Hole, Massachusetts, and a stable of eager playmates. But when Lindsey wakes up in rehab with no memory of how she got there, her world is turned upside down. Her roommate, an HIV-positive teenage prostitute named Maggie, is the most volatile patient on the ward. The facility is plagued by disturbing thefts. And another theft unfolds when her competitor, an engineer named Karen Battersby, discovers and steals Lindsey's astonishing new invention from her Woods Hole lab. Lindsey and Maggie must face the consequences of past transgressions if they hope to deal with present perils and ascend from the desolate world of the Bottom Dwellers.

PENMORE PRESS
www.penmorepress.com

# The Chosen Man

## by

## J. G. Harlond

**From the bulb of a rare flower bloom ambition and scandal**

Rome, 1635: As Flanders braces for another long year of war, a Spanish count presents the Vatican with a means of disrupting the Dutch rebels' booming economy. His plan is brilliant. They just need the right man to implement it.

They choose Ludovico da Portovenere, a charismatic spice and silk merchant. Intrigued by the Vatican's proposal—and hungry for profit—Ludo sets off for Amsterdam to sow greed and venture capitalism for a disastrous harvest, hampered by a timid English priest sent from Rome, accompanied by a quick-witted young admirer he will use as a spy, and bothered by the memory of the beautiful young lady he refused to take with him.

Set in a world of international politics and domestic intrigue, *The Chosen Man* spins an engrossing tale about the Dutch financial scandal known as tulip mania—and how decisions made in high places can have terrible repercussions on innocent lives.

PENMORE PRESS
www.penmorepress.com

# BODO
# The Apostate

Donald Michael Platt

In a time of intolerance, following your conscience is a dangerous choice...

"In the meantime, a credible report caused all ecclesiastics of the Catholic Church to lament and weep."

-Prudentius of Troyes, Annales Bertiniani, anno 839

On Ascension Day May 22, 838, Bishop Bodo, chaplain, confessor, and favorite of both his kin, Emperor Louis the Pious, son of Charlemagne, and Empress Judith, caused the greatest scandal of the Carolingian Empire and the 9th century Roman Church.

Bodo, the novel, dramatizes the causes, motivations, and aftermath of Bodo's astonishing cause célèbre that took place during an age of superstitions, a confused Roman Church, heterodoxies, lingering paganism, broken oaths, rebellions, and dissolution of the Carolingian Empire.

PENMORE PRESS
www.penmorepress.com

Penmore Press
Challenging, Intriguing, Adventurous, Historical and Imaginative

www.penmorepress.com

CPSIA information can be obtained at www.ICGtesting.com
Printed in the USA
BVOW04s0051150516

448062BV00008B/13/P